The View From Plum Lick

By
David Dick

*Illustrations
by Jackie Larkins*

First Edition Soft Cover, June 1, 1992
Second Printing Soft Cover, September 1, 1992
(As ISBN 0-9632886-0-1)

First Hard Cover Edition, May 1, 1997

Copyright 1992 and 1997
by
Plum Lick Publishing, Incorporated
1101 Plum Lick Road
Paris, Kentucky   40361-9547

Cover design by Stacey Freibert Design

Cover and book Illustrations by Jackie Larkins

Other books by David Dick

Follow the Storm
Peace at the Center
A Conversation with Peter P. Pence
The Quiet Kentuckians

ISBN: 0-9632886-6-0

Library of Congress Catalog Card Number

97-91895

for
Lalie

Contents

PART ONE

PART TWO

PART THREE

EPILOGUE

FOREWORD

All across America there have lived those sentimental souls who have longed to return to their ancestral roots, or to their own Plum Lick Creek branches. Few of them, however, have so pleasant an ancestral haven to claim as their very own as David Dick of Bourbon County, Kentucky. With the soul of a poet, the eye of a seasoned Grecian shepherd, and the down to earth reality of a Kentucky dirt farmer, he writes from a deep spiritual affinity with his land and of his place on it. The tempo of his narrative is set by the turnings of the land and seasons. David and his wife Lalie have settled themselves on this quiet rural corner of earth to spin out the years of their life webs of allotted time. They have accepted the joys of their domain on the one hand and responded to its demand on the other as dedicated tenants.

No matter how isolated or secluded a farm may be there never occurs a day without incidence. Whether it be lambing, plowing, setting crops, or simply whiling away the lazy summer evenings, something, expected and unexpected is always happening.

David Dick writes about the flow of life on the Plum Lick Farm with the graceful casualness of the country days themselves. Plowing, setting tobacco, lambing, being awakened at night by the baying of coon hounds, or just whiling away a soft evening beneath a maple tree, all are a part of life along the creek. The author details the occurrences of incidents, minor and consequential, with the grace and spiritual attachment of an Elizabeth Madox Roberts, of Wendell Berry, or a James Still and Jesse Stuart.

David Dick integrates the memories and history of the ancient ancestors who traveled the country roads and worked the Plum Lick fields before him. He has had moments of taking spiritual stock of his own life and that of his beloved Lalie. Lalie has shared a full partnership in life on the land, the lambing season, the fortunes of the farm, and, especially those precious moments when the course of life is celebrated in more dramatic fashion in sitting by wood fires listening to the chirping of a chimney-stack cricket. Always on a farm there are the dogs, the cats, and animal pets. They too are sharers of the land and its generous largess. Even the cricket in the bathtub holds warranty title to a niche and seasonal date in the old house which has sheltered so many generations of his ancestors.

David Dick savors for his readers' vicarious pleasure those precious moments when winter surrenders to spring and there suddenly is new promise of life in the sheep fold, the tobacco bed, and along Plum Lick Creek. Spring literally tumbles into summer, and summer into fall when it is tobacco cutting and housing time. Then comes the anxious moment of waiting for rain enough to bring the golden leaf into case and the taking advantage of an early market.

In less physically tangible fashion, but even more soul broadening for the author was that moment when a toddling grandson greeted him as "grandfather." This was a bonding. The seasons and the cycles of the land reached out to include the human occupants in their unrelenting embraces. There on the land the grandson built his castle and soiled his hands with the honest dirt of the ancestral seat, an act which hopefully will be repeated through many generations to come. Reading David Dick's book is actually an exercise in taking a vicarious stroll along a narrow country lane, stopping around every turn to savor a new scene. Only a dedicated steward of so pleasant a site on earth as Plum Lick Farm in Bourbon County could inscribe on paper for his readers the sacramental experience of lifting a two year-old country ham down from the joist of a country smoke house.

Dr. Thomas D. Clark

PREFACE

The telephone rang at our home in Dallas on my 50th birthday. It was John Lane, CBS News Vice President.

"I want you to stay in Dallas for now."

It was then I knew my chances of a permanent assignment in New York had all but vanished. After 14 years as a newsman for CBS News, it was becoming increasingly clear my clock was running out on becoming another Dan Rather or a Charles Kuralt. Just being a regular first team player for the Tiffany Network was becoming increasingly difficult.

There had been three Presidential campaigns, the Jonestown massacre, uncounted tornadoes and hurricanes, and civil war in Central America. "Following the storm," as I used to call it, was obviously going to grant me a death wish some correspondents and cameramen seemed to possess, but I was beginning stubbornly to resist. I was coming to understand that CBS News was consuming me like a fire. Until my 50th birthday I had been convinced I would die with my boots on. During all those 14 years I could see no other way.

After the phone call from New York I decided to begin planning my retirement by the time I was 55, the earliest possible moment to leave the network with a modest pension. In 1982, my second wife, Lalie, resigned from Revlon in New York to come home to Dallas to start our new family. But, that was the year CBS sent me to El Salvador, Nicaragua, Guatemala, Mexico, Argentina, Uruguay, Israel and Lebanon.

I carried with me a central thought. It was the green and the dream of Plum Lick in Kentucky, where somehow I knew I was destined to live the best years of my life with Lalie and our as yet unborn child. Having this sense of place made Beirut bearable at a time when it was so horribly broken by civil war.

In all my years with CBS News I had never turned down an assignment, but I knew almost everything has an outer limit, and it was certain to me I was fast reaching mine. I saved and counted watermelon seeds from Israeli fruit stands as I fantasized living and loving on Plum Lick. I sketched floor plans for a possible homestead, not knowing at the time, that in three short years, I would be sitting in a rocking chair on the front porch of an ancestral house by the side of

Plum Lick Creek in Bourbon County, Kentucky. Nor did I think that my desire to return "for a few years" to my alma mater, the University of Kentucky, would lead to the directorship of the UK School of Journalism.

Little did I imagine in my wildest dreams that Lalie's uncle, Audio Gray Harvey of Jackson, Mississippi, would buy the land adjoining my original inheritance and resell it to us on terms unavailable anywhere else. On June 30, 1985 I worked my last day for CBS News. I wrote in my journal:

"I suppose you'd have to say, we've grown up considerably. Some things just take longer to accomplish."

The entry for July 1, 1985:

"...the first day of independence from CBS; the first day as associate professor in the School of Journalism at the University of Kentucky."

The *View from Plum Lick* is the story of what happened in the following seven years, our living and loving within the reach of John Donne's twin compasses, the anchoring of the "fixt foot" on a piece of land purchased 200 years ago by my great-great-great grandfather, Joshua, in the valley of the Plum trees.

David Dick
May, 1992

J. LARKINS

Plum Lick and the hills surrounding the ancient creek in the valley are like John Donne's compasses, anchoring our identity.

"If they be two, they are two so
As stiff twin compasses are two,
Thy soul the fixt foot, makes no show
To move, but doth, if the other do.
And though it in the centre sit,
Yet when the other far doth roam,
It leans, and hearkens after it,
And grows erect, as that comes home." [1]

"THE FIXT FOOT"

<p>lum Lick lies in a part of Kentucky so quiet the silence is sovereign beneath the jet trails by day, the star treks by night. The view from the valley inspires clearer thinking. There's no guarantee the result will be wisdom, but the chances for it are favorable.

The location of my retirement from 26 years of broadcast journalism—19 with CBS News, seven with WHAS Radio and TV in Louisville—requires a map and some imagination. Several directions will do, which is one of the joys of living here. It's not a one-way street, a cul-de-sac or any other kind of dead end. Though the fixed foot of our twin compasses is here, Lalie and I are free to move in any direction—we understand the importance of returning home.

The county is Bourbon. Plum Lick is tucked away in the far eastern part of Bourbon on the watershed dividing the Inner and Outer Bluegrass regions. Most road maps show a crossroads in Bourbon called "Plum." The intersecting roads are officially designated KY 57 and 537, but the local residents call them many names: "Levy Road," "Levee Road," "Cane Ridge Road," "Little Rock Road," and "Bunker Hill Road."

It's best not to undertake a journey in the middle of the night. Outsiders are almost certain to become hopelessly lost. There's an inner web of roads in this area not appearing on most maps. While the neighbors are friendly, it's as difficult to give directions for getting out as it is for getting in.

Anybody ever down this way might want to stop for a little refreshment—where the Ale-8s are the coldest—at Workman's Grocery, about all there is to metropolitan "Plum." Ray and Lou Ellen take turns presiding over the daily proceedings, which is mainly the morning and afternoon sessions of local farmers and commuters to jobs in Lexington and surrounding communities. The County Judge Executive, "Bugs" Hinkle (everybody, even "Bugs" himself, calls him "Bugs"), farms a stone's throw away. "Bugs" stops in frequently, as well as other candidates for public office, and the conversation has been known to turn political once in a while. More times than not, the talk is about the weather, welfare and women roughly in that order (when Lou Ellen's at the house, and Mayor Ray is holding court).

The earthquake of 1988 was worth a round or two of talk. Mayor Ray got his picture on the front page of *The Bourbon Times*, as he recalled how Plum plum shook. Usually those in attendance at the morning and afternoon sessions sit in a half circle with an opening for newcomers to enter. It may sound and look like a fish trap, but it isn't. Unlike the maze of roads in the area, it's as easy to step outside Workman's Grocery as it is to step in. Nobody will twist anybody's arm about staying. A stranger will almost certainly cause silence at the start, but hardly anybody should be put off by it. Just don't come in talking loud. That would be bad manners, and the silence would become worse—in fact, most would get up and go find something else to do. Plum Lickers don't admire loud talk, any more than dogs and sheep like to be yelled at.

Lou Ellen says not nearly as many people drive out now from town to Plum to talk and eat baloney and crackers, even though the place has become almost a regular item in Dick Burdette's column in the *Lexington Herald-Leader*. Well, he's written something about the place at least two or three times. When he's down to nubbins he calls up Plum to see what's happened lately.

It's just as well. Lou Ellen and most of us around here would probably be put off by too much traffic. We're more than willing for "progress" to occur mainly between Lexington and Nicholasville in Fayette and Jessamine counties. Those two counties are so homogenized, they ought to merge into Fayamine or Jessette. They could throw in Scott for good measure, and call it Fayaminescott or Fayscotamine. Most of us down here would rather stay plain old Plum in Bourbon.

As for four-laning the road between Paris and Lexington, in the heart of the Inner Bluegrass, Judge "Bugs" and most others are for it. A few Inner and Outer Bluegrass purists are in favor of "improving" it, but not much more than that. There's a big argument about whether it's important to save trees, stone walls and horse farm entrances, not to mention the horse farms themselves.

It's been a tough, emotional subject for decades, and the final outcome is probably best left to the courts. Some of us have a few more things to worry about than whether the Paris Pike is four-laned. But when it is, which it probably will be one of these days, we'll toast progress with some Ale-8 and hope everybody will drive like they've got good sense. Plum was never intended to be a thorn in the side of progress.

My own view from Plum Lick is about a mile and a half upstream on Plum Lick Creek. That's the direction great-grandmother Cynthia's grandfather Joshua traveled. In the late 18th century the creek bed or the banks, depending on the weather, was the road. Four-laning was not an issue then. Folks considered themselves lucky to have a small piece of one lane. Today, our access is from the one and one-half lane Plum Lick Road to the south.

But from the other end, to the north where the Big Dipper tips downward as if to pour, the part of the land just before you come to our place is called Joshua Meadows. It was named by my second cousin, once removed. Old Joshua would be right pleased that 200 years after he came into the Kentucky wilderness, his great-great-great-great granddaughter, Anne Armstrong, the owner of Joshua Meadows, would be a member of the Legislative Research Commission staff in Frankfort.

Anne helps ride shotgun on legislation the way Old Joshua kept an eye out for tomahawks when Kentucky was "the dark and bloody ground." Anne and I can show you the spot less than a mile down Boone Creek from Plum, where Daniel Boone's brother, Edward, was killed by the Indians.

My family and I live a quarter of a mile up stream from the log house still owned by Anne, where Joshua and Polly Sr. lived 200 years ago. My wife, Lalie, our daughter, Ravy, and I live about a quarter mile beyond the deserted old house where Joshua's grand-daughter, Cynthia, took up housekeeping with John Houston Crouch. They were my great-grandparents. The logged house with its giant chimney and its ghosts of two centuries gone by is wearing away with each passing winter. Our place, built by John Houston's brother, Isaac Shelby Crouch, is where we've chosen to live in as much solitude as possible.

The Isaac Shelby Crouch house has its share of shadowy memories too. Isaac and John Houston were two of the founders of nearby Little Rock Christian Church. Isaac, the more flashy of the two, favored fund-raising to build the church. Great-grandfather John thought that

XVII

sort of thing tended toward sin. He was partial to individual sacrifice and has probably turned over in his grave several times about the Kentucky Lottery.

The two cantankerous brothers were also leaders in the establishment of "Plum Lick Turnpike," a primitive toll road of the time, but their disagreements were many and would eventually lead to splits in their branch of the Crouch tree that wouldn't heal 'til hell froze over.

Our place, dating back to the mid-19th century, includes views from down in the bottomland, or up on top of the hills. It depends on the quality of the thought. Wherever it occurs, the main thing is the willingness to listen good. Sometimes, especially on star-filled full-moon nights, voices seem to whisper to us, and we answer back from time to time: Joshua and Polly Sr.; William and Polly Jr.; John Houston and Cynthia; Bill and Laura; Samuel and Lucile; Big Ike and Little Ike; Mary Louise; Kitty; Margaret Jane (Aunt Mug); Jim; Idelle; Houston; Clark; Elizabeth; Anna D.; Troup and Alpha; Hilton and Margaret; and other good people now living close by.

Come sit a spell. We'll talk, some...

PART ONE

MA BOYD

Old Blue sputtered and ran out of gas on the Bunker Hill Road in front of Mrs. Timon Boyd's house. I'd been meaning to stop many times, but I always seemed to have other matters on my mind. I'd kept saying to myself, I ought to get to know the lady who wears the bonnet.

I'm convinced God made me run out of gas in front of her house. There's no other explanation for it because Old Blue's last gasp was right there on that spot by the side of the road. I had been so caught up in solving the problems of the world I forgot the Lord moves in mysterious ways, and when Old Blue says empty, Old Blue means empty.

As it turned out I was mighty glad God made me run out of gas because otherwise I might not have had the conversation that I did with Ma Boyd.

Ma stuck her head out of the window of her house and indicated she was curious as to what was most likely my problem. I told her I'd run out of gas. She said her son, Coleman, would be back directly, and would I like to come in and sit a spell? Ravy, who had just turned four years old at the time, was with me and she and Ma hit it off right from the start. Ma Boyd was 87 years old in 1987—born at the beginning of the 20th century, looking toward the start of the 21st. Her hands clasped the top of her cane, which she used to steady herself in the heat of a summer day. Her dress was simple, fresh and clean; her bonnet shaded the sides of her peaceful face. You don't see

1

many ladies in bonnets in 1992 in Kentucky, but when you do you're like as not to say to yourself, isn't that a picture? To me, there's something reassuring about ladies in bonnets.

Ma Boyd and modest contentment seem to go together—haughtiness, vanity and pride replaced by more pleasant and durable values. As it's written in Proverbs, "Pride goeth before destruction and an haughty spirit before a fall." Something similar might be said about modern man running out of gas. Sitting on empty has a way of getting a traveler's attention.

Ma and Ravy found a common meeting place at a plate full of cookies. Ma likes to hand them out and Ravy has never been known to be shy about reducing the cookie population. While Ravy ate cookies, I listened to Mrs. Timon Boyd.

"I was born just across the hill" here in Montgomery County..."The farthest I've ever been from home?...well, that would have been the trip to Cleveland, Ohio when I was ten years old...that lake fascinated me." That was the summer Thomas Edison demonstrated talking motion pictures. It was also the year Mark Twain, O. Henry, Edward VII, King of Great Britain, Winslow Homer, Florence Nightingale and Leo Tolstoy died.

Ma married Timon Boyd in the Little Rock Christian Church parsonage when she was 17 and he was 20 years old, the same church John Houston and Big Ike had helped build from scratch.

"I don't believe I've heard the name Timon before," said the visitor who had run out of gas.

"It's a name from the Bible, Acts VI, Chapter V," said the little lady with the sweet face from beneath the freshly washed and starched yellow bonnet. "I really miss my husband—everybody loved him. But, I know he's at rest. We worked and saved to own our farm. We didn't buy fancy clothes, but we always had plenty to eat."

Ma recalled Timon was 82 when he passed away. They had started out with chickens, cows and hogs; they raised tobacco and corn back when people paid $2.50 a day for housing tobacco and putting up hay. Ma washed on a board until "...the motor gave out. Electric came through in '46, or maybe '47," almost 40 years after Edison invented talking pictures.

"Didn't have fans?"

"No, didn't have fans."

2

Ma went on: "One year tobacco sold for two and a half cents a pound, and a neighbor went to crying. Timon told him, don't cry, I've got a wife and two sons and they'll make it some way."

Ma worked "as hard as any man," said her young son, 65-year-old Coleman, who joined us on a warm afternoon in June.

"Did you ever have to spank Coleman when he was a child?"

"Didn't believe in spanking, but had to once or twice. I talked to them mostly."

Great-granddaughter Jennifer and great-grandson Bo came in from catching a big butterfly in a Mason jar, and they sat close to Ma.

"What kind of advice do you give your great-grandchildren?"

"Be good, mind your parents and study hard."

Ma leaned forward closer to Bo's face and said, "Do you behave, Honey?"

Bo smiled, and Ma said, "Well, bless you."

"Where do you go to church?" asked the visitor, who by now had forgotten about gasoline.

Ma said, "I don't anymore, but I'm a member of Peyton's Lick Christian Church." Peyton's Lick is over several hills from Plum Lick.

"Do you watch television?"

"Watch every Sunday morning, but they don't preach like they used to. Seems like they all mostly beg."

When Ma quit the Little Rock High School after two years to marry Timon, she canned preserves and helped kill hogs. "But, we always had dessert, too."

"What kind of dessert?"

"Mostly cake."

"What kind of cake?"

"Any kind of cake. Jam and coconut."

Ma and Ravy exchanged birthday cards in 1987 since their birthdays are on the same day—June 15. They shared their birthday cake and I haven't stopped thanking the Lord for making me run out of gas in front of Ma Boyd's house.

TWO CALVES BETTER THAN ONE, FOUR CALVES BETTER THAN TWO, SOMETIMES

S hortly after hearing of the blessed events I drove around from Plum Lick to the Levy Road past Joshua's final resting place, across Boone Creek, which usually in August is behaving itself, up the hill past the rock outcroppings on what used to be the Old Flanders Place to the little house now occupied by the Tolsons.

Mrs. Tolson and the family dog came out to make acquaintance.

"Understand you all have had two sets of twin calves."

"That's right," smiled Mrs. T.

"Thought I'd come over to see them."

"They're out back."

"Everything all right?"

"Just fine."

"Their mammas took 'em?"

"Yes, they did," smiled Mrs. T.

We walked together up a ways to the barn. Mr. Tolson stepped out as pleased as could be. And why wouldn't he what with two sets of twin calves and their mammas accepting them to boot?

"Heard about your two sets of twin calves."

"Yep," said Mr. T. His smile outdid Mrs. T.'s.

"You ever had twin calves before?"

"Been farming ever since I was big enough to," said 62-year-old Mr. Tolson, as he led the visitor in between two tractors. Mrs. Tolson headed on back to the house.

"I was born on Long Branch about ten miles above Frenchburg in Menifee County, where my daddy was a farmer and a storekeeper. Moved to Bath and then to Bourbon."

"Big family?"

"Seven boys on a straight."

"On a straight?"

"In a row about two years apart."

"No girls?"

"Youngest was a girl and the oldest was a girl. Seven boys in between."

"Children of your own?"

"Two girls and two boys."

Mr. Tolson led the way around the slope on the creek side of the barn.

"There's the twins." He smiled all the time.

Four calves hugged the ground like they might fall off. Their mammas stood close as if to say, we'll catch you.

"Found the first set on Friday and the second set on Sunday. Those two with the brownish color were by the Limousin bull."

"Wouldn't mind seeing him."

"He died of pneumonia this past Spring. Right down there by the creek."

"Sorry to hear it."

"I tried to doctor him, but the vet came out and said he was too far gone."

"What was the other bull?

"He's Angus with some Bremmer in him."

"Are the calves bulls or heifers?"

"All bulls."

One of the calves stood up and went to nurse. The mammas eyed the visitor as if it were all right for Mr. T. to be there but strangers were a different matter.

"That one's techy," said Mr. T.

"S'pose it's luck?"

"Sorta lays in the bulls," said Mr. T. as we turned back to the house. "They used to have to sell the cows, afraid they wouldn't own the twins. The boys thought they wouldn't take 'em but they did."

"How's farming been to you, Mr. Tolson?"

"Used to be could make money. Some years, seems like we just swap dollars."

"Well, I'm going to ask about it up at the University but it seems to me I heard that bull twins might be valuable because there's a chance they'll pass along the twin trait."

"I may wait on banding them," said Mr. T.

HEAD RECAPITULATOR

H ad a bull named Billy Joe. Had a bull named Elvin. Had a bull named Head Recapitulater. Billy Joe wore out. So did Elvin. Head Recapitulator was another story.

I have to take you back to the George Wallace campaigns in 1968, 1972 and 1976. The Governor's chief press secretary most of the time was Billy Joe Camp. His assistant was Elvin Stanton. I always said, when I retired from following Governor Wallace around and returned to Plum Lick I'd name my chief bull, Billy Joe. The assistant bull would be Elvin. After they had worn out (Elvin's feet went bad on him), I brought in one of those "exotic" breeds of bull and named him Head Recapitulater. I had used to lie awake at night on the campaign trail, dreaming of retiring and having a bull named Head Recapitulater.

It was one of the Governor's favorite stories:

"There I was on election night in the grrreaaaat free state of Maryland. It was 1964 and I'd run in some primaries, and I'd done pretty well. In fact, I'd won a couple in Wisconsin and Indiana, and now in the grrreaaat free state of Maryland the returns were coming in and I was running ahead.

"I was watching television and you know what those reporters were saying? They were saying, 'What has come over the people of the grrreaaaat free state of Maryland?'

"And they called the mayor of Baltimore onto the television. And you know what he said. He said it was 'saaaadddd.'

"And then they called the head recapitulater onto the television. And you know what he said. He said, 'We've got to recapitulate the vote.'

"And they did recapitulate the vote. And after they had recapitulated the vote, George Wallace was running behind.

"I still don't know what 'recapitulate' means but I'll tell you this: if anybody ever tells you they're going to recapitulate on you, you better watch'em, 'cause they're about to do something to you."

I paid good money for Head Recapitulater. He was some kind of bull. He bred everything on the farm and then started traveling to see what else needed to be done. He went through the fence so many times, we were plum worn out tracking him down and walking him home. He sort of had the attitude that "This is what I thought I was supposed to be doing." One day, Bill Gilvin put Head Recapitulater inside the tobacco barn and closed the door on him. As Bill walked away, he looked back to see the whole side of the barn coming out like taking tissue paper out of a box. He opened the barn door, and couldn't be blamed for thinking, "To heck with this."

I called Wayne Shumate, the fellow who sold me the bull.

"Help."

"What's the matter?"

"Pleeeasssee let me bring this bull back to you. Keep him, sell him, I don't care what you do with him. We can't handle this Head Recapitulater any more."

We were lucky to get him delivered with the truck still in one piece. It was like driving down the Stringtown Pike with a case of dynamite and somebody sitting on top of it, smoking a cigar.

Later I had a phone call at my office at CBS in Dallas.

"Mr. Dick?"

"Yessir."

"We hate to tell you this, but we had a little problem with your bull."

"What happened?"

"Well, we couldn't keep him corralled either. The last time he broke loose he traveled all the way to the next county. By the time he got to Millersburg, the only way we could catch him was to pin him between two semi-trucks. We took him right on down the road to the stockyards. He's hot dogs by now. We'll be sending you a check. Won't be much. Real sorry."

I was relieved the beast had not wound up in a schoolyard and wiped out an entire population of first graders. The words of George Corley Wallace came back: "If anybody ever tells you, they're going to recapitulate on you, you better watch 'em, 'cause they're about to do something to you."

7

"NARD"

T he sight of Bernie Nudelman in July of 1989 riding into Plum Lick on his super motorcycle brought back so many memories we couldn't possibly recount them all but we tried. The last time I'd seen my old friend "Nard" was in Guatemala during the coup of 1982. Seven years hadn't changed him much. His 6'6" frame, give or take an inch, was still as rugged as ever. The huge gentleness was still there. The generosity flowed as it always had. The first time I'd seen this splendid giant of a man had been in a dusty Rio Grande valley town.

A green, inexperienced network correspondent was on the George Wallace campaign plane in 1968, and, waiting in the crowd was "Nard," a veteran stringer television cameraman for CBS News. The crush of people was so great the smaller cameramen were pushed out of position, but the tallest shooter of them all hoisted his shoulder-mounted film-and-sound camera to his head, hooked it there, pointing it like a coal miner's lamp effective as if he'd been hanging from a blimp. The memory came back of my first real blimp ride with Bernie (we called him, "Bernie," "Bern," "Nard," and just plain "Nudelman") when we had a little time to kill one day in Miami. Those were the golden years. It was also the time of the crash of the Eastern L-1011 in the Everglades. We covered that too.

Bernard Nudelman was born in Jacksonville but Miami and Dade County, especially Coconut Grove, became his home, a launch pad for virtually every country in Latin America. He had filmed Castro in Cuba, Somoza in Nicaragua, Torrijos in Panama, Peron in Argentina, Stroessner in Paraguay, Pinochet in Chile and Papa and Baby Docs in Haiti. Traveling with "Nard" through Central and South America was helping to live a legend. His trademark was cool in times of chaos, and chaos was his meat and potatoes. He could charm the socks off a cobra. On the 1972 Christmas Eve when I arrived in Managua to cover the earthquake that killed an estimated 20,000 people, "Nard" was waiting for me at the airport. He had already interviewed President Anastasio Somoza.

"Here," said "Nard," smiling as he handed over the film.

The other members of the original Nudelman crew were "Hennie" Adyr and Dick Martin. In the old days they were as unlikely a three musketeers as you'd ever want to come upon in the middle of a star-crossed night. Yet in the midst of the worst of calamities they'd have just about everybody feeling better within sight or sound…they were the essence of the art of not taking yourself seriously.

"Remember the whore house we slept in the night after the earthquake?"

"Yeah, but where were all the whores?"

"Remember the Doberman pinschers guarding the place?"

"Remember the time you tried to ice skate with Cornelia Wallace in Milwaukee?"

"I remember you and Hennie laughing your asses off."

"Remember the good times at Sans Souci in Haiti? Oh, and remember when I fell through the roof over my swimming pool and it didn't have any water in it?"

"Remember the last run of that little train, what did they call it? the 'Mountain Goat' at Sewanee?"

"Remember Jonestown?" Sitting in the rocking chairs on the front porch on Plum Lick more than a decade later, sipping tequila, watching the sun going down over the old Hedges place where Cynthia's in-laws were born, studying the worm turning in the bottom of the bottle, memories floated back.

"Remember it was right after that we did that "day-in-the-life-of" a shrimper off the coast of Maryland? I had all those bandages around my broken ribs, and the shrimp boat was pitching all over the place?"

All his bones would have to ache after 22 years with CBS News, seven years with NBC News and one year with ABC News covering Latin America as if it were his own back yard with these little "problems" out there to quiet down.

"Damn it, LaSoufriere is erupting again," I said in 1976 as I pounded on Bernie's door at two o'clock in the morning at the hotel in Basse-Terre, Guadeloupe. "Wake me up first thing in the morning," said the huge man standing there in his underwear, filling up the doorway. Of course there was nothing to do at two o'clock in the morning, but Radio News had called from New York, wanting an instant report. Bernard Nudelman had more sense than try to placate the radio news desk in New York at some outrageous hour of the night when it was obvious the best thing to do was to get a good night's sleep. He'd leave stupidity to correspondents. And then there was that night in Key West when Bernie had something more important to do than to fret over the possibility of a hurricane. It was the big guy's birthday, and he was determined to celebrate it—to hell with hurricanes or anything else that might spoil the fun.

"Nard" stayed two nights on Plum Lick. He had dropped in to check out his old buddy. He seemed pleased, climbed on his Honda and headed back toward Miami.

The first night he called from Grundy, Virginia.

"Had a great time up there on Plum Lick."

"So did we. Please come back."

"...YESSIR, MY FRIEND"

The shepherd had the bad sense, again, to take a trip out of Kentucky in the summer of 1989. It was one of those commitments I had felt compelled to keep, compulsion being one of my major flaws. The Southern Newspaper Publishers Association had invited me to Atlanta to attend a symposium (a fancy word for "meeting," or as some of us say down here on Plum Lick, a little "get together.")

It took me the whole morning to get my show on the road, and it wasn't until midday I was eating a franchised hamburger on the south side of Lexington. The south side of Lexington reminds me in places of most of the reasons why I'm so content to live out my days here on Plum Lick where I can actually hear birds singing in the giant Water Maples, without artificial air conditioning. I can feel the soft breezes blowing in my window. When it rains here it's not an inconvenience, it's a part of the great hydrologic system. The peaceful quiet along Plum Lick Creek is as sweet as balm of Gilead.

Of course not everybody likes this sort of thing and that's why I'm here and so many thousands of others are on the south side of Lexington. The only person I encountered between the south side of Lexington and the Kentucky-Tennessee state line turned out to be the link I needed to reconnect me to a reasonable level of sanity. I had pulled into a Stuckey's Pecan Shoppe at Exit 25 on I-75 at Corbin. Usually when I present myself for a franchised hamburger or self-serve gasoline I feel like the orphan child who doesn't have a friend in the world. Talking through one of those drive-through microphones to humanoids is about as satisfying as trying to communicate with alien forces in outer space. It's possible that I'm the problem, but I'd rather think not. It's only warmth I crave. Warmth is what I received from Mr. O. W. Sloane at the Stuckey's Pecan Shoppe. O.W. said he was born in 1918.

"I'll do it, my friend," he said, when I suggested I would pump my own gas.

"That brought her up, my friend," he said, after adding a quart of oil to my old station wagon.

"It's my pleasure, my dear," he said, after giving a child two suckers.

"It's my pleasure, my friend...yessir, my friend," O.W. said as I handed him my money.

"Business good?" I asked.

"Yessir, it is, my friend."

I found myself saying something which I don't ordinarily feel inspired to say when trying to communicate into drive-through microphones with several of the present crop of humanoids.

"You are possibly one of the friendliest persons I've met in quite a while."

"I was raised that way, my friend; my father was a minister, my friend."

Possibly they teach such strategies in schools of management and business and economics, but I imagine it's relatively rare. Although I didn't ask him, I'm pretty sure Mr. O.W. Sloane did not graduate from Harvard Business School.

The drive from Kentucky to Georgia was the normal interstate sameness. They're here to stay. There's no turning back. Super highways are in. Country roads are out. Well, not exactly. Both worlds are possible in Kentucky, and I give thanks on a regular basis that I can continue to live on a little country road with barely passing room.

Interstates are fine if you're in a hurry, but country roads are best when you've time to slow down for more interesting possibilities. As for the traffic in Atlanta, they can have it and their airport too.

I managed to arrive on time for the educators' meeting near downtown Atlanta, but I don't remember anything that stood out as much as Mr. Sloane at Stuckey's. The participants at the meeting talked about cooperation between academics and professionals, and I left as convinced of the importance of it as I did when I left home. I wasn't sure that driving all the way to Atlanta made any difference that could not have been achieved by writing a letter to the same folks.

I decided it was time to do something that could not be done anywhere but in Atlanta. It was time to go visit somebody special—my old friend, cameraman Laurens Pierce. He shot the footage of the attempted assassination of Governor Wallace, miles of footage of the Reverend Martin Luther King Jr. before the world knew or cared who he was, presidents, potentates and piddling folks. Pierce was already a legend before the heart attack that killed him, and I was long overdue in making a pilgrimage to his grave. I had not attended Pierce's funeral (we all called him, Pierce, seldom did we call him Laurens), and I regretted it. I owed him more than I'd ever given back.

I stood by his marker on a slope of green in Arlington Memorial Gardens, and I remembered the thousands of miles we'd traveled together from 1968 to 1978 for CBS News. For the first time on my return to Atlanta, where I'd lived and first met Pierce, I said: "My friend...yessir, my friend."

PIERCE

I had probably learned as much from Pierce as I had from any one person I'd ever known. Pierce was a student of the confrontation. He knew its possibilities and he considered them virtually limitless. The essential nature of Pierce's handling of the confrontation was that he was always able to take normal situations at least one step beyond the point that average, conventional people are able to conceive or execute. Pierce viewed the world and all the characters who strutted upon its stage with approximately equal contempt, and once he had finessed them over the line into an area where they had never been before he delighted in opening them up for autopsy.

For example, "maple syrup" had to BE maple syrup. Real cream had to BE real cream. If an ice cream parlor in Memphis had a sign on its door stating that business hours ran until midnight, there'd better be somebody there at 11:59 scooping ice cream. This may strike some as silly, others might view it as quixotic—those views would only serve to increase Pierce's contempt for inconsistency and lack of courage to stand up for what was right.

Pierce's trademarks were his glasses resting on his forehead and the mobile phone he carried with him at all times. If the door was locked at the ice cream parlor in Memphis, and if there were police inside eating ice cream and flirting with the ice cream maids, Pierce would whip out his trusty mobile phone and call the president of the company, rouse him from a deep sleep and ask him if he were aware he had a store in Memphis refusing to let a customer come in.

Pierce was a master of obtaining what he had been told would be his at a motel or hotel upon check-in. If the arrangements were less than he had been led to believe, out would come the mobile telephone. To the disconcernment of the front desk clerk, Pierce would whistle the exact frequency triggering the mobile phone operator, a work of art I've never seen duplicated.

"Hello. This the President of Holiday Inn? Possibly you are not aware of a very unfortunate situation we seem to be having at one of your locations...yes indeed...you wish to speak to the clerk? by all means..." (handing over the phone to the distraught clerk)..."Your president wishes to speak with you."

On one occasion, on a Delta flight from Atlanta to Knoxville, (or was it Chattanooga?) Pierce became embroiled in an argument with two flight attendants, one pilot and one gatehouse supervisor after being told there was no seat for him in the first-class section, one of the stipulations in the cameraman's union. After receiving no satisfaction from the stewardess or the gate agent, Pierce was on the mobile phone with the Director of Public Relations for Delta Airlines. By this time, one of the cockpit crew members had insisted that Pierce stand outside the plane in order to make the phone call. They said the radio activity would be a security problem. The flight was delayed about 30 minutes while Pierce was being accommodated and by the time we arrived in Tennessee the pilot was beside himself. He asked me who Pierce thought he was. Lamely I replied, well, sir, he's a very good cameraman, and he's under a lot of pressure. To which the captain responded, well, I have to fly this plane and see that it arrives safely, and I'm under a lot of pressure too. The next time something like this happens, I'll throw the whole bunch of you off MY airplane."

Anticipating the pilot was going to file a report with his office, I called Brian Ellis, the CBS Southeast Bureau chief in Atlanta and told him what had happened. He in turn called New York. Pierce, his confrontational tactics and the maddening mobile telephone had finally succeeded in hitting a fan that would not turn off. It was one of the few times I ever saw Pierce lose. He was suspended. He was mortified. And he blamed me for not only not standing up for him but for turning him in as well. He spent his suspension time trying to prove that Delta flights always left 30 minutes late from the Atlanta Airport. While I knew I never had Pierce's courage or his determination or his total commitment to professional newsgathering, there was a limit to how much others could take of his prescriptions for what ailed the world. Like many network news cameramen, Pierce was an enigma, a collage of inconsistencies: petty yet professional; lovable, yet as venomous as a jug full of cobras as occasions seemed to demand; courageous as any junkyard dog and filled with raw energy. It was all those colliding characteristics that combined caused Pierce to be the only cameraman to record for history the shooting of Governor Wallace in May of 1972.

On another occasion in North Carolina, Pierce poured the yellow of his egg into the ashtray at our breakfast table.

"Why did you do that, Pierce?" I asked.

"Because I'll do everything I can think of to discourage people from smoking."

"Mr. Pierce," the front desk clerk would try to explain, "It is past check-out time, and we're going to have to charge you for another day."

"If you insist on charging me for another day," Pierce would reply, "I'm going to call 'my room' at 3 o'clock in the morning, and if there's anybody in there, I'm going to be sure you refund my money."

"Mr. Pierce, you can't just return this new car you bought 15 minutes ago."

"I don't like the way this car drives. I want my old car back."

"Now, Mr. Pierce, you know we can't do that."

"You'll be hearing from my lawyer. In the meantime, THIS car is yours."

"No, it's not."

"Yes, it is."

"No, it's not."

"Mr. Pierce, we're not going to give you the keys to your old car because it doesn't belong to you any more."

"Then keep them both, suh, I do not want your car."

"Sir, you owe tax on this bottle of brandy you're bringing from Mexico into Texas."

"I do not owe it, and I will not pay it."

"Then we must confiscate this brandy."

"Get your supervisor in here. This is a constitutional question."

"What do you mean you're not going to pay to enter the Massachusetts Turnpike?"

"I'm a resident of Alabama. You have no right to make this assessment."

"C'mon, Pierce, it's late—let's pay the man like everybcdy else."

"You can pay him. I'm not going to pay him."

"Now Mr. Pierce you cannot come down this hallway, this is as far as you go."

"Now, you look here, suh, just because you're the Secret Service, doesn't mean I can't do a simple thing like walk over there and pick up those bags."

"Mr. Pierce, you're no different from anybody else."

"I'm GOING to pick up those bags."

"It's too dark in this restaurant."

"Excuse me?"

"I said, it's too dark in here. Turn up the lights."

"Pierce, what's all this talk about the Governor's plane leaking oil?"

"It leaks oil. I would think the pilot would care about that."

"It's more of the same old negative reporting."

"If the plane doesn't leak oil, it doesn't leak oil. If it does leak oil, it does leak oil."

Working with Laurens Pierce was a tuition-free, all expenses paid liberal arts education.

When Arthur Bremmer's arm came through the crowd and fired five shots at Governor George Wallace, Pierce was the only photographer to capture it all.

For that, he won an Emmy. He should have had a roomful.

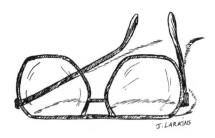

J. LARKINS

BREAKING CAMP

There they are: the faces of Arnie, Melba, Marilyn, Patrick, Martha, Carlos, Tommy, Ken, Jack, Kathy, Jim, Julie and David in front of a white board fence on the edge of Dallas, the faces of the Southwest Bureau of CBS News. The framed picture hangs above a bookshelf between the two windows overlooking the Kentucky hills, where the sun sets and the moon and the evening star shine.

The words above the faces, "Happy Trails, David...May 18, 1985," written against the huge Texas expanse, appear as skywriting against a backdrop of fundamental change—the beginning of the end of the glory years at the Tiffany Network.

It had nothing so much to do with the departure of David, but quite a lot to do with the advent of the bean counters, the corporate number crunchers on patrol duty at the beginning of the decade, prowling through the dark corners of hotel coffee shops in San Salvador, Managua and Guatemala City. They searched for dollars misspent against a landscape of human tragedy. They were the bottom liners, representing the corporate marketeers who a century before would have been well pleased with profits generated from banana republics and benign dictatorships. They would have relished the concept of law and order with patriotic fervor. Before mid-20th century, the Andrews Sisters would reap profits from "Managua, Nicaragua is a Wonderful Town," "Drinking Rum and Coca-Cola," and "Working for the Yanqui Dollaaaaaar."

In the late 1970s and the early 1980s, the bean counters, panting for more profits or at least bottom line respectability, and the newsgatherers, faulted for paying combat drivers too much, met on uneven playing fields. The bean counters could pull the plug, and did. The newsgatherers would put their lives on the line day after day in Leon, Masaya, Esteli and Matagalpa, places where most bean counters seldom ventured. If they did, they'd probably pay almost any price to get the hell out. Yet, they questioned why the company's representatives were in these hellholes, spending the shareholders' money like drunken sailors. Every morning of the civil wars in Nicaragua and El Salvador, the newsgatherers would go out to bring back the news, never asking or caring whether it would mean increased or decreased corporate dividends. Some, like ABC's Bill Stewart, didn't come back. He was assassinated. Bill is buried in Ashland in eastern Kentucky.

Looking at the faces on the wall: there's Arnie, the genius of electronic newsgathering devices; Melba, who started her career as bureau den mother when Dan Rather was still a local boy in Texas— she's no longer bridging the gap between the newsgatherers and the bean counters...Melba, one of the sweetest women who ever lived, is answering telephones in Heaven, still wiring money by Wu-Wu (Western Union); Marilyn, who once reminded a colleague, a future college professor, who sought to correct her usage of English, "I don't *want* to talk like a white man." She was the electronic editor, who regularly saved newsgatherers' and anchor people's hind ends by working under the most extreme pressure imaginable to put their pieces together and feed the polished finished product to the satellite. To the counters of beans, she was just another member of the union to bargain over at contract time.

Patrick was the cameraman, who would get you the shot you needed when you needed it; Martha went on from Dallas to report the bloodshed in South Africa, Austria and Iraq; Carlos lost out in the counting of beans, and wound up back in the minors.

Jack, who could mystify the best of the bean counters, is out there somewhere in the land of the consultants; Tommy could be down in Houston stringing lights for fancy outdoor birthday parties; Ken is probably some cameraman's right-hand man in Dallas-Fort Worth; Kathy was last heard from producing for the CBS Evening News in New York; Julie doubtless went on being pretty; and Jim, the "Known Liberal," is probably on a ranch somewhere in the west, driving his pickup truck into another sunset, while sipping a cool one.

Where have all the bean counters gone? Gone to numbers, every one. True, the financial wizards get a bum rap from the idiots who have no appreciation for two plus two always equals four. But, possibly a greater truth: whenever it comes down to bean counting as an end in itself, for some of us old die-hards it's time to break camp and head home to Plum Lick where people grow beans and don't waste time counting them.

SADIE

Let me tell you about Sadie King. She knows her beans.

I drove out the Fogg Pike in Montgomery County to see if Sadie could teach me a thing or two about growing. Since Sadie has been gardening for the past 43 straight years, I figured she might know a little something about it. I found out she knows acres about a lot of things. So, I listened.

"Find yourself a chair, I'm puttin' on some bread, and I've got to watch it."

I sat there in the back yard and looked at the bowl of green beans and the firm tomatoes sitting on the table, and then I looked out across Sadie's garden and hated myself for being so lazy. Sixty-six-year-old Sadie King came bounding out of the kitchen, and informed me this was going to be a "short visit." But as soon as she sat down in front of the bowl of beans, which she called "white half runners" I figured she was really in a mood to talk.

"All I do is try to get the garden turned in fall, and disk it all to pieces."

"I hear fall gardens are sometimes better than spring gardens," I ventured cautiously. Sadie shook her head politely but there was no mistaking, anybody who thought fall gardens in this part of Kentucky was a good idea still had something to learn about frost times and signs of the moon.

"Can't fall garden here. Can't predict frost. Used to be the crickets hollered and then you had six weeks before the first frost. Now the crickets holler year 'round. Don't plant past the last of July. Might harvest, might not."

"What's your favorite vegetable to grow?" I said, seeking safer ground.

"Beans."

"How many different kinds of beans do you grow?"

"White fall beans, striped fall beans, white half runners, greasy grits, red bunch beans and john beans—don't ask me why they call 'em john beans."

"Why do they call them white half runners?" I knew I shouldn't have asked the question no sooner than the words went floating across the table.

"I don't know, they just call 'em white half runners."

I resisted the temptation to ask about greasy grits. "How do you cook beans?" I asked, sagely, as if I knew how to cook anything.

"Medium on your electric stove. Cover with water. Boil down dry. Don't pour off water because the beans'll be mush if you do. I use pure lard."

"Do you put meat in with your beans?"

"Sometimes."

"I save all my seeds," said Sadie as she, barefooted, led me out to the garden to show me how she didn't bother to pole her beans. She plants corn and beans at the same time and lets the beans use the corn for poles. Ingenious. Practical. Waste nothing, want nothing.

When Sadie King came to Montgomery County from Knott County, she brought her bean seeds with her. I bit my tongue to keep from asking her if anybody had ever called her Sadie and the Beanstalk. Sadie grew up near Kite, which is close by Wayland in Knott County. Her mother lived to be 83 and her father lived to be 94. "I was raised by an old-fashioned mother and daddy. They could tell time by the sun."

The little girl who grew up to become Sadie King inherited her parents' reliance on the signs of the moon.

"Plant on dark nights—no potatoes."

"How do you think the moon makes that happen?"

"I don't know. It's an old rule you follow, passed along from generation to generation. It's all people had to go by."

Sadie goes down to Monarch Milling Company in Mt. Sterling every year to pick up her calendar, which lists all the planting days according to the signs of the moon.

"Plant when the sign's in the bowels—you get nothing. Plant when the sign's in the heart—nothing. The twin signs are the real time—that's the arms."

There's something else you ought to know about Sadie. She doesn't go to the County Fair. That would be like carrying beans to Boston. You might say, she is the County Fair and has been for nearly half a century. She's her own blue ribbon, if you know what I mean. Sadie was raised in the Old Regular Baptist Church back in Knott County, but she believes there are "good people in all churches." The gospel according to Sadie is, "Live for the Lord, serve him in your own house rather than a big church."

Serious gardening has a way of hooking you up rather directly with the powers of creation, meaning no particular offense to assorted intermediaries. As for ministers returning from the dead, Sadie says, "The Lord don't work like that." Of course, that's one gardener's opinion, and I'm pretty well persuaded she not only is entitled to it but probably is right to boot. Likewise, Sadie doesn't have a heap of faith in doctors. "I don't believe in going to the doctor for every little thing. I don't go to the doctor 'less I have to."

Since it's the nature of gardeners to move on from tomatoes and potatoes to consider the universe, Sadie and I fell to talking about raising children and the present generation taken as a whole.

"What would you have done if your child had sassed you?"

"I would have slapped him clean across the room."

Sadie spent three years in the 8th grade, and never went any farther. Her parents would not allow her to go live at Alice Lloyd or the Hindman Settlement schools in Knott County, which she said she would have had to do in order to go to high school. Nevertheless, she managed to send her three children to college.

"How?"

"Scholarships."

Of course, you have to talk with Sadie for a while to understand how frugal she's been all her life. She hardly ever goes to a store to buy anything. Buying fruits, vegetables and meat in a store would be for Sadie like trying to buy fresh air. You don't need a college education to understand that.

Sadie King had given me during our visit a lot more learning than I had a right to expect. Unfortunately, teachers such as Sadie are not as easy to find as they once were. As I walked away, I heard her saying, "If you get lonesome call me—I can talk country all day."

"MR. BILL"

Mr. Bill is gone.

The Kentucky he left behind will endure. An octogenarian, whose vitality and boyishness shone like a determined light, Mr. Bill passed away last Friday night. I felt his unmistakable air and manner when the sun rose again on a June morning in 1987 on Plum Lick.

William H. Rogers was my stepfather during my formative years from the age of 4 to 14. My mother, Lucile, was his second wife. They met and married after their first spouses had died in their youths. Wonderful as those days were for me at Mt. Auburn in Bourbon County the friendship we shared after I became a man was like a sprig of mint in our silver julep cups.

I seldom pass a mint bed along Plum Lick Creek that I don't remember a strong Kentuckian, a steadfast Bourbon Countian for whom life was always brisk and challenging. Bourbon whiskey is like that too, but the touch of mint provides its distinctive flavor. "Mr. Bill," which is what I always called him and would never think of calling him anything else, was no more perfect than I or anybody else is perfect. There were those who did not like him just as there are those who don't like me. It's impossible to be liked by everybody just as it's impossible to please everybody.

"Son," said Mr. Bill one day, "Get an education because that's the one thing nobody can take away from you." That single remark was probably the most important thing the man ever said to me. He would die, but those words would live and because he said what he did I would go to college with my mother's added encouragement, a little piece of my real father's insurance policy and, later, the G.I. bill. I would earn degrees in the humanities. I would become a correspondent for CBS News, and, in the latter years of my life become a college professor, but mainly I'd become a shepherd on Plum Lick. Lalie and I would have a house full of books. We would read aloud to each other. The quality of our lives would become the fruit of the learning planted by "Mr. Bill" at his farm about five miles as the crow flies from Plum Lick.

Mt. Auburn has looked out over a knoll to the west of Brush Creek since before the Civil War. To that little ribbon of water I used to run as a boy to play along the miniature banks. I'd pretend it was a mighty fine river, and with small pieces of wood I'd run my own steamboat races. I was the starter, I was the crowd cheering along the way and I was the judge at the finish line, which I called "Victory Island." I was Huck Finn one day and Tom Sawyer the next.

Through all the past 200 years, back into the preceding millenniums, the water of Brush Creek, on one side of the ridge dividing the Inner Bluegrass from the Outer Bluegrass, and on the other side the water of Plum Lick Creek have met in the south fork of the Licking River. From there they've rolled on together to the Ohio, the Mississippi and the Gulf of Mexico.

Mr. Bill had a favorite walking horse, a fine bay mare with a splendid blaze on her forehead. Early one summer morning a storm moved across Mt. Auburn. I happened to be lying in bed, looking out the upstairs window of the huge old house, when a bolt of lightning struck a tree on the nearby southern hill, a powerful flash as real in my memory today as it was four decades before. I remember hoping there'd been nothing taking shelter beneath the tree. But in a little while I learned Mr. Bill's bay mare had been standing there. He accepted the loss quietly as a man of iron on the outside, a softer man of deep hurt inside.

There were other more common horses and mules living and working at Mt. Auburn. I put distance between myself and two of the tall, long-faced mules, because when they laid their ears back you could feel a vicious kick coming. The air would whistle with it. My own favorite work mares were Bird and Belle, who pulled the wagon when we harvested corn. Being a little boy of not much physical consequence, there was only so much important work I could do on the farm: use the team to pull the drag over harrowed ground; spread fertilizer; drive the sled when the ground was too muddy or mushy for wagon wheels; round up sheep to be sorted, dipped, clipped and castrated. Bird and Belle were always patient with me when I struggled to put the harness on them. They pretty much tolerated me all the way to the fields, especially the cornfield and back and forth to the silo. They never tried to run away with me when it was time to head back to the barn at the end of the day. I never mistreated Bird or Belle and they seemed to enjoy such light hands on their reins.

I was 4-years-old with memory hardly started when Mr. Bill and my mother, Lucile, were confronting the tragedies of their first marriages, getting married again, and after 10 years, separating and divorcing. For young children in families about to be divided, life is difficult to understand. Perhaps the children born of my first marriage—Sam, Deborah, Catherine and Nell—will one day know the meaning of the fixed foot on Plum Lick, the quality of life shared with my second wife, Lalie, and the love that includes respect and admiration for their mother, Rose, my first wife. Not until I had clearly identified my sense of place—Plum Lick—could I grow with better grace and total commitment to all things springing from the good earth.

Lucile is gone now, a beautiful, impressionable, passionate, sensitive girl, having both Neal and Crouch in her genes. She looks down on me from the portrait above our bedroom fireplace on Plum Lick, and I can still hear her favorite words of encouragement to me: "Your time's coming." But, she'd also add with consummate Crouch clarity, "You'll never live down there," reflecting her desire to escape Plum Lick, where she was born in harder times at the beginning of the 20th century.

The last time I saw Mother, moments after she'd died in the Bourbon County Hospital, I kissed her on the forehead. There was a peaceful expression on her face that I had never seen before. The last time I saw Mr. Bill, I helped him from his car and walked with him to his house in Paris. The deaths, separated by years, were joined in my adult mind as symbols of the passing of parents. Forever after I would bear entire individual responsibility for myself.

For nearly four decades, Mr. Bill and Martha Lair, his third wife, had been married, and they had raised their own family. Each of us, every one, my stepbrothers, Warren and Billy, my sisters, Jane and Florence, and later Mr. Bill's and Martha's Matt and Dorothy, went out from the big house overlooking Brush Creek, which had sheltered sorrow and happiness and the shaping of children for a century and more. After my first marriage ended in divorce, Lalie and I started our own new family. We came to be senior citizens with Mr. Bill and Martha, our paths crossing and re-crossing from Dallas and New York to Mt. Auburn and Plum Lick from 1978 to 1987, discovering more about ourselves than we ever thought possible.

Early on the morning of Lalie's and my 14th wedding anniversary— April 15, 1992—Martha Lair Rogers died peacefully in her sleep. The family gathered on the eve of Easter in the North Middletown Christian Church, and "Amazing Grace" filled it up.

LOST

On the south side of Lexington in August of 1990, I was, as Mr. Bill would say, a lost ball in the high weeds. Only, there were no high weeds—high trees lined a street of substantial homes where the old guard lived as well as many members of the academic community of the University of Kentucky and Transylvania University.

Some of us country folk down on Plum Lick count the day a total waste if we aren't lost at least once. I stopped to ask for directions from a man near the front brick entrance to a splendid home.

The man did not seem to be happy. Even lost, I was still in a good mood.

"Sir, I'm lost."

The man stared back.

"Sir, I'm looking for the home of a friend, but I'm so completely turned around, I can't seem to find it."

The man did not seem to care one way or the other.

"Do you know where Carriage Street is?" I asked.

"No."

"Well, do you have a telephone book I could possibly use to check

25

and be sure I have the right address?"

The man rose to a standing height of about 5'11", went into the house and returned with the phone book. As I was leafing through the pages of names and addresses, I felt the urge to compliment the neighborhood.

"This is really a very nice street."

"I've lived here 30 years, I don't know anybody, and I don't want to know anybody."

Even lost souls have the breath taken away by such a sad state of affairs. It contrasted right sharply with the community picnic held the day before at Bunker Hill, just up the road from Plum Lick.

Sweetpea Florence was talking about getting his tobacco in; Ray Hedges was proud as could be about his new artificial hip, which had taken care of his arthritis; Darla Carpenter had sold 373-1/2 inches of advertising for *The Bourbon Times*; Paul Lyons was filling up plates with barbecued pork; Betty Sue Florence was gathering bits of comings and goings for her newspaper column; the Billy Dales were encouraging their granddaughter to smile for the camera; Plum mayor Ray was forecasting the first frost; George Arnold was standing as straight as he did when he was a young man; Bill McCarty was fishing out a boiled potato from an iron kettle; Bill Gilvin was tuning his fiddle; Lucille Hedges said, "Why, you walked right past me without saying anything;" Elaine Hinkle was seated quietly near the Jones' open barn door; Rose Jones was commenting on the offer to sell Bunker Hill Grocery; Roger Wilson was standing not saying very much on the edge of a group of farmers; a volleyball game was in progress; youngsters were kicking a soccer ball up and down the side of the hill by the tobacco patch; small children were competing to see who could lead the walking infant on her early steps.

The music carried from the top of Bunker Hill down the way to Plum Lick, and everybody was pleased in a community that knows who its neighbors are, and wants to keep it that way.

"MISS SUDIE"

iss Sudie was waiting. She was seated with her legs extended in front of her. On the wall above her head were the words: "Let us run the race that is before us and never give up."

"I've lost my sitter," Miss Sudie said as she carefully draped a scarf across her legs, finally rebelling after 91 years of use.

"Do you know of anybody who could sit with me?" she said with a mischievous, crinkly turn of mouth.

Her 61-year-old former sixth grader said he'd be on the lookout for somebody, but he felt guilty because he knew his words were more talk than commitment. He didn't even wrestle with the possibility that he might sit with her from time to time to pay her back for all the things she'd taught him in the sixth grade at the North Middletown Consolidated School: where the Rock of Gibraltar is located, why Australia is a continent, what a triangle and a rectangle are, why Joyce Kilmer should have said, "poems are made by *folks* like me instead of *fools* like me," what it's like to build a bird house and how good it feels to know you've weaved a basket.

"I get letters from New York to California. They don't say they learned to read or write, not one. They always remember the birdhouse and the field trips. Basket weaving was doing something they wanted to do. When they saw the finished product, it was good."

Miss Sudie seemed tired of everything except talking about 50 years of teaching—beginning in a one-room schoolhouse on Stoney Point in Bourbon County, the school attended earlier by John Fox, Jr., the author of *The Little Shepherd of Kingdom Come* and *The Trail of the Lonesome Pine*.

Miss Sudie was a youngster of 24 to whom a travelling salesman said one day on the playground at recess, "Lady, can you take me to your teacher?"

"You're looking at her," replied the young lady, the salesman discovering Sudie Boardman could be a Rock of Gibraltar. All funny business would be found out and dealt with quickly—like the 10-year-old boy who chewed tobacco and hid a spitting can beneath his desk. Miss Sudie spotted the dreadful plot and took the little boy to the cloakroom for a switching. The child said, "Miss Sudie, if you won't switch me, I'll give you all the frozen apples I have."

"Did you switch him?"

"No."

"Did he bring you the apples?"

"Yes. They were soft as mush after falling to the ground and freezing."

There were 30 students in eight grades in that one-room schoolhouse, including little first grader Foster McKinney, whom Miss Sudie invited to sit in her lap to keep him from being "stepped on" by  the bigger boys. After two years at Stoney Point, Miss Sudie began her 48-year career at the North Middletown Consolidated School. The sixth grade was her sovereign domain. Students knew better than to try to steal her thunder. It was blue skies when folks behaved, stormy weather when they didn't.

"Jimmy Thomas had worried me all morning. I'd taken it as long as I could. We were in that little building up on the hill, the one they call the chicken coop. It was a hot day. I had Mr. Gentry's paddle hanging on the wall. I took it down and started walking toward Jimmy. He saw me coming, and he jumped out the window. It worried me to death. I thought maybe he'd broken his arms and his legs. I finally got him corralled, and I said, 'Jimmy, why did you jump out that window?'

"He said, 'Miss Sudie, when I saw you coming at me with that paddle, I had to do something!'"

"Allen Gordon's mother came to school and told me 'Allen's afraid of you.' I said, 'Why, we're good friends.' Allen's mother said, 'Whatever you're doing, keep on doing it.'

"One day, I was explaining how the 1812 earthquake changed the course of the Mississippi River and the map of Kentucky. Melvin Stewart put his hand up. I said, 'Yes, Melvin, what is it?' He said, 'Miss Sudie, did it keep you awake?'

28

Miss Sudie's entire body shook with the telling of the earthquake story. Her student of 1942, visiting with her in her nursing home room in 1991, asked her what she thought was the best strategy for teachers in 1992. "Be understanding. Be kind. Be pleasant. Give them a chance to learn on their own. Don't poke the learning down their throats. One time I stood at the door to ask the departing students what they had learned. "What did you learn, Johnny?"

Johnny Claypool said, "I didn't learn nothing."

I said, "Well, we'll see what we can do about that tomorrow."

On the day I stopped by to see her at the nursing home, Miss Sudie told me, one of her hundreds of graduates: "I just wanted to be a good teacher."

Miss Sudie died last year. As the funeral procession was making its way from Paris to the cemetery in North Middletown, at the top of the hill where the Harrod's Creek Road comes in, a yellow school bus came around the curve in the opposite direction. The driver stopped the bus and waited as the small motorcade headed home.

BEER, LIMBURGER CHEESE AND GALLSTONES

From time to time, along come blessings I hadn't counted on. Each of the three times I have accepted invitations to teach non-fiction classes at the Writers' Workshop for People over 57, I've always thought, as I've driven out the tree-lined lane to the Carnahan House, I should have paid them instead of the other way around.

The University of Kentucky's Council on Aging has sponsored this annual event for the past 25 years. For a solid week at the Carnahan Conference Center on Coldstream Farm, students from more than 20 states attend lectures, participate in readings, meet individually with the faculty, improve writing skills and enjoy the good company of old and new friends. The abilities of the students have been underwritten with enthusiasm and commitment. Age is often like that. Especially after 57.

From Lillie, who after six years of grieving now wants to write about her love/hate relationship with her husband lost to cancer and confusion, to Jamie, who has written the history of a small town in Madison County, these determined souls have much to give back to their instructors and their readers.

Seventy three-year-old Ken saved my life. About ten years ago, Ken ran two marathons. He credits his aerobic exercise with overcoming what otherwise would surely have been terminal cancer. It also saved him from a colostomy. When his doctor recommended it, Ken said, no thank you. One conversation with Ken at the Writers Workshop for People over 57 convinced me, two years off from running is unforgivable and quite possibly fatal. Being 50 pounds overweight is likewise no small sack of potatoes to be carrying around, even while lying down, much less walking, or the Lord knows, running. Nutrition, said Ken, goes hand-in-hand with exercise. While most of us were at the daily trough for lunch, Ken was relaxing with a book. Ken is a beautiful writer. He's calm, and he's confident. He has much to say about the possibility of living beyond 100 years. No, not a broken-down-gone-to-hell-in-a-hand-basket 100 years old, but a strong, yet graceful bound-for-glory 100 years old and more. Who is to say we have to hang it up when we're 57, 67, 77, 87, or 97? It was Ken who inspired me to decide to retire from UK in the year 2000, when I would be 70 years old, giving me about 30 years to become a good shepherd on Plum Lick, thanks to Ken.

Then there was Irma from Cincinnati. Oh, that wonderful, always smiling, Irma. How could I bring myself to tell her that I really thought her "information-giving through free verse" most likely would not enjoy an audience any larger than the few who would compliment her because they wouldn't want to hurt her feelings? So, I listened. That's one of the techniques I stressed in my three years of lecturing at the Workshop: the willingness to be a good listener, not to come rushing in on a person or place, unwilling to let the students be their wonderful selves. Irma told me about her gallstones—about her love for Limburger cheese, onions and beer. I encouraged her to write about that as non-fiction prose rather than the information-giving through free verse, which she had hoped might save Indians from ecological disaster and the entire world from nuclear destruction.

"Just give 'em Limburger cheese, onions and beer and write from within your own experiences," I quietly and politely suggested to Irma. Did she ever! When we read it to all the other students, they applauded and Irma stood up and took a bow. Irma smiled in spite of her Parkinson's disease. "I think I better take another pill," she said, when her shaking threatened to run away with her. "See there? I'm not shaking anymore," said Irma, who wanted more than anything in these precious, never to return moments, to write and write and write.

My new friend, Timothy, explained what happens when a cow loses her cud. It's nothing like a human losing a piece of chewing gum. There's a simple, dictionary definition of "cud:" "food brought into the mouth by a ruminating animal from its first stomach to be chewed again." In other words: no cud, no cow.

"There are 72 ruminants in the world," explained Timothy (or, did he say 73?), including the kangaroo. Imagine, Kanga chewing her cud while patting Roo on top of his head. The importance of the cud to the cow is just one of the stray but significant bits of information in Timothy's storehouse of knowledge from which he will draw as he writes his book on the grasslands of Kentucky. From Big Bone Lick in Northern Kentucky to his tree farm in McCreary County near the Tennessee State line, Timothy will trace the evolution of that God-given plant life without which all grazers would be as dead as dinosaurs. Timothy is an agronomist, retired from the University of Kentucky, who at this time in his life wants to stop appealing only to academics, and begin reaching out to you and me about the priceless heritage beneath our feet (where concrete has not yet covered it over).

John is, as they say, a piece of work. He's a gravel-voiced tax attorney from Woodford County and he plays a mean mandolin. He's writing a genealogy of his Scottish forebears. John seems a wee bit fey, but don't be put off by that. He's one of Bobby Burns' men for all seasons, more what you might say, "bluff"—good-natured outspokenness and unconventionality—the sort you'd like to have along on a craggy, cold night, when a portion of cheer might warm your innards. John could strum his mandolin and we'd all be patting our feet, keeping time as if happiness were absolutely meant to be. And after we'd taken our cups of kindness we were in a proper frame of mind for the singing of Auld Lang Syne. Ah, what a fine joy it was in the evenings at Carnahan House.

John is as bluff as Anne is gentle—Anne, who taught my childhood sweetheart, Barbara Insko, in the third grade at the old Paris High School in Bourbon County. At that time I was learning my multiplication tables at the North Middletown School.

"What was she like then, Anne?"

"A sweet child," said Anne. Anne wants to write about her strategy for handling misbehaving children in the classroom. Her technique involves storytelling in which the misbehaver is placed in the role of the childhood villain. "It worked for me," said Anne with a serene look on her face.

Helen's writing about "The Hat" was the turning point in the fortunes of an immigrant family. We'll want to read about it when Helen is published, something she dearly desires.

"Be Still My Heart" was a wondrous piece written by Alma and read aloud to the entire workshop—a conversation about God and the meaning of life, a conversation between a well-meaning husband and his equally earnest wife as they sit by cups of hot tea in the twilight of their years.

Poetry, fiction, non-fiction and children's literature—those were our main roads taken. But as the maze of unmarked, unmapped country roads near Plum Lick, we crossed back and forth, warm in the knowledge that fences may be made to keep cows and their cuds at home, but writers, especially after 57, resist the notion that if it isn't nailed down, roped in or fenced for privacy, it isn't worth foolin' with.

Lillie hurried back to St. Petersburg to learn how to use a word processor for the first time; Henri returned to the desert southwest to rewrite his women-in-prison story; Ken went home to Louisville to run, to eat sensibly and to write professionally; and dear, sweet Irma returned to Cincinnati to prepare for her gallstone operation and the clear as crystal prose she will write about it. I kissed Irma on that last day, and she kissed me back. I said, "You're a wonderful woman, Irma," and she said, "Thank you."

IN A DUSTY LIBRARY

call came from a nice lady who said, "I've had two notices that my subscription to The *Bourbon Times* is running out, and I've about decided not to renew because I'm recovering from eye surgery."

The publisher of a small-town newspaper does not take lightly a problem with a neighbor's eyes or the cancellation of a subscription. I reached for the telephone.

"Hello, Mrs. Shannon?"

"Yes?"

"I was thinking about your eye problem and your conclusion that you might be canceling your subscription, so how about you not worrying about it and let me come over there and read the newspaper to you?"

"Nobody's ever offered to do anything like that."

"Be glad to do it."

I shut down the word processor in my office at UK, went straight to my car and headed for Paris. A reporter for The *Bourbon Times* said it sounded like an important story to him, so he came along to take a picture of a newspaper publisher reading his newspaper to a lady recovering from a cornea transplant.

"Here on the front page we have: a story about a sale on the courthouse steps; Pumpkin Day plans a little uncertain; North Middletown going to have its first community fest; Horseshoe Drive residents hope for better luck curbing drainage; county judge comes with plan to decrease drainage woes."

"I'd like to hear about the Horseshoe Drive residents."

"Many people living along this peaceful, horseshoe-shaped neighborhood have dealt with a persistent water and sewer drainage problem for years."

We moved on to the editorial page and read an angry letter concerning the coverage of a fatal head-on car wreck, followed by the editor's response. The lady nodded but reserved judgement.

"Understand you enjoy the column 'Our Kentucky.' "

"Yes, I do, especially when you write about education. I think you ought to write more about education."

The reporter, who had quietly been taking pictures, packed up his camera and left to make another deadline, leaving the publisher and the lady to savor the end of the day. Her interest in education was becoming clearer. Her late husband for 20 years had taught political science at UK. Jasper Shannon had been Malcolm Jewell's predecessor as head of the department. Dr. Shannon had moved on to the University of Nebraska where he had spent another 15 years.

"We always knew one day we'd come home."

"To Paris?"

"Yes."

We stopped reading the day's newspaper and began strolling through a past including a visiting professorship at Western Kentucky University.

"He didn't think much of retirement," said the lady with the soft eyes and the sweet face. She began to talk about the library upstairs.

"Do you suppose I might see the library before I leave?"

"If you promise not to look at the cobwebs."

"Promise."

As we turned for the stairs, I saw the late Dr. Shannon's picture on top of the piano. I recognized him: robust, eager, inspired. I'd not had a class with him, but now since I was a professor myself, I wish I had. I preceded the lady up the winding staircase. At the top was the library.

Books lined the walls from the floor to the ceiling. They were double-banked on the shelves. The mustiness of the room was more pleasant than the freshly-cleaned Margaret I. King library at the University of Kentucky: volume after volume on the administrations of Eisenhower, Nixon and Johnson and before. The world wars, the Nazi era, the founding of nations and the birth of a commonwealth, all were there.

"On this side of the room is the desk where he worked when he was an academic, and on the other side of the room is the desk where he worked when he was a farmer."

I began to see myself. I began to see the time when others would visit my library after I was gone. I began to see my young wife having a problem with her eyesight. I began hoping if she enjoyed reading and said she was thinking of canceling her subscription, the publisher would drop everything he was doing and drive out at once to Plum Lick to go over the front page news with her, read the editorial page to her, both the favorable and the critical. Most of all, I hoped the publisher would come prepared to talk about education.

SAM CLAY

Sam Clay was a Kentuckian's Kentuckian. He was a tall, kind, sensitive, intelligent 20th century man who lived on Cane Ridge. I'd see him on the edge of his grand and spacious front lawn, and he'd be pruning trees with his chain saw, or he'd be mowing or he might be watching birds.

My first recollection of him goes back to the late 1930's on those cool late summer afternoons when he'd be boarding the George Washington in Winchester. He looked like a Mr. Smith or a young Mr. Lincoln on his way to the nation's capital. But, he was Sam Clay of Bourbon County heading back to Princeton to continue his education in the classics, studies having much to do with validating trees and chainsaws, lawns and mowers, birds and watchers, his studies living proof of the argument for the liberal arts education well pursued. The reporter for *The Bourbon Times*, which Sam helped create, called him the "Renaissance man" at the time of his death. His education had enabled him to become a better farmer, banker (he was Chairman of the Board of Bourbon Agricultural Deposit Bank), singer in the choir of the North Middletown Christian Church, environmentalist and friend to the members of his community in Bourbon and the other 119 counties in the commonwealth.

We watched him board the trains to the East each year, because we were there to say "goodbye" to Billy, then Mr. Bill's youngest son, who'd be on his way back to Philadelphia where he attended a special school for the hearing impaired. We liked the idea that Sam would look out for Billy, and we knew he was not only in good hands, but that Billy and Sam would have fun together.

In the last years of his life, I took Sam Clay down to see our farm on Plum Lick, so much smaller than his, not nearly as richly blessed with financial support as his. You'd have thought our farm was every bit as important as his. When we looked out across the steep hills above Plum Lick Creek, he seemed as excited and pleased as if he were seated at the Keeneland Yearling Sales. He told me once how his father had made a conscious decision early in his life that he would not become involved in the horse industry. It always impressed me that someone as wealthy as Sam Clay would continue his father's tradition of sticking to basic farming: cows and grass and grain, some sheep from time to time.

The North Middletown Christian Church was so full for Sam Clay's memorial service I considered myself lucky to be seated with Lalie in the balcony in the year 1990 when once again we heard our old friend from Cane Ridge described as a "Renaissance man."

That's what Kentucky and the rest of the nation need in the 21st century as much if not more than anything else: more renaissance men and women like Sam Clay.

BUCKEYES AND HILLBILLIES

The drive up to Cincinnati from Lexington is fast. It used to be slow. Back 50 years ago, US 27 near Falmouth had a killer of a hill. Car radiators moaned and groaned with grapes of wrathness. Some boiled over and gave up the ghost. But, now, it's all different. It's very modern. Interstate 75 cuts through the hills of northern Kentucky like a chain saw through warm butter. That's OK. It's hard to argue with this kind of progress, yet sometimes the progress thing has a jarring downside.

As Lalie, Ravy and I were riding up the escalator to the main lobby of the Westin Hotel at the corner of 5th and Vine in Cincinnati to attend the annual Scripps-Howard awards banquet, I tried to tell them we were actually passing through the space that 50 years ago was the RKO Albee Theater. I gave up trying to recapture the memories of Esther Williams swimming through my fantasy world of spectacular movies, Sonja Henie skating in flashing patterns lifting me up from the narrow framework of my rural Kentucky heritage and Bogart, Greenstreet and Cagney keeping me on the edge of my seat in that palace across the street from Fountain Square. Bob Crosby and his Bobcats provided live entertainment on one amazing afternoon between double-bill movies. I was in Heaven. Dear, cantankerous Aunt Florence took me to see Walt Disney's "Fantasia" in that grand theater, and the memory of the experience is still warm in a special and secret part of my heart. It's probably just as well I wasn't around when they brought in the wrecking ball and tore down the Albee.

I would have cried. Now, past 60 years of age, the tears hang on the rim of my telling of this story, the same pain I feel whenever I drift back to warm afternoons at Crosley Field, remembering Wally Post landing a home run on the roof of the laundry across the street, Ewell Blackwell's sweeping side-arm pitches making it seem he was always throwing to third base instead of home plate. They and Frank McCormick, Mike McCormick, Lonnie Frey, Ernie Lombardy and Harry "The Hat" Walker were all my original boys of summer. Maybe, one

37

of these days I'll see a Reds game in Riverfront Stadium. I just haven't been in a big hurry about it.

Whenever I reluctantly fly someplace in these A-CBS (After CBS), shepherding days of my life, I usually stop and marvel at the mosaics moved from the old railroad terminal in Cincinnati to the Greater Cincinnati Airport in northern Kentucky. It brings back the sounds of steam whistles, the smell of swirling soot on steel tracks spanning the Ohio River and the contrasting cultures on each side. After my birth in Good Samaritan Hospital in Cincinnati in 1930, after the death of my father, Samuel I, in 1931, after the return of the family to Kentucky in the depths of the depression—Lucile left a widow before she was 30 years old with three small children, heading back to the Bourbon County where she was born—the occasional trips back to the Queen City to visit with Aunt Florence and grandmother Nellie made me a victim of the taunts: "Hillbilly!"

I hated them for it. I hated the little boy who accosted me in a public park one day, and said, "Give me a lick of your ice cream cone or I'll knock the pee out of you." I hated myself for giving in to him. I hated it whenever fun was made of Kentuckians who had gone north looking for factory work and not finding it, or losing it after a short while, had fallen back to the riverfront on the Cincinnati side where they lived in Hoovervilles. Years later, I would not be pleased with my hero, Louis Bromfield, whenever he spoke unkindly about "southern dirt farmers," which he frequently did.

We used to play a game. Whenever the family piled into the car to drive from our home on the farm in Kentucky to spend a few days with Aunt Florence and our grandmother, "Monnie," on Hollister Street in Cincinnati, there were two main events. One was to stop for a candy bar and a soft drink at the "Halfway House" in Williamstown; the other was to see who would be the first to spot Carew Tower on the Cincinnati skyline.

On the March, 1991 trip to Cincinnati, the child in the car didn't play the game. The chain saws had opened up the warm butter of the northern Kentucky hills, and the suspense was no longer possible. Carew Tower and all the skyline of the Queen City burst into view without surprise.

GEESE

T he trip not taken is sometimes the best. I had thought I would be in New York City this week, because there'd been an invitation to attend a seminar on new communications technology. A lapse in human communications resulted in postponement, and for that I am profoundly grateful, because otherwise I would have missed standing with Lalie watching 40 geese fly over Plum Lick. I would have missed the awesome sound of the honking as the southbound October travelers realigned their formation, fine tuning the "V" as expertly as magna cum laude graduates from air controllers' school.

We watched the geese come up over Bunker Hill, arch high over Plum Lick Creek and drop over the horizon like softly falling thistledown. Then they were gone. But, we were not left lonely. We turned our attention to the pig lot, watching Blue trying to communicate with one of the hogs by biting him on the snout. Three cheers for swine stoicism, which pays Blue Heelers no never-mind.

Lalie and I, who have invested so much of our time traveling from one end of the country to the other, from one end of the Western hemisphere to the other, putting our lives in the hands of over-worked air controllers and over-wrought, wildly honking cab drivers, walked hand-in-hand the short distance from the hog lot to the sheep shed, where we stood wordlessly, allowing our thoughts to wander in silence as the sheep moved peacefully back and forth in the little lot behind the garden. On our return to the house I picked up an armload of firewood, while Lalie gathered in some kindling. We walked up the knoll together and placed the wood in the hamper by the side door. It would be there for a cold night not yet upon us. If we had been geese we would not have been bothering with firewood, of course.

We would have been up there in formation, moving on unassisted to the warmer parts of the hemisphere. We would have been looking down on earthbound mortals—honking, but not at poor souls trying to cross 5th Avenue in New York City, or Plum Lick Road in Kentucky. Our honking would only be enough to encourage smooth, orderly flight patterns, no mindless, idiotic honking for the sake of honking. We wouldn't need sophisticated technological communications systems. We'd be relying on our most basic and time-proven instincts. For one thing, we'd be tasting the air, feeling it rush along our exquisitely feathered undersides, fueling our internal homing systems with full freedom to take us where our most serious compulsion was directing us. Sometimes it seems to me, when I look skyward from the valley of Plum Lick, there's a supercharged, computer-driven, satellite-connected, network-contrived, stereophonically-encased artificiality, which has all but replaced a good many simple pleasures of life still there for the sharing if only we'd slow down and be ready for them.

Wendell Berry's essays are fundamental reading for all those concerned about population shifts from rural underpinnings to urban superficialities. Yet, it was fate more than it was Berryian commitment and courage that postponed the trip to New York City; it was our true selves discovered that accepted it with good grace and gave us unexpected extra time to listen and respond to our own more primitive, yet reliable and noble communications systems. This may be a poor, even unacceptable substitute for telecommunications mavens, who've grown more accustomed to the cutting edge of technology on the magical brink of the 21st century, but for us on Plum Lick it quite exceeded an even exchange.

It was the joy of hearing geese honking instead of short-tempered, neurotic cab drivers transporting their desperate, nerve-frayed passengers.

It was deeply-felt admiration for creatures so skilled in navigation, so strong-willed and determined to set the right course, and then to stay with it serenely. We hoped the hunters would be few, the hunted triumphant. It was the fun of watching the puzzled look on a dog's face when upon biting into a hog's snout, the result was about the same as if it had been a stone wall. The hog's communications skills clearly left the hound undone. It was the peace and quiet experienced while watching a small flock of sheep searching for just one more sprig of dried grass during a season of drought. It was the satisfaction of gathering firewood for the hearth, where words are spoken simply and only as needed. It was the warmth of sitting quietly together before the flames of Water Maple, Locust and Wild Cherry.

JONQUILS

L alie asked me to go looking for Jonquils here on the farm because we don't have as many as we'd like around the house. Something told me not to take a shovel or be in a hurry about these Jonquils. It was something other than just plain laziness—taking Jonquils from one place and putting them in some other place presented itself quietly as a matter of no small ethical consideration.

There weren't any sirens going around the corners of my conscience, or bells ringing loudly somewhere deep in my subconsciousness. Yet, I instinctively knew it's one thing to pluck a single Jonquil, raise it to your face softly to enjoy the subtle fragrance, then to walk slowly away with the watery-green stem turned tenderly by your fingers, perhaps to be taken home to your loved one so as to say with a warm smile, "Brought you something." It's quite another thing to spade up Jonquils wholesale from their freedom to be sentenced to live in slavery for the rest of their lives. It would be about the same thing if one were to cage the first several robins of spring as it would be to go out to harvest Jonquils, at least that's the way I feel about it. Robins and Jonquils are two of the sweetnesses of life in Kentucky, gentle harbingers of the birth of the season of promise. Something told me on this day in early Spring just to go and be on the lookout for Jonquils—yellow bells, we used to call them when we were children. Oh, we used to delight in discovering a whole field full of yellow bells, didn't you?

And wasn't it fun to lie among the tall stems and look straight up at the blue sky over Plum Lick, your Plum Lick? The earth was just beginning to warm up enough to entice us to lie on our backs and feel the earth beneath us, holding us in the palm of its dependable hand as it whirled through the vastness of the universe. And when we looked in the other direction toward the heaven within the Jonquil itself, past the delicate fabric of the six yellow-white petals, past the deeper yellowed cup containing the six sentries flanking the inner-most reproductive organs—then we knew the private joy of intimate discovery.

On this particular day on Plum Lick I found more than I had ever expected I would. Perhaps, it came as a result of a certain measure of maturity, something born of experiencing much joy and sorrow. Wayne, the farm manager, and I were moving cows over to the Old Jim Crouch Place. When we passed the big abandoned well, covered with a huge tree trunk to keep children and other varmints from falling into it, I noticed off to the side, a large, nearly geometric design of Jonquils. Perhaps, I said to myself, they are watchmen, protectors in uniforms of yellow, but not nearly so much standing guard as serving as reminders of what had once stood in the center of their configuration. There had been a home here, once—a tenant house, not unlike the one Wayne and his family lived in. In fact, parts of the former house had been used to build the new tenant house closer to Plum Lick Road. Now the former house was all gone—except for the Jonquils. I dared to step inside to the center. The flowers did not protest. It is not their nature to fight. Their strength lies in their beauty and their roots. Of course, an invading army of tractors and plows could destroy them. But, there'd always be just enough left over to assure that the yellow bells would in time reclaim their rightful places.

Though every trace of the old house had disappeared, I stepped upon the front porch and went through the doorway without first knocking. I didn't think anyone would mind. I stayed a while in the living room and looked to the east toward Plum Lick Creek. What a fine place to have watched the sunrises of all the seasons of a lifetime. I stayed only a little while in the bedroom, because it didn't seem proper to linger there where there'd been so much love and birthing and dying.

Probably by now the north window would have been left open at midday to allow the breezes to enter from beneath the Water Maples. The Water Maples are still there, growing old gracefully and proudly, not having been raped with chain saws all in the name of no falling limbs and whatever other reason is given for this kind of butchery.

I stepped into the kitchen and wondered about the smells that must have issued from it: fried mush cooking; old ham and red-eye gravy; hot biscuits and honey; the full aroma of coffee. I stepped back outside. I said to myself, this would be a day no Jonquils would be picked—not even one.

"WHO'S ALL GONE?"

T he crumbling house sitting downstream from the Isaac Shelby Crouch house, around the bend in the creek, seemed in even greater disrepair when the sixth and seventh generations stopped by on an afternoon. "This is where your great-great-great-great-grandfather and your great-great-great-great-grandmother lived."

"Maybe a stranger lives here now," said Ravy when she was five.

"Well, nobody lives here anymore," said her father as they walked up the hand-hewn stone steps of the late 18th century house, where Joshua, the patriarch, established his homestead, when Kentucky was very young: the doors locked now; the metal fasteners, rusted; the wood on the front porch crumbling; the windows, broken.

> "All the countryside is marked
> With broken stonewall fences;
> The gayly swinging garden gate
> Has fallen headfirst down."

The lines had been written by me nearly 50 years before when I was a student at the University of Kentucky, the land grant college in Lexington. Even then, I was pessimistic about urban sprawl and rural decay.

"They're all gone," said Ravy, wise before her time.

"Who's all gone?" tested her father to be sure he understood the child's emerging reasoning.

"My grandfather and grandmother," said Ravy as if fathoming the generational connections more clearly than her father. Had Joshua and his Polly Sr. heard? Had their grandchild, Cynthia, awakened for one brief moment as the sixth and seventh generations walked hand-in-hand around the outside of the bedroom fireplace? There were no sounds other than the sharp, clear conversations of the early spring-time birds in the giant Water Maples in the front yard. Only that, and the distant purr of Wayne's tractor as he worked the corn ground in the adjacent bottom land along Plum Lick Creek just before it spills into Boone.

How many times this fertile soil has been plowed there is no counting, but it's now past 200 years since Joshua came here from Delaware and paid with British crowns to purchase the land in the valley of the Plums. Wayne, the new young man on the iron horse, amused himself by keeping close watch for Indian flintstones to add to his collection. He climbed down from the tractor to let it idle a while, to cool off from the long pulls up and down the bottom land.

He lit a cigarette, and joined Ravy and me for a drive to the top of the ridge stretching westward from the old house. Up there, the air was cool from the recent cold snap, the land seeming to be resting a while from its sudden springtime bursts of energy. From the highest elevation the sixth and seventh generations could draw unto themselves a part of themselves, the view stretching from the Plum crossroads back up Plum Lick Creek, winding its way along limestone embankments through Joshua Meadows, as it has done for thousands of years, tens and hundreds of thousands of years.

We three—Wayne, Ravy and I—spoke little up on the ridge. We returned to our work of the day, Wayne to continue the plowing of the bottom land, me to write *The View from Plum Lick*, while Ravy slept downstairs in her great-grandparents' bed in the house around the bend in the creek.

BILLY'S COW

I was considerably relieved after watching Billy Dale's cow die, to see on the late news I'd been passed over as the one to lead the reform of Kentucky's school system. The death of a neighbor's cow and the subject of education are linked. The inability to understand the one leads to confused thinking about the other. If I had been named for the awesome responsibility of education reform task force coordinator, I probably would have aggravated those who fail to see the necessity of individual imperatives and aspirations. I'm talking about the tendency to try to average out everything. The noble quest for equality eventually damages the quality of education. Equality of opportunity is praiseworthy, but it as everything else has its downside. If all you do is take the brilliant and mix it with the dull, what you inevitably have is mediocrity, an idea I acquired from UK Chancellor, Robert Hemenway.

Billy's cow was not mediocre. She was a beautiful red with a large white band around her shoulders. Billy and his wife had raised her, and she'd become a pet. Late one recent afternoon, they'd gone out to check the herd, and that's when they made the discovery. The cow was quietly choking on an apple.

Dr. Roland Ratliff was called from Mt. Sterling. "I said to myself on the way down here, this is either going to be the easiest call, or the hardest one." He pitched in and helped move the whole herd from the pasture behind our house to the barnlot, and from there into the holding pens. The cow with the apple stuck deep in her throat was not yet in the distress that was to follow when the air passage would become tightened by the swelling. We put her into the headgate and secured her there. Dr. Ratliff inserted a length of pipe into the cow's mouth to hold it open, and through the pipe he manipulated a smaller tubing with which he tried to dislodge the apple.

It wouldn't budge.

"I'll have to operate."

"Maybe it would be better to let her go, Doc."

"She has no chance that way. By operating you have some chance."

J. LARKINS

"You do what you think is best."

Dr. Ratliff took off his shirt, put a pinch of tobacco into his mouth and went to work. Mrs. Dale went up to our house to seek a bit of relief from the anguish. Billy and I stayed to help in any way we could. The operation was a marvel of human ingenuity, years of experience and a sound veterinarian education. Trying to find one small apple inside one large cow, in an area as murky and dense as a swamp is a job to be wished on no one. Dr. Ratliff located the apple, but still he could not move it.

It was near the cow's heart. The doctor sewed up the incision in the cow's side, and tried one more time to force the apple loose by working from her mouth. Time was running out. The cow was breathing hard. Dr. Ratliff had his arm up to his shoulder in the cow's mouth and throat. Several times he yelled with pain when the desperate animal clamped her mouth shut, as she too was in pain.

"I can't get my arm out!"

Billy pulled harder on the cow's tongue, and she finally turned loose of Dr. Ratliff. He walked around, rubbing his numb arm now drained of all strength. He had done everything he possibly could. We watched as Billy's pet cow breathed her last. A hush fell with the coming of night. Dr. Ratliff gathered up his instruments. The Dales went to their house, and we to ours. It was not a good time for talking.

That's why when I heard on the late news that I'd not be heading up the reform of the Kentucky school system, I was appeased. I needed to put some distance between the death of Billy's cow and the inevitable squabbling about improving something which should have been done years ago. Almost everything seemed petty when compared to the loss of one fine member of the natural order.

I'll say this: what we need in our schools is the concern I saw in Billy's eyes as his pet cow closed hers; what we need in our schools is the determination I saw in Dr. Ratliff's face as he probed for one small apple lost along a dark, unfathomable bovine passageway; what we need in our schools is the love and the patience I felt as I watched Billy's wife climb into their pickup truck and head down the Plum Lick Road; what we need in our schools is a renewed commitment to caring in all we say and do.

"THANK YOU VERY MUCH, DOCTOR."

Thoughts had turned to thistles. Arriving at the main gate, there they were again, green spikes annually threatening to take over the pastures of the farm.

"I'll be back with my grubbing hoe, you sons of guns, just as soon as I change my professor's clothes for my peasant's rags.

Inside the house, clothes flew in all directions. In less than a minute

I was out the back door and headed for the machine shed, where I'd left my favorite grubbing hoe on the bed of the 1962 Chevrolet farm truck. The first interruption in the best laid plans to eradicate thistles was the good news: the Super C tractor had come home again from the hospital in Mt. Sterling, the plows could once again take their rightful place, and when the ground was dry the former CBS News correspondent would be threading the needle of the rows of corn and tobacco.

"Billy called," came the voice of Lalie from the house.

"You've got a cow trying to have a calf. He's been trying to get the cow in all day. Couldn't do it. He's on his way down here."

I climbed on the Super C and moved it into the machine shed, took a fond look at the grubbing hoe, and said to thistles wherever they might be: "Only thing that's saving you right now is a cow trying to have a calf."

Old Blue, the pickup truck, responded to the call of the ignition. We drove down the lane to open the gates and waited for Billy to arrive. He had his wife, Eleanor, with him. Maybe three of us could get up the cow.

"Where is she?"

"She's way over by the Crouch place."

Two pickup trucks forded Plum Lick Creek, and we drove to the back part of the farm. There she was, tail up, straining, frustrated with a day of lying down, getting up, lying down, getting up, moving in a tight circle of mashed-down grass. She responded to the three of us walking her toward the barn. Two times, she balked at crossing the creek, and we sloshed back and forth more like trout fishermen than cattle trail bosses. "The calf's probably dead," said Billy.

"Yes, But, maybe not."

On the third pass, the sleek, black, purebred Brangus cow, five years old by the number branded on her hip, submitted and headed up the lane. We moved her into the large holding pen, then the smaller one and finally through the chute to the headgate, where she was restrained. Billy tried to pull the calf, but all he could purchase were two feet, enough to tell that the sire had been the Limousin bull, judging by the red color. Billy looped twine around the feet, and used the come-along, but it wouldn't work.

"I believe it's a breach, " said Billy.

47

We loosened the twine and called the vet. Dr. Russell Skinner was at home in Mt. Sterling, but agreed to come right away. We positioned Old Blue, so the headlights would be of a help for by then darkness had closed in. We waited. We talked about the rain. We talked about the remote possibility that the calf might still be alive. We talked about the cow that had died because she'd choked on an apple. As soon as Dr. Skinner arrived, he went straight to work. First he determined it was not a breach.

"Is the calf dead?"

"Yes."

The calf's head had been turned down and back. That had been the trouble. Dr. Skinner kept working to save the cow. The doctor and Billy manipulated the professional calf-puller and finally removed the long, red, lifeless form. Dr. Skinner administered antibiotics to the cow and made her stand on her feet again. We released her from the headgate and turned her into the barn lot.

"Walking will be the best thing for her," said the doctor as he packed up his equipment and medicine.

"Thank you very much, Doctor, for coming out from home."

"You're welcome."

Lalie and I sat on the front porch for a little while before going to bed. The night closed in tighter. It was quiet for miles around.

SACRED COWS

Wayne and I stood in the driveway of the farm manager's house. We spat into the dust as if that would do any good. The main subject of our conversation was the cows. Even one of the golden retrievers killing a lamb and bringing what was left of it to the house as if to win a prize was not dismaying us as much as the cows.

When the cows cross the pasture the dust rises to meet them. The drought of 1988 has wrung the moisture from the land. The cows' moanings echo from hillside to hillside. The sheep don't seem to mind so much the dusty taste in their mouths, because they're such low grazers anyway, but the cows seeking and preparing their daily salads become more restless as each day passes without substantial rain.

Wayne and I talked about the unthinkable. We wondered if the drought had progressed to the point where it made better sense to sell off some of the breeding stock. We speculated as to whether cattle prices, which had been so high would begin to fall so low. We feared the bottom might fall out. We had to decide whether it would be better to sell now before the real heat of summer set in. If we waited and tried to ride it out, it might be too late. Panic selling and a run on the market could lead to ruin. But, do we sell some of the Revlon and Governor Wallace girls, the blue bloods, the registered Simmental-Angus cows named in a moment of fun after some of our former colleagues and friends? The bulls—Billy Joe, Elvin and Head Recapitulator—had long ago gone to the slaughterhouse. No one had wept for them.

The drought treats the bulls and the cows equally—they both need water to drink and good grass to eat. When the creeks and the pasture begin to dry up, it's time to make a tough decision. The brutal reality is, when it's time to go it's time to go. The only question is when? Wayne and I pondered some more, spit in the dust some more. It takes years to build up a dependable breeding herd. It's neither simple nor easy to buy replacements exactly when you want, at the price you think you can afford. Your own herd is as disease free as you can make it, but what you bring in are usually unknowns. You may be introducing all the problems you've managed to avoid for years. And yet, the day dawns when something has to be done. The heat is oppressive from Plum Lick to Montana. The Mississippi River drops to record lows. Barge traffic stalls. There's a stillness across the countryside. The cows and the calves crowd together in patches of shade. The cattleman prays lightning won't flair from an overheated sky and strike a tree where the Revlon and Wallace girls have sought relief.

Wayne and I made the decision.

Sell.

"Everything?"

"No, I don't say sell them all, but let's sell some."

"I'll have them up tomorrow."

"I'll call the truck."

The next day, some of the Revlon girls and some of the Governor George C. Wallace girls rode to town to the stockyards.

The calves were split off to be sold separately. Nobody liked the idea. But there was no other way that made sense to Wayne and me.

The weather forecasters had been calling for a "20% chance of rain." That of course means, there's an 80% chance that it won't rain. Then they raised it to a "40% chance of rain," which still left a 60% chance it wouldn't.

We picked up our checks from the stockyards, and we were neither pleased with the already falling prices nor with the fact that some of the best of our breeding herd were gone. Maybe our bankers would be happier. They deal in numbers. We deal in numbers and something else—animal husbandry.

As if Melville's Cosmic Joker were working overtime, playing games with us, after the cows and calves had gone to market, a wind began to stir a little before midnight. Rain began to fall. It came up through the alfalfa bottom and gave the crops and pasture a little drink. It didn't start Plum Lick Creek flowing. It didn't penetrate deeply enough for that. The Cosmic Joker just cooled us off for a time.

Lalie and I went out on the front porch to show Ravy the spectacular display of lightning bugs in the bottom land after the shower had moved through. It was a dazzling sight as diamonds discovered where least expected. Still, there was something missing: our old friends, the cows.

"Cows aren't sacred," I thought aloud.

It sounded hollow.

LIGHTNING BUGS

The performance by the fireflies each evening in the bottom land in front of our house is as spectacular as any show we've ever seen on Broadway.

Showtime is about 10 p.m. No reservations necessary. No pricey cab ride from and to the hotel. No fancy dress in the rush to see and be seen. No panhandlers. No horns blowing. No police on horseback. No dirty streets. No frowning ushers. No tickets, please. We sit there on the edge of creation, you and I, and we say, there is no place like this place. This is the place where we want to live out our days.

"Look at the lights sprinkled through the trees."

"It's like Christmas."

"People actually pay for these lights at Christmas time!"

"Look, the lights are going on all the way to the top of the hill!"

Pumpkin, the Australian Shepherd, nuzzles up to the side of you. The bonding deepens. The satisfaction of lives lived decently and simply is immense and as varied as the lights of the fireflies sparkling all around.

"They are more beautiful than diamonds."

"Look, they're falling now from the tops of the Water Maples."

"This one doesn't seem to be doing so well," you say, as the tiny creature crawls across your thumb.

"Stop squeezing it," I say to be playful.

"I'm not squeezing it," you reply, refusing to be done in by pranks. The firefly slips from your thumb and falls, exhausted and confused to the freshly mowed grass.

"Look at all those males out there, trying to attract all those females," you say from your wealth of endless pieces of information stored so as to be ready if needed.

"You mean, all those lights are males?"

"Maybe half of 'em."

"And, the other half are females?"

"Yep. It's a mating ritual."

Why would the Creator do it that way? No answer. But, the performance continued. It would seem they could have danced all night. There was no intermission. There was no applause. There was no need of music swelling from the orchestra pit. In fact, nothing at all was needed beyond the simple but awesome display of lights as far as the human eye could see.

> "There was a time when meadow, grove and stream,
> The earth, and every common sight,
> To me did seem
> Apparelled in celestial light." [2]

As if Wordsworth's "Intimations of Immortality" were enveloping us in a glorious crescendo, we turned to each other, not wanting to stay for the final curtain. As we arose to go inside the place of our retirement, we looked directly overhead through an opening in the overlapping Water Maples. There was the reflected light of the Big Dipper of the constellation Ursa Major, tilted downward toward us.

———————

One of the fireflies came inside the house. It must have been looking for its mate. From our bed we watched Tinkerbell light the room.

"The fire-fly awakens; waken thou with me," wrote Tennyson, stirring lovers—in a television-saturated time—to want to read more.

> "Now folds the lily all her sweetness up,
> . And slips into the bosom of the lake:
> So fold thyself, my dearest, thou, and slip
> Into my bosom and be lost in me." [3]

The beauty of Tennyson's The Princess is mainly lost, because society in the United States of America in 1992 typically finds its identity, its concept of "beauty" in the brain-burning images transmitted by towers dependent upon audience ratings—who is watching what, when, where and only possibly to what effect. Tennyson's leather-bound, gold-tipped pages, sadly, have little and often nothing to do with human communication near the end of the 20th century. It was the advent of one firefly, that single Tinkerbell, from out the millions lighting the night outside our windows that caused me to turn to Tennyson. Surely, in that there's a miracle more powerful than a hundred television towers pulsing with messages of every kind.

> "Sunset and evening star,
>   And one clear call for me!
> And may there be no moaning of the bar
>   When I put out to sea,
> But such a tide as moving seems asleep,
>   Too full for sound and foam,
> When that which drew from out the boundless deep
>   Turns again home." [4]

One firefly here on Plum Lick helped us better understand the depth of our love, its destiny, and its ultimate meaning.

SPEAKIN' OF RAIN

T he crossing on Plum Lick Creek was bone dry. It looked almost as barren as it had most of last year during the bad drought. The cattle were restless. The #10A cow had figured out how to worry the horseshoe latch off the gate at the end of the lane coming from the pasture. She had been leading the search for anything greener, even if it were just something different to break the monotony of the summer heat. The sheep's heads hung low as they nibbled at the last sprigs of weeds in the lot behind the barn. The nodding thistles had lost their green vitality, their thistledown had departed weeks ago on their journeys, which will result in mass seedings in the spring of '90. The tobacco plants were hunkered down, their roots as yet unable to make the connection with the fertilizer and lime that had been spread there earlier in the year. The coolness of the late spring and early summer nights, and the unusual moisture back then had triggered the blooming mechanism. Up and down the roads of the Plum Lick area, tobacco crops were producing their flowers too soon. Farmers scratched their heads and wondered what possibly could go wrong next?

The television weather folks were not, as they say down here, "hollerin' rain" much less "speakin' of rain."

"Great weekend shaping up. No rain in sight. You all enjoy yourselves this weekend."

The usual urban dialogue bore no relationship to rural needs. Those of us who don't golf, don't tennis, don't fish, don't hunt, don't boat, don't surfboard, don't skateboard, don't ski, don't skydive, don't softball, don't do much except work while the sun is shining—we entertain ourselves during dry times by anticipating the blessings of wet times.

Good news for the television weather folks is more bad news for most of us down on Plum Lick, and the other way around is true. Our good news is mainly the city feller's bad news.

"What's the weatherman say?"

"He says no rain."

"That's bad."

"That's not what he said."

"Right. Tell me when he says it's bad, because then I'll know it's good."

Fact is, many of us around Plum don't put much stock in weather forecasts on television. Anytime somebody says there's a 50% chance it'll rain, you'd think they'd know there's a 50% chance that it won't. It doesn't take a whole lot of imagination to figure that out.

Whichever side of the 50% the weather falls on, we don't think in terms of umbrellas. Carrying an umbrella down here makes about as much sense as going swimming with shoes on. As dry as it had been, and as much as we had been needing rain, when it rains we walk around in it, look straight up and let the sweetness splash on our faces.

"Listen."

"I hear it."

Rain was beginning to fall in the early morning hours. The wonderful sound for which we'd waited so long had finally descended upon the roof of the Isaac Shelby Crouch house, as it had so many times before during the past 139 years. Television was not a factor in 1850, nor was it now, because the screens were dark, the transmitters off in the wee hours of the morning.

Pure water ran down and along the gutters, mingling with the leaves of last year. (We'll have to clean those leaves out one of these times.) The breezes through the giant Water Maples in the yard blew the moisture through the open windows, across the bedroom, one of the main advantages of not having artificial air conditioning.

Without words, Lalie and I embraced. The essence of the break in the weather brought us together in tenderness. There was no 50% commitment. Such is the wonder of living on the land, where the falling of rain is not a matter of inconvenience, but the recognition of necessity. The rainfall filled the cistern, replenished the crevices leading to the underground sources from which the submersible pump pulls the lifesaving water up to the livestock trough, to the spigot in the barn, to the taps in the old house where we live out our years.

"Isn't it beautiful?"

"Yes," sighed Lalie.

And the rain kept falling.——— ———

The rain came, just as we were flopping around on the brink of despair. It proved one more time we're often short on faith and long on impatience. It also reconfirmed Kentucky is a land of four seasons, none too extreme, none too prolonged. While there was no minimizing the severity of the drought of '88, the great hydrological system was still working, and—as long as we work with it—we'll be all right. When the first drops began to fall after weeks of no moisture, an Aquarius was awakened by a Pisces well after midnight.

"Do you hear it?"

"Yes."

The Pisces ran outside and walked around in the falling rain. The Aquarius stayed in bed and let the sound of the heavenly drops drive him back into a sleep both deep and sweet. The Pisces, the more extraverted of the two, let the delicious water outside fall upon her hair, bringing a smile to her face where there had been etched the demarcations of deepening drought. She sauntered beneath the Water Maples as the dried rose bushes fluttered in the unaccustomed dampness. As the Pisces turned to return to the warmth of our bed, she saw and heard water hitting the tin roof over the screened-in side porch. All was reassuring.

The sheep that had been miserably hot were now miserably wet, and they'd be smelling more like sheep than ever before. The out-of-season lambs would wonder what in the dried-up world was going on. What is this stuff falling out of the sky? Why, it's rain, my dears, it's rain, said the super-heated rams, who appeared to have had about as much drought as they could handle while at the same time attending to normal chores.

The cows and their calves and the bulls were bending their heads away from the direction of the rain sweeping across the brown and bare hills. Unprogrammed and untroubled by anything so much as resembling connected thought, the bovine animals would wait out the storm and with the coming of dawn they'd begin another day of constant search for the slightest hint of vegetation. If a calf cavorted in the rain it would say more about young energy than a respite from drought. The cattle take their days as they come, unsurprised by anything except a sudden visit by hungry dogs or varmints or humans wanting to drive them to holding pens to load them up and take them off to slaughterhouses. Even then, their lack of understanding is especially pathetic.

The next morning there were actually puddles here and there in Plum Lick Creek, not nearly enough to start the stream flowing again. There were too many crevices to fill, too many sinkholes for the water to gurgle down, too many subterranean rivulets to recharge. In due time when the hydrological system was ready, the creek would begin moving again across the flat bedrock surface.

"Look at the greening over there," said the Pisces to the Aquarius as they drove through the countryside. It was true the desperately needed rain was quickly having its effect. Although brown and seemingly dead, the grass was responding almost instantly. The weeds were having a field day. A few days after the initial rain, hardly a drought-buster, clouds again formed, the sky darkened and there was more water from the heavens. The hydrological system was at long last giving back that which it had drawn up from the Gulf of Mexico, the water that had run down all the valleys of Kentucky on the way to the mouth of the Mississippi River. There'd been much talk about the Greenhouse Effect, changing global climate patterns and considerable doomsday predictions. The reality lay somewhere in the middle of the extremes—paradise forever on the one hand, a dry and deserted planet on the other.

The time to save water is when there is plenty.

THE THUNDER BABY

The Father of the Western Wind came calling at the Isaac Shelby Crouch house on a hot July night near the end of the 20th century. The big Water Maple at the northwest corner of the 1850 house had been one of the anchors for the matrimonial hammock handcrafted in Guatemala, purchased there after the bloodless coup bringing Rios Monte to a brief and hapless reign.

On the night of a full moon rising over Plum Lick, young lovers might have thought that Water Maple would have withstood another century of rain, sleet, snow, ice and hot summer night thunderbolts. It would be more poetic and make a better story to say the lovers were at home that sweltering night in July, that they were shamelessly making love in the matrimonial hammock when the Father of the Western Wind came calling. They were in town putting out another issue in the brief life of the hapless *Montgomery Times*.

Nobody was at home except Turk, the dachshund, and Tigger the cat, when the departed spirits of Isaac and his long suffering wife, Sarah, and the Prathers who came and lived there later, and the Hopkinses who followed them—all came home, returning on the flying coattails of the Wind from the West to make something of a statement.

The fury of the wind bore the hurt and embarrassment Big Ike had known when the 19th century Shorthorn cattle mania came crashing down on his head, and there had been a noisy, whiskey-soaked auction 100 years ago out on the training track in front of the house, where the corn now grows, silently.

In the next century there would be a funeral in Isaac's house for the elder John Prather, who had also fought and bled tears to hold on to the land along Plum Lick Creek, where the giant Sycamores still say "No" to the Father of the Western Wind. Water Maples by their nature are more fragile, or so it's believed. In fact, the root system of the Sycamore is often more shallow than one might suppose. There's a balance in the Sycamore overcoming shallowness.

Old Man Prather was more Sycamore than he was Water Maple, and he had pleaded with the bankers, had cried unashamedly before them not to take his land away from him.

"Can you live on your hogs, your chickens and your garden?" they had wanted to know.

Of course he could, and he did, with the help of his able sons. A determined man with a loving wife and loyal sons and daughters by his side has been known to be unbent by the strongest of winds. Year after year, the Prathers had turned over the profits from their main crops to the bankers, and the family had survived—and so had their land. Thus, it was on the day of Mr. John Prather's funeral, the final day for a patriarch of Plum Lick, farmers and friends came from miles around to pay their respects to a man of such an indomitable spirit.

Old Man Prather had returned that hot, sweaty night in July as the century was grinding down as if to say, Water Maples are pleasant and refreshing, but my Sycamores down there by the creek are more stubborn and longlasting.

If any spirit returned from out the past, Mr. Emmett David Hopkins

57

would have certainly been among them—Mr. Emmett with his mane of splendid white hair, Mr. Emmett with his voice as soft as a woman's, Mr. Emmett with his body broken by a tractor rearing up on him. He had worked too long that day, he was very tired, more tired than he realized, and he had put himself in harm's way on one of the steep hills to the west near the middle tobacco barn, the direction from which the strongest winds usually sweep in. The tractor had come over on him as he was mowing into the late hours of a torrid summer day.

"Make hay while the sun shines," his father's words were probably droning in his mind. He miscalculated. Or, his attention slipped away. He may have dropped the front wheel of the tractor into a groundhog hole that wasn't there last year. Maybe he was thinking about a storm that was brewing beyond the western ridges.

The tractor came over on him.

In those split seconds when a man sees his entire life pass before his eyes, there was still time to act instinctively. One quick move involving no more than a quarter of an inch probably saved his life. Mr. Emmett lived, but until the last day of life, the man with the magnificent white hair and the soft woman's voice, walked with a limp. In the big house today there's a hook above the bathtub, where Mr. Emmett attached a rope with which to pull himself up and let himself down into the water, gently.

The mighty wind of July, 1987, came rolling in from the Rock Ridge Road, where Ben Dalzell—Benjamin Franklin Dalzell—had lived, had sat on a perch as much as a porch, from which Mr. Ben claimed he could see on a clear night all the way to the Ohio River—the Ohio River, some 70 miles away as the buzzard flies and the hawk screams and horses' nostrils quiver and sheep bleat with their heads hung low and the mockingbird plays tricks on an old man's imagination.

"Mamma, the Thunder Baby's crying."

"That's all right, child—you've nothing to be feared of," said great-grandmother Cynthia to her frightened son, Jim—Jim, who never grew up quite right, Jim who became a burden to his brothers and sisters and cousins, Jim who needed help with his land later in his life, Jim whose 100 acres lay now in the path of the approaching storm.

In her brief life of childbearing, eight children in all, Cynthia who lived not quite to her 35th birthday and died at the end of the Civil

War, knew the fear that could seize a child's mind and leave an unerasable mark.

"Mamma, the Thunder Baby's crying."

"Hesh, now, child, the Thunder Baby has good reason to be a-crying. God in heaven is moving His furniture around is all," whispered the childlike Cynthia, old before her time.

The air, as close and sticky as the rank weed along Plum Lick Creek, had turned cool, too cool not to cause great-grandfather John to look up from the hay field and decide it was time to come to the house. As accustomed as he was to lightning, he jerked his head each time in the direction of the flashes knowing if he saw it he was all right. It would be the one he did not see that would bury him six feet down.

The sky was black with clouds folded over at the top like an undertaker's coffin. The wind rushed from the crossroads at Plum. It rolled up the bottom land until it reached Big Ike's house—Isaac, most likely too busy with his Shorthorn pedigrees to be out in the hay field where he should have been if he had any practical sense whatsoever.

"Daddy, the Thunder Baby's crying."

"Now, Jim, it's just a thunderstorm," said John, as he washed his face from the pan by the back door.

The summer storms that have moved across this land during the generations following Joshua and Polly Sr., have all been different.

Then came the moment when the almost 80 mile-an-hour wind wrenched the aging Water Maple from out the ground. It popped the trunk two feet up, laying the length of the tree on the roof of the house, inches from the big stone chimney. One of the long, slender limbs near the crown of the maple stabbed like a spear through the upstairs window. Glass skittered across the floor.

Turk, the dog, and Tigger, the cat, cowered in uncommon brotherhood beneath grandfather Bill's bed downstairs, until the Thunder Baby hushed and went back to sleep.

SOMEWHERE

T he rainbow stretched from a point east of Plum Lick to the southern edge of Mt. Sterling. Broad and vivid, the only discernible colors—red, green and yellow—arced in smooth brilliance, a sign of promise for a tired traveler heading east on Interstate 64. There was a break in the technicolored archway, the cloud formation fracturing the phenomenon at the top causing the seven basic colors—violet, indigo, blue, green, yellow, orange and red—to cascade earthward again, completing the arc.

The moisture providing the bow with its substance was ahead toward Owingsville, while the sun was in its descent toward Frankfort and Louisville. The focal point seemed to be near the Montgomery-Bath county line, where it fused the countryside burning it in yellowed, hot gauze. The temptation was to go to that very point, scoop up the mirrored and refracted raindrops, and splash it all on dry and colorless face and arms. The thought arose to run to the end of the rainbow, not to discover a pot of gold, but to surrender to the rapture of a brilliant moment before it evaporated.

Something there was that cautioned, "Yes," this rainbow is especially for you, and do enjoy it from the vantage point where you have the good fortune to be right now, but, "No," don't try to capture it as you would have grabbed in the cup of your little hand the phosphorescence of a lightning bug when you were a child. Don't try to imprison it as you did that chipmunk that had scampered in complete freedom, that small, tan creature with the black stripe down its back that quickly died in your senseless captivity. Many things are not meant to be touched, much less contained. It has taken more than 60 years of living to learn this fundamental lesson, which applies to so many matters, human and non-human.

It often comes down to the issue of private ownership, the basis of free enterprise. The important distinction lies in the extent of the ownership. It's true you and I own certain pieces of the commonwealth (including the stewardship of our unique selves), but in a larger and much more important sense, we all share in the commonwealth.

That's why it does matter whether you or I litter our highways, whether you or I pollute our streams, you or I foul our air. We are a commonwealth of individual ownerships within a nation of ownerships. This is not the occasion for selfishness, for that leads to territorial disputes. About 130 years ago, the ownership of humans by humans played a major role in leading to a monstrous civil war, the outcome of which signified the end of institutionalized slavery in the United States of America.

The rainbows playing themselves out across the Kentucky sky are much more than a coalition. They far surpass black, white and tan issues. They signify in colors usually not perceived by the human eye, the riches of human, economic, political, sociological and environmental possibilities. Who can say what the violet, indigo, blue, green, yellow, orange and red (with all their gradations) mean? It seemed to one Kentuckian turning for home down the Plum Lick Road that this one rainbow communicated challenge, courage, hope, longevity, inspiration, determination and strength, as we head as a commonwealth and a nation toward the wonders of the 21st century.

THE BIG SYCAMORE

About this time of the year in Kentucky—mid-August—there's a malaise that sets in. You can see it just about everywhere, and you can feel it. From the limp leaves on the Water Maples outside our window, to the mournful calling of a weary cow across the way, it's not necessary to look at the calendar to understand this is the time when the sun beats hottest, the breezes are thinnest and human frailties are most fragile.

Nothing is immune. Just when you go to thinking, well, there's the giant Sycamore down on the creek—an ancient tree standing tall and majestic, like some magnificent sailing ship with its prow pointing westward—just when you go to thinking that, something very surprising may happen.

"There's the big Sycamore, Mama," cried out Little Jim as the family on horseback rounded the bend of the creek on a hot mid-

August afternoon a century and more ago.

"Sure is, Jim," Cynthia might have said.

The young girl who had spent her short life childbearing, and who would be remembered generations later as Great-Grandmother Cynthia nudged her riding mare on up the dry creek bed.

Jim rode behind her.

Sycamores are wonderful places for family picnics.

"Meet 'ya down by the big sycamore," Isaac Shelby might have said to his brother, John Houston, "We'll rest and talk a spell."

Sycamores are reliable places for honest talk about cattle prices and the like of that.

"Would you carve my initials here, just for me?" said a young girl to her splendid young man.

"Why, sure," he'd doubtless reply, "Why, sure, no trouble at all. Say now, how's this look?"

Sycamores are just right for lovers' initials and hearts with arrows cut through them. We, as five generations gone before us had come to depend on that sycamore as a kind of reaffirmation that there are some things and some people who endure despite all adversities.

When I said Old Man Prather was more Sycamore then he was Water Maple, it was a sign that I didn't understand as much as I thought I did about Sycamores and Water Maples. While the Sycamore is one of the most massive trees in the United States, heights varying from 100 to 175 feet and trunks 3 to 8 feet in diameter, the root system can be deceptively shallow. Water Maples, on the other hand, are smaller. Sometimes called the Red, Scarlet, Soft, Swamp or White Maple, the Water Maples we love but outsiders often curse usually grow 40 to 70 feet in height, with trunk diameters of 2 to 4 feet. Depending on the location, Maples may have a root system superior to the Sycamore. Yet, while the Water Maple's wood is soft, the Sycamore is hard, so hard it is used to make butcher's blocks like the one Mr. Bill gave me before he died. At the time when one of our summer's sudden heat-inspired storms had torn down one of our best Water Maples from out the front yard and laid that favorite tree over on top of the house, I remember thinking, thank God for the Sycamore.

That thought's comfort lasted only to the night I was driving up the lane toward the old house, and I looked across to the Sycamore for some much needed encouragement, just a little reassurance that no matter what else might have gone wrong that day at the University, the giant Sycamore would make things right again.

In the early evening darkness I could see there was something terribly wrong. The tall, silver sailing ship's masthead was not reaching for the horizon. Her pennants were not fluttering with the sea wind. Her long and graceful hull was not awash with frothy sea spray.

Everything was upside down.

My breath caught. Numbness set in. No words formed on my lips. There was nothing to do but go look closer.

I opened the gate to the lane leading down to Plum Lick Creek, and I drove slowly to the place where the Sycamore had stood for decades. Apparently, another heat-generated, heat-driven, heat-insistent midsummer storm had moved suddenly up the creek from Joshua Meadows with some kind of sibling madness determined to wreak havoc. The entire Sycamore—its several mammoth forks—was no match for the wind. The base, which included what I had been led to believe was the massive ancient root structure, had been brutally wrenched from the ground with Jack the Ripper violence. What had been the broad foundation of the Sycamore was now perpendicular to the creek bank, and what had been flush with the earth was now two stories high in the muggy night air.

Cynthia's great-grandson walked around it. John Houston's great grandson had all thought stripped bare. Little Jim's grandnephew was speechless. But, there was no anger. There had to be acceptance. After all, there it was. It could not be put back. At best, it would become firewood.

The sixth generation learned that which it should have known all along: nothing on this earth is forever. Even the earth is not forever. Certainly, I am not forever. My beloved wife, Lalie, is not forever. Nothing that we hold dear and precious on Plum Lick is forever. Our loving should be now while we have it. We ought not to despair because we have limited time in which to do our loving. The impermanence is what makes everything meaningful. Only those things with definite time frames possess the meaning needed for lasting value. All open-ended matters have a natural tendency to drift off into nothingness. A sense of urgency well-equipped with sharp expectancy is necessary, even vital, if life is to reach satisfying maturity.

Old Man John Prather, who lived in the big house four decades ago, was indeed more Sycamore than he was Water Maple, and yet his muscle and might, his determined fortitude, were not eternal. His grandson, Johnny, our neighbor now, who was my schoolmate in the Little Rock, Kentucky schoolhouse, has grown tall and straight; yet, I suspect he understands his own mortality—as I did mine upon the passing of our giant Sycamore that hot summer of 1987.

SHELBY

Since I won't be sitting on millionaires' row at Churchill Downs for this year's Kentucky Derby, I'll settle for a stroll down Plum Lick Creek, where on the bank slightly downstream from the old Sycamore stump there's always a fresh supply of mint. I'll take the dogs with me if they're in the mood for it, and I'll gather up two handsful of the green, heady sprigs, hold them like bouquets for a time, and then saunter with a smile on my face back in the direction of the house. I'll walk over the bottom land, where over a century ago there was a training track—there's nothing left of it now, not even the slightest trace.

If it hadn't been for cousin Shelby Crouch, namesake of the builder of the old house we call home, I would probably never have known about the old track. On that day Shelby stopped by, we sat on the side porch and sipped a glass of bourbon. Maybe, it was two. It was the last time I saw Shelby. I failed to go see him after I'd known he was dying of cancer, failed to take the tape recorder to have him tell me about the legendary "Black John" Crouch and "Lyin' John" Crouch. What Shelby didn't know about the Crouchs of Plum Lick, wasn't worth telling, and it's almost certain he added his own vivid imagination. Even now, the mere mention of Shelby's name causes knowing smiles on the faces of those who knew him. I chose to believe him, mostly.

The last time he stopped at the house and swung in the side porch swing, Shelby wasn't clear as to whether we were talking about thoroughbreds or standardbreds, but I imagine it was the latter. Race horses and our steep hills on Plum Lick on the rim of the Outer Bluegrass are not exactly made for each other. Even standardbreds are today in the shortest of supply. Mules, too. Come to think of it, aside from a nag or two here and there from time to time, we aren't in the horse business on Plum Lick in the latter years of the 20th century. Even the venerable inner Bluegrass thoroughbred establishments are hard pressed to survive. Calumet had its bankruptcy sale in 1992. The way Shelby told it, his namesake shouldn't have been in the horse game—that and the Shorthorn craze.

In the mid-19th century in Kentucky, it rivaled speculation in Holland tulips, and other pyramiding schemes. According to Shelby, while my great-grandfather John was living a pretty plain life down creek, brother Isaac was going hog wild like many others in Shorthorn cattle. Newspaper accounts at the time in the *Western Citizen* and the *Kentuckian Citizen* of Paris had almost as much news about the comings and goings of Shorthorns as they did short people. Everything was fine until the inevitable day of reckoning.

Shorthorns hit the skids, and prices turned down in the direction of rock bottom. Great-granduncle Isaac Shelby "died a pauper," said Shelby as he and I sipped our bourbon.

"That a fact?"

"Buried in a pauper's grave."

We paused a bit as the breeze stirred on the side porch of the house, where Isaac and his wife, Sarah, had started housekeeping over 150 years ago. The house had changed over the years with each generation passing through—the Crouchs, the Prathers, the Hopkins, the Windleys and the Dicks, but the pleasant memory of the young couple lingered around the homeplace facing west toward the paired hills to the south and the north, hills as smooth and graceful as a woman's full breasts.

After Big Ike was buried in the pauper's grave, Sarah somehow managed to get out a tobacco crop on the only piece of land that didn't go under the auctioneer's hammer, and when she collected her money she had her Ike moved from his pauper's grave to the middle of the North Middletown cemetery in Bourbon County. After Sarah died, she was buried there too.

Shelby never came back. He was like a ghost that had appeared, drunk his bourbon neat and departed as smoothly as he had appeared.

Most Derby Days I'll sit in one of the big rocking chairs on the front porch of the old Crouch house with Lalie, and we'll sip our mint juleps and we'll look westward toward Churchill Downs. The view across the bottom land where the training track once felt the pounding of hooves now is as silent as the grass shrouding any reminder of what once was but is no more.

"About time to go in and watch them break from the gate."

"If you insist."

After the "fastest two minutes in sports" is viewed on television, the Plum Lickers returned to their rocking chairs, clinked their glasses and toasted the winner of one more Run for the Roses.

TWILIGHT AND EVENING STAR

On most warm and sometimes muggy nights we can be found sitting in our rocking chairs on the westward-facing front porch. We like first to watch the setting of the sun, then the descent of the evening star. We think it's Venus, but we don't worry so much about the exactitudes of astronomy as we do the peace of mind it provides. Since astrology holds no interest for us (the fact that one of us is Aquarius and the other is Pisces is nothing more than an occasional cause for smiles), we focus our attention on the distant planet, and loosen the reins of our earthly imaginations.

Our concerns go far beyond Plum Lick.

While we have no desire to travel on interplanetary missions, we do care deeply about our immediate neighborhood, about the Commonwealth of Kentucky, especially in its bicentennial year, about the great free nation of which we are a part, about our Western Hemisphere and about the whole planet earth as it spins in perfect rhythm 93 million miles from the sun, the star that is the source of all our light and heat.

We see more clearly because of the dependability of the sun and the evening star. And what we view as the most important necessities of our lives, if they are to be meaningful at all, is the education of mankind. We take that to mean the stimulation and development of mental and moral growth at every level of society. If the blue collars must behave, so must the blue stockings. Education should not be the province of the rich at the expense of the poor. We find elitism in all its forms to be repulsive. It is not compatible with the rhythms of the sun and the evening star. Universal truths are for everybody if they are for anybody. The challenges and the responsibility fall upon those who have received education to distribute it every day without fail, without reservation of any kind.

There was a time not so long ago in our United States when it was considered illegal to allow a slave to learn to read and write. The elitist reasoning was quite simple: slavery and intellectual freedom were a conflict of interest. In order to preserve a slave system it was essential to keep the chattel as mindless as possible. It's crucial for the people of Kentucky and all former slave states to understand the absence of intellectual development within the public school system will inevitably result in forms of slavery, as real as shackles on both wrists and ankles. It may not seem that extreme, but one of the outcomes of a lack of education is the inability to see anything very clearly. Illiteracy and unenlightenment in all its forms are addictions. Even if we know we are committing errors, we seem powerless to resist fatal attractions. Too often we have lost control of our individual power systems.

For us in our rocking chairs on the front porch of a house built about 200 years after Bacon wrote the "Advancement of Learning," our inspiration these summer nights on Plum Lick comes both from above and from beneath. We have taken the time to view the setting of another sun, followed by the setting of another planet, and we have looked introspectively at ourselves.

We abhor slavery in any form. Bondage to indifference and disinterest at a time when our places of education, whether on our front porches or in our classrooms, desperately need reform becomes an addiction no planet can either afford or sustain.

After the sunset there comes the sunrise, and we must be up and out of our rocking chairs, we must be taking care of business: professional, vocational, agricultural and industrial—but, we give business a dirty name if we omit the cause of the educational dimensions of our lives.

The view from Plum Lick tells us not to dismay. There's a new day coming. Optimism is the water springing from beneath, coupled with the universal knowledge descending from above. The sun, the evening star and our human nature—the work of the Great Creator—are the  ultimate sources of our inspiration and salvation.

IT NEVER RAINS IN CALIFORNIA

Chubby's plow turned the rich soil of the bottom land, where a century ago the training track for Big Ike's horses resounded with high-reaching hooves, the guttural noises of the riders, the soft voices of the women watching from the rails. The dirt is dark now with the fertility left by the sheep from the house to the Plum Lick Road in the year 1991. The cycle of grass to crumbled loam is a filter of elements and a lifter of spirits for the couple growing older as they watch from the kitchen window.

"How's it look to you, Chubby?"

"All right," said the young plower to the older man, who had left the warmth of the kitchen. He rested his right foot on the bottom plank of the fence encircling the old house. It is the foot, the fixed foot, that feels stiffer when the aging grandson arises on March mornings from Grandfather Bill's honeymoon bed.

"Our minds must've been running on the same track. I called over to your house, and your wife said you were headed in this direction to plow before it rains."

Chubby smiled. "No telling when it might be dry enough again to plow."

The older man looked up at the clouds forming off to the southwest, the point of the compass responsible for much of the rain that falls on Plum Lick. "I won't hold you up, Chubby."

The young man with the plow turned the small Ford tractor back toward the road. He did it instinctively, not needing the literary artifice of *The Plough* for his teacher. Edgar "Chubby" Lovell, a Kentucky plower 200 years after the dark and bloody ground became the Commonwealth, did not look back. As Richard Henry Horne wrote in the 19th century, so Chubby did on the cusp of the 21st: He plowed deep and straight with all his powers, and the right wheel fitted itself to the furrow as a foot to a well-worn shoe. The twin plowshares knifed through the soil, laying it over as perfectly as a long peeling from an apple.

The older man turned back to the house. He picked up a few pieces of Water Maple limbs and stacked them along the way. When he re-entered the kitchen, the smell of slowly cooking fried mush greeted him at the door. It was good.

The news from California on Charles Kuralt's "Sunday Morning" was not good. In 1991, Californians were not having the problem of hurrying to plow before rain came. Out there, Chaucer's "Droghte of Marche" continued, deepened, dividing rural and city folk in open and bitter hostility. The farmers in the San Joaquin Valley needed water for the production of food and fiber for all of the state, much of the nation and international populations. The urban dwellers in Los Angeles and many other non-rural communities needed the food and fiber, but they didn't seem to understand it takes something as simple as drops of water to make it happen.

A major part of the problem is overdevelopment. The crisis is compounded by southern Californians who've been kidding themselves into believing their part of the state is something other than a desert. It's one thing to overdevelop. It's quite another thing to overdevelop a desert, a reality not fully appreciated until the rains stop falling. While rainfall is hardly controllable, development is manageable. It becomes a feat to see how many cities of the angels can fit on the head of an arid pin. No matter how many land developers, public relations experts, public office holders and mortgage lenders become involved, the fact remains: the rain comes or it doesn't come, and man has to live with it. Complaining and fault-finding won't produce so much as one drop of water—maybe a tear or two in Hollywood, but they are salty.

California is only one example of what can befall the human condition. There are reports of as many as 22 million people in Africa facing starvation due to drought and civil strife. The older but not necessarily wiser Plum Licker looked out the window at the plowed ground with rain beginning to fall softly on it, and he said to himself, "Plum Lick is a paradise, but what is happening in California and Africa could happen here. Californians and Africans didn't think their paradises would turn into Hells, but they were wrong."

One week later, a look through the bedroom window across the way toward little Plum Lick Creek was like standing on the bank of the Ohio River, staring at flood time. "Look at that water out there," I said through sleep-crusted eyelids.

Lalie unlocked the front door and stepped outside. I followed, my bare feet tingling at the dampness of the uneven front porch. Even my sleeping right foot was coming awake sooner than it normally did. We stood, silently watching the flash flood rolling, spreading, filling the freshly plowed bottom land with brown, dirty, foaming, churning water that hours before had been rain falling steadily throughout the early spring night.

Pumpkin, the Australian shepherd, was still tied to the headgate by the loading chute, where she'd been left by mistake the night before. After I dressed, I waded through the water and the mud to rescue Pumpkin. She was grateful for the warmth and the dryness of the floorboard of the pickup truck. The two ewes penned with their lambs two nights before were peaceful. There was not time to put out ear corn or hay. The sheep would have to wait until nightfall, I thought as I leaned on the stock barn gate to better watch the wet weather runoff coming down in torrents.

The sound of the rain falling on the tin roof of the stock barn was as pleasant a sound as could possibly be in a world of artificial, industrial noisemaking. There's something plainly sweet, I thought through the webs of my irrevocable aging process, about the first spring rain, yet, there's something rueful about a flash flood, something reckless, something terribly menacing.

When I returned to the house, where I live out my own dream of 100 years, I looked toward the bottom land once more, to the tobacco beds again. The water that had covered one-third of one of the four beds now covered all but one-third of all four. Sometimes, nature will have nothing to do with man's creations.

A drive to the Plum crossroads found the "Mayor of Plum" standing with his hands in his pockets in front of his grocery store. He and a friend were watching the water rising almost to the bottom of Boone Creek bridge.

"We've lost the tobacco beds, Ray."

"May not have to re-seed them," smiled back his Honor.

"May have to," was the look on the friend's face.

"Can I get to Judy (the next crossroads) on Bunker Hill Road?"

"No way," said the Mayor. "You'll have to go to Sharpsburg, and back in that way to Mt. Sterling."

The drive across county lines from Bourbon to Nicholas to Bath to Montgomery was flirtation with flash floods. Finally, the sun began to break through. The rain stopped. New buds on the boughs of Dogwoods, Purple Plums and Tulip Poplars were popping open. There was the first hint of the humidity that becomes a fact of life in Kentucky with the approach of summer. There's something about the first flash flood of spring to stir innermost feelings too long sleeping, a cleansing to awaken a sullen heart.

FARM "HAPPY TALK"

At the beginning of another year, Wayne and I had sat at the breakfast table by the back window, and looked out in search of any green tufts of grass. From here to the Plum Lick Road and beyond there was the first subtle but unmistakable change in the ground color. The slow warming process had begun, and with it had arrived the harbingers of Spring.

I was sipping hot tea, and Wayne was finishing off his Ale-8. He saved the last swallow in the bottom of the bottle for a place to dust his cigarette ashes. We had some happy talk. It wasn't the Happy Talk that would win us any anchor positions on local TV. In the first place, we didn't rule out some raucus March winds or a few surprise April snows. We were just soaking up the last week in February, taking it for what it is: a time for some of the trashier birds to get a running headstart on the prima donna robins by poking for winter-drugged earthworms; a time for jonquils to be rubbing their eyes, preparing for the big push to the surface; a time to dust off the salted-down old ham and hang it high in the meathouse.

Any one of these pleasant thoughts would take too long to talk about on television, especially when leading into the weatherperson part of the news. Many of these folks make a big thing out of sunshine being good, and rain being an inconvenience at best.

Wayne and I know better. That's why when Wayne caught the recent warm spell he went out and did some plowing. The pulsating earth—thawing, refreezing, receiving moisture in the form of both rain and snow, basking a while in the brighter sun, shivering in the coldness of the night—becomes more fertile with each changing condition. It is not made to order. Nature doesn't take roll cues. Wayne and I like to think of ourselves as part of the system, not bystanders wishing it would do our bidding.

Lalie was doing her bidding at an auction in the area (she came home with a set of 19th century salt cellars) when Wayne and I took Ravy out to look at the first calf of the season. That's an event a good many miss these televised days. There's hardly any substitute for the real thing. We piled into the four-wheel drive pickup and headed down the muddy lane toward the creek, running full now with the blessed rains and snows we've been having (the ones lamented regularly by the Happy Talkers).

This is the same creek that was bone dry so much of last year, and probably will be again this coming summer. But now we smile to ourselves and deeply rejoice as the accumulated moisture of the valley gurgles over the rock formations; and the water pushes on downstream toward the Licking River and the deep and wide Ohio and Mississippi Rivers.

Some of the cows had crossed over to Joshua Meadows but on a fine February day such as this we are less mindful of the sanctity of fences. Both the cows and the water seem to know it's all one world. The fences are at best temporary structures having little to do with the reality cutting across the centuries.

Wayne leans out the pickup and calls the cows back to our side. They mind better than the water.

"Skee-ow, skee-ow...suckcalf...skee-ow," and the cows look up from last year's corn field. They come back through the fence they've worried down, and we let the herd take its time reforming. Wayne knew better than to try to call back the water, nor to rail at the falling of the rain producing it, nor to bemoan its passing through the gap toward its juncture with Boone Creek. Likewise, the new heifer calf born on Valentine's Day fell from its mother's womb, and later this year will be forever separated from her. The job is now for the mamma cow and the heifer hugging close to her udder, and the joy is for us to watch it happening.

We talk with great wisdom about genetic engineering, the impoundment and hydroelectric stratagems for the water—while some of us are paid to Happy Talk no matter the silliness with which it is done—but to miss the miracle of life, both in the heifer calf and the onrushing water, is to miss what it truly is all about.

It had been a splendid evening in August of 1991 when we drove over to be with the folks at the annual Harrison County Conservation fish fry. The ocean perch cooked up by the Berry Lions Club was about as fine as eating ever gets. The cornbread, pinto beans, cole slaw and iced tea were enough to make a hungry man and his family feel like they'd found the glory land. The people were friendly, the way you'd expect them to be, and they all seemed determined to conserve the soil, water and trees in Harrison, a county rich with blessings. Chapel Mastin's invocation spoke to the importance of the work at hand.

Julie Ritchie, chemistry and physics teacher at the Harrison County High School, was presented with the teacher of the year award, which only seemed right since she'd already received the same honor for the entire Commonwealth of Kentucky. Leon Dennis, who retired the past January after 15 years as a district board member, received a special award and the applause of the audience at the Rural Electric park on the edge of Cynthiana.

The tree awards were won by Vickie Drakeford for Oaks, John Sosby for Black Locust, the Rollins children—Nathan, Stephanie and Jason—for the Sugar Maple, and Jami Fain for Pine. Everybody in Harrison County was encouraged to sign up at the local ASCS office for cooperative efforts with the Division of Forestry on a cost-sharing basis.

Since I was the invited speaker, I talked about what had happened in the last decade to the Mahogany trees in Haiti, an ecological disaster involving mass migration from the rural areas to the capital city, Port Au Prince. The people ripped out the trees from the countryside: they sold them to furniture makers; they used the wood to build fires to warm themselves on the cold, barren city streets; and they used the Mahogany to carve obscene human forms to sell to cruise boat tourists. Many of the tourists thought it was funny, the exaggerated male genitals barely concealed behind a moveable shield.

Port Au Prince, with a population approaching at least a million people, needed more electrical power for lights as well as the energy to lift drinking water from deep wells within the city. The turbines of the hydroelectric dam, built in the area of the rape of the Mahogany trees, became silted after the run-off of top soil. The lights went out in Port Au Prince, and there was no power to raise drinking water from the deep urban wells. The United States sent in tree seedlings in an effort to reclaim the hillsides surrounding the reservoir, fast filling up with what formerly was life-giving earth, but the effort was thwarted by hungry people.

They ate the seedlings.

I described what we had done on Plum Lick in the mid-80's to find our own water. I talked about the drilling of the three wells, and what it had meant to our lives. Of course, we may have been simply lucky, a one in a million throw of the dice. Yet, instincts tell us, no, it was a calculated gamble with odds in our favor. Once striking something more precious to us than oil or gas, it became our challenge to use the water carefully. We decided to be unselfish, too. We made it available to our neighbors at no cost to them. The important thing is, we think, we looked first to ourselves for a solution to the problem. We told ourselves we didn't want to be the problem, we wanted to be, if possible, the answer to the problem. We remembered what Booker T. Washington had said in *Up From Slavery*: "Put your bucket down where you are."

UNIVERSALITY OF THE SOIL

Looking at the ad in the newspaper did not bring the expected tear to my eye. I knew the day would eventually come.

"Think of it this way," I said to Lalie, my innermost soul connection, "We never owned it in the first place. That's right, we never did. Well, we paid the taxes, and we decided how the land would be used or abused, but we never owned it in the sense that we could dictate terms from the grave—in perpetuity, as the lawyers say."

The voice on the other end was as always, silent, waiting, listening, cutting the "owner" more eternal slack.

"What I've come to understand is a sense of stewardship," said the farmer.

> "They're the lords and owners of their faces,
> Others but stewards of their excellence.
> The summer's flower is the summer sweet,
> Though to itself it only live and die." [5]

Shakespeare's words, unowned, looked back from the Sonnets' page.

"I have planted, Apollos watered; but God gave the increase...Every man's work shall be made manifest...Stewards of the mysteries of God." [6]

The Apostle Paul's words, unowned as well, rose up from The First Epistle to the Corinthians.

Oh, doubt not the American farmer's belief in ownership of land, or his support for the free enterprise system. Much beyond that, he or she who "owns" the land defends it with every ounce of energy, every particle of principle within rational thinking—yet, there comes to most the realization that, indeed, the soil goes on as the stewards enter and exit the stages of life.

The Little House Up the Hollow, and Grandfather Bill's and Grandmother Laura's first housekeeping place on the side of the hill will one day succumb to a summer storm or a winter cold. These evidences of an earlier time will pass from view for they are as mortal as the stewards of yesterday.

The soil survives. It breathes.

"Civilization is built on six inches of topsoil, and enough moisture to raise a crop," said our friend, John Heick at a recent Farm Bureau meeting. As expressed by the late Professor James A. Shear of Montgomery County, Kentucky, in fact, all the water there ever was, was here in the beginning; and all the water that is here now is all the water there will ever be.

"Joe called and said he has a prospect he's taking down to look around our farm."

"That's good!"

Talking in this way did not produce tears that might have taken their toll, because Lalie and I had carefully thought it through. We were healthy. We were sane. We were selling one parcel of land in order to secure "ownership" of another, the sort of thing that had occurred again and again, each time a replenishment for realtors, attorneys and county clerks who make their livings tracking transactions.

The view from Plum Lick does not disappear with the passings of the owners. We who occupy the old Crouch house downstream a ways from Bill's and Laura's place, upstream a ways from John's and Cynthia's place will continue to arise each morning of the remaining days of our lives, and we will see the contour of the lovely hills stretching into the distance and we will rejoice at the coming of the new "owners," in much the way Margaret and Hilton Windley felt when they handed over the keys to us in 1985.

The nice thing about a sale is that it produces new neighbors and new possible relationships. Not all will be made in heaven, of course, but the soil has endured much human badness. The important thing to remember is the universality of the soil, the stewardship of it and the responsibility for placing it in new hands.

J. LARKINS

THE REVEREND DICK AND NELLIE

Plum Lick taught us a lesson this spring. Winter has a mind of its own. It won't be told what to do. None of our seasons conforms to the artificialities of the calendar. It's as if we need to be reminded the attempt to calendar the world and all the weather that's in it is a feeble business at best.

In April of 1987 came the heaviest April snowfall ever recorded here by the weather bureau. We estimated four or five inches on Plum Lick. A neighbor up the road said it was more like six to eight. Over in the mountains of eastern Kentucky it was not uncommon to hear of 15 to 18 inches. But there we go again, trying to quantify something giving neither two hoots nor 17 hollers whether it's counted. We don't seem to be satisfied unless we talk about it in terms of numbers.

Boob tube babies and ageless couch potatoes are more comfortable with and reassured by electronic weather maps and other technological wonders of the video kingdom. Television anchor folks turn from happy talk to head wagging. The sneak snowstorm in April of '87 finessed, outflanked and fooled all of us. Down here on Plum Lick there was much head-scratching over whether young plants were "in the cruck" and whether the ground had "spewed," both certain signs of untimely death. But the incurable optimists among us looked upon  the whole episode as the laying down of a warm white comforter upon the land, protecting the plants, tucking them in on this "unseasonable" night.

No sense fighting it. Here on Plum Lick there are four seasons, each one as cantankerous as it is splendid. There's no reason to be bent out of shape about it. Everything occurs in good time. If we cooperate, it mellows our minds, soothes our souls, works wonders on our unwillingness to let go and allow the seasons to carry us forward to the next natural phase of the year.

Caracas, Venezuela, where Lalie and I spent a hellish year in 1978—the year of Reverend Jim Jones and Jonestown—likes to boast of its "Eternal Spring." Sounds fine, and for a while it is fine. No winter, summer, no fall—just "Eternal Spring," the ultimate of what some seek in Florida, like a battalion of Ponce de Leons lusting for "Eternal Youth" down in the saw grass. Caracas's "Eternal Spring" is boring and Ponce de Leon's fountain of youth turns to leathery skin on Miami Beach, both as deceptive as the Rev. Jim Jones' promise of "Paradise on Earth."

Give me Plum Lick. Give me four or five inches of snow in April just to keep me on my toes. We all need our little humbling experiences. It cuts us down to manageable size, reduces our hat dimensions and reminds us we are after all a little this side of immortality. I've decided, therefore, to have nothing to do with "Eternal Spring," "Eternal Youth" or "Eternal Anything." I especially want to watch out for evil pied pipers, like the Rev. Jones, when they offer miracle cures and a free all expenses paid trip to glory land.

Rev. Coleman W. Dick, my grandfather, never had the opportunity to be an electronic minister. He never raked in thousands, much less millions of dollars. He never saw a Rolls Royce, much less drove one. He never led more than 900 people to Guyana and convinced them to drink poison. My grandfather at the beginning of this century was a simpler Kentuckian in a simpler time of the commonwealth. If he were living now, I would like to think he would be working for the Lord quietly in some little country church, such as the North Middletown Christian Church in Bourbon County, where he was the minister when the 20th century began its troubled way.

Coleman's wife, Nellie, my grandmother, whom we all called "Monnie," was never bedecked with diamonds. She glowed from a sweet and simple complexion. She never glittered. Nellie was totally blind most of her long life. Yet, her ability to see was remarkable. She was born Nellie O'Malley Cralle, April 10, 1860 in the Elizabethtown jail, where her father was the jailer.

Nellie's first remembrances were from the latter days of the Civil War. Her gentle nature was to include the combination of old south and new north characteristics, much as it does today in Lalie and many other southern women, the "steel magnolias" who have Scarlett's ability to be a friend and a comfort to blacks and whites on a level not political or self-serving, but filled with love for humanity.

It would never have occurred to Nellie to help establish theme parks or prayer towers, and if her husband had come home with such an idea she probably would have said, "Now, Coleman, what in the world has come over you? Have you lost your marbles, or what?"

Coleman and Nellie were disks in the backbone of the religions of their time, she quietly supportive while he delivered his upright sermons unadorned by televised theatrics, unassisted by sophisticated wireless microphones. Coleman, still a young Disciples of Christ minister when he died at the age of 49, used a specially bound Bible his daughter, Florence, handed down to succeeding generations.

Before she died at 95, Aunt Florence told how her father had turned his Bible over to a black man, an old bookbinder who removed every page one at a time, then rebuilt the entire volume of Old and New Testaments so every other page was lined for sermon notes. On many pages, the ink had faded. At best, Coleman's handwriting was scrawled. There had been no word processor to correct his misspellings or justify his right margins.

"It takes a pretty warm preacher to keep from freezing in some churches...In old days of the church one sermon used to convert 3,000, now temperature is so low it takes 3,000 sermons to convert one member...There has always been a rivalry between heart and brain. Bible is full of heart, never mentions brain once...Every house has a best room. Some call it the parlour, but all have it. Here is the best carpet, furniture, pictures, a few choice treasures on a mantelpiece. All things not in common use, set apart as a little better are taken to the parlor. It is the room of honor of state. Here we receive our friends. That's pride! You were never farther from the truth. It is striving after the ideal. It means refinement, culture. Woe to the family that has no best room. The Lords' day is the parlour of the week. Oh, all days are alike, and all places are alike. By no means. Suppose the shoemaker should bring his tools in the parlour, carpenter his saws and shavings, the cooper, the cook. Glad to see you but I've got a little work I'm bound to finish.

"These things all right in their place, but take them out of the parlour. All labour honest but let us have one day free from it. Shop is honorable and a man should be a Christian there, but not a good place to worship. The week is a house, and Sunday is the best room. If the Lord's day is a day to be dreaded, something wrong in your training. Don't avoid it—sorry when it comes, glad when it goes. It is manhood's day. Today I'm not a toiler, servant, hired man. No taskmaster over me. I'm a man, a free man, and belong to myself and wife and children and above all to God."

HOME

The absolute auction sign in the narrow front yard of the 19th century Kentucky heritage home in the crossroads community of North Middletown meant the old Turner-Dr. Bean house would once again be sold to the high bidder.

The original Turners and Beans were all gone, remembered only by their names framed on the living room wall next to one of the three front doors. Other families had followed, each leaving individual marks of stewardship—the heights of sister Jane's children—Ann, Harry III and Liza—were recorded on the frame of the door leading from the bathroom to the kitchen.

Grandfather Bill Crouch and Grandmother Laura Neal ("Lala") moved from the farm on Plum Lick during the days of World War I to take up housekeeping in the Turner-Dr. Bean house. As a child I'd thought my grandparents had always owned it. I didn't understand they too were just passing through. Grandfather tended his vegetable garden here, and he had a pheasant run. Grandmother made lye soap in a wash tub in the back yard. She and her Bill resisted 20th century attempts to modernize their lives. They had left Plum Lick, but not the country ways that had served them as well as they dared to dream. Grandfather's gravity flow water system didn't need electricity to make his tomatoes and cucumbers as juicy as the earthiness of his speech.

After Bill's and Lala's only daughter, Lucile, lost her young husband, Samuel I, she came home to the Turner-Dr. Bean house. She brought her three small children with her—Jane, Florence and David—and the big old house found room for them all. David's first remembrance of life was dropping his baby bottle to the floor on the sun porch. I remember crying. But I don't remember Grandfather Bill dying. It would be too much too soon for a young grandson to comprehend. I'd be shielded from the grief at both my father's and grandfather's funerals. Most of what I would have would be their names written on stones above their graves 300 yards away in the North Middletown cemetery. But in the passing of the years, there would be no escaping the sight of Grandmother Lala's frail body lying in her casket in what later would come to be known as "The Rally Room."

It took that name years later after a Saturday night party that had included beer drinking and piano playing and late night calls to the more temperate in town, reminding them that it was the eve of "Rally Sunday" at the church, catty-cornered across the street on the edge of the cemetery. Those were the years of learning to play "The Darktown Strutters' Ball," "Boogie-Woogie Bugle Boy" and "You'll Never Know" on the upright piano in "The Rally Room." The piano bench would become a good place to hide cigarettes.

At the end of her second marriage, Lucile had returned home again to the old, sagging, but seemingly indestructible house on the corner of Church Street. Left behind were the ten years at Mt. Auburn when she was married to "Mr. Bill." It had been a frustrating and embittered time for the young woman at mid-life, but she had enough Crouch blood to see it through with her head high, her priorities in as straight a line as one of her father's potato rows. When Rosemary Clooney recorded "This Old House," Lucile smiled a deep smile and believed the song had been written for her.

In time, Lala's oldest granddaughter, Lucile's oldest daughter, Jane, and her three children found safe haven in the Turner-Dr. Bean house. Another generation—music on hot summer nights of pubescent years that tested the patience of the most forbearing—passed in and out of the doors, up and down the steps of the structure that was always home to those who needed it.

After Lucile followed Lala, and Jane followed Lucile, another stewardship ended, and it was time to call the auctioneer.

On the inside of a closet door upstairs there were still visible the corners of rejection slips accumulated by a would-be poet. On a nail leading down old stone steps past original logs to the cellar there hung a U.S. Navy pea coat, moldering until a few days before the absolute auction. The unrequited poet had returned to take the coat away to have it cleaned if not to be worn. I smiled at the thought that it might fit. I knew damn well it wouldn't. Out in the back yard, near the spot where the old coal house used to be, there was an unmarked grave. That was where a boy's dog was buried. Tom West, the black man who in the 1990s hitchhiked from Bourbon County to the Veterans' Hospital in Lexington whenever he needed to go, dug the grave 50 years ago. It was Tom, and no one else, who helped a devastated little white boy lay Dusty to rest.

The absolute auction of August, 1988, went off as scheduled on a pleasant Saturday morning. The boy, who had become a man, listened as the auctioneer, Eddie Burke Williams, started the bidding. I wished I still had need of the old Turner-Dr. Bean house, but I didn't. Someone else had a greater need. The buyer was a young man soon to leave the Coast Guard. He had plans. He was excited about the possibilities. He wanted to fix the old house up, some.

A new generation was about to pass through.

LEAVES

T he yellowing of Kentucky has begun from Ashland to Benton, from Covington to Corbin. It begins with a paler green. It's most noticeable after turning off Bunker Hill Road onto Plum Lick. The foliage on the driver's side is the first sign of the gradual shift of seasons. Even in early August, the leaves are in their greenish-yellow stage, which means one thing. In only a few weeks it'll be September again, and by then most of the green will be replaced as the autumnal equinox approaches. "A time or period of maturity verging on decline," may be a definition acceptable to some, but for one Plum Licker there's no "decline." It's better to look for the positive in the seasonal alternation, otherwise despair damages the human spirit. The leaves of summer, slowly losing their greenness as their supply of life-giving photoplasts shuts down, become the stuff of which new generations are created. Neither leaf nor mankind should find despair in that.

Another sign is in the wood stored behind the meathouse. It's time to bring it closer to the back door, where it'll be dry for the annual celebration of the lighting of the fire on the bedroom hearth on the first cold night of autumn. The essence of the wood—Sycamore, Water Maple, Black Walnut, Cherry—that once was a tree with life abounding, soon will be ascending heavenward.

Days and especially nights have become cooler with the freshness of the changing air currents. A light comforter on Grandfather Bill's and Grandmother Laura's bed feels deliciously pleasant to tired souls. The humidity that left hang-dog looks on "Blue" and "NCAA" melts away, leaving the critters in more agreeable frames of mind. The grateful dogs roll in the grass. When the full moon descends they howl with full-throated dedication, releasing long months of pent-up, hot breath. The flock of sheep had been standing in mournful number, clustered, their heads bowed as if in somber prayer, looking like pilgrims poised to meet their maker.

"Why do they look like they're praying, Wayne?"

"Face flies," answers Wayne as if wondering how anybody could miss something so obvious.

But now from time to time the sheep begin to look up in late August. The cycles of estrus are starting, and the Dorset rams look longingly through the gate. The cattle have begun leaving the woods during the day, their refuge less needed now. The cows and calves are among the first to realize the scorch of summer is slowly shifting toward cooler moments.

The yellowing of the countryside is most noticeable in the tobacco patch. Wayne and Judy and their hired help have been moving through the fields, wielding the cutting knives, spearing the plants onto the sticks, handing up the green-turning-yellow leaf to the wagons. As the day passes, there's a procession to the waiting curing barns where one by one the sweating workers hoist by hand the sticks through the tier-rails to the top. The annual ritual represents a major passage of time, signaling the transition from summer to fall. The yellowing process is gradual. There's a pale green phase that pulls Summer gently and smoothly into Autumn. The fiery reds will arrive later when the Canadian air masses push the colder temperatures south of the Ohio River. But, in September there's a lingering of the life that springs annually—rose bed by the side gate and the Clematis on the walls of the coal house—while now weary of summer heat, the flowers with their fragrance have begun nodding their heads, seeking a time of rest.

"Do you hear them?"

"Hear what?" comes the sleepy reply before sunrise.

"Geese,"

"What?"

"Geese." The distant clamor slides by. The sleepers, reveling in the coolness of the September morning have not the resolve to go out and search the sky to greet the southbound travelers. It's a mistake that may be forgiven, but there's no guarantee of it.

End-of-summer rains descend. The moisture that had been needed so desperately in mid-season now moves up the valley as if to say,

"I'll come when it suits me." No, it wouldn't talk that way, even if it could. There is no vengeance at work in this. Only humans are capable of thinking of the possibility of trying to get even, settle old scores, seek advantage.

Wayne and Judy and their young son, Bobby, and the unborn child she carries, leave the tobacco fields for a while. They and their hired help have hung the last of the sticks of Burley that was cut. They've watched the skies, smelled the air and heard the weather reports.

"They're hollarin' rain," says Wayne, a much more imminent warning than merely "speakin' of rain."

The timing of the housing of the crop has been just right. Were it not so there would be sticks of tobacco standing or falling over in a field fast becoming deep in mud. The unharvested part of the crop is having another long drink, and the yellowing will pause to let the pale green catch up.

All over Kentucky, the scene is repeated as the commonwealth looks to changing its garments. There's wistful resignation present that makes us more at peace with ourselves. The passage of summer has lifted the heat of anxiety from the burdens of another long day of work.

"The air doesn't smell like this in any other place in the world," Lalie sighs as we turn toward home after midnight.

"You're right." And, I think to myself how marvelous it is to be a Kentuckian living on Plum Lick.

Autumn in Kentucky is probably much like what Heaven is apt to be. I'm making little selfish prayers that the Good Lord will let me stay here on permanent assignment. Of course, I'm in no position to dictate terms, but maybe it's no sin to state a preference.

Where else do the evening breezes blow so softly? Where else does the early morning fog drift so lightly? Where else does the full moon rise more magnificently? There are some places in the world with their intrinsic beauty: St. Vincent, Guadaloupe and Barbados in the Caribbean; the coasts of Ireland; the eastern shore of the Mediterranean; the Big Bend of Texas. Still, for me, there's no other place possessing the grace and the excellence of Plum Lick.

Autumn is one of the reasons. It was always my mother's favorite season, and the passing of summer was always an occasion for her to give thanks. For Lucile, not even the Dogwoods of spring could compare with the refreshments of autumn. Though spring symbolized birth and new possibilities, and autumn emblemized death and dog days remembered, the fall of the year was the time Mother held closest to her heart. Each morning the dew has settled in the bottom land along the creek, enfolding in cool mistiness the footprints of old Joshua. Through all that time, the mists have moved through this cooling season of the year. Joshua's granddaughter and after her, her granddaughter, my mother, came to accept this changing of the guard as a special gift.

The wind stirs more strongly in late September, and the leaves try their first and last wings of flight. A covey of doves takes wing, too, catching mortals by surprise unless they're there with hunting sacks or garden baskets to gather in a harvest. Some of us would rather allow there to be unchecked free flight of bird, leaf and thought—yet, from time to time we say yes to the workers who've toiled all summer, who want to bring to their tables the rich, wild tastes of small, murmuring, gray-bellied fowl, or the high-bounding white-tailed deer in the woods to the west.

The woodpile behind the meathouse will soon be moved, log by log, to the box by the side door to season a few more precious days before the building of the first fire of autumn. That is the time when the friendly crackle of the flames and the slow, easy warmth of the fireplace will bring unhurried smiles to our faces. Cloud, the new white cat, will experience her first warming time at our feet by the edge of the black marble hearth. The wind will play at the chimney opening, and the leaves from the giant Water Maples will strain and snap and swirl toward our bedroom window.

We've never been rakers of leaves or hunters of doves or deer, and we're not sure why. Maybe it comes of the joy of observing abundance and the life well-lived, rather than the taking of something more marvelous when left untouched. Still, we understand the harvest theory—whether it be doves, deer or dandelion wine—and we know too many leaves in our gutters and our gardens present a problem only gathering will cure. So, we live out our reasonably efficient autumn days, remembering to savor as much of the sweetness as possible. Perhaps, we mellow with the nature of the time of the year.

We can't detach ourselves from the events unfolding for generations as far back through September mists as Joshua and the founding of the commonwealth 200 years ago. While some things differ so very little so as not to be noticeable, and some things we'd prefer not differ at all, even apparent sameness embraces infinite variety, as the snowflakes flying later in fall. Each will carry its own imprint, its own identity. Each will have its own twin compasses.

Lalie and I sense the fragile nature of our mortal lives. We recognize and accept how we've begun, how we've grown, how we must eventually accept our ultimate departure from all that is so beautiful to behold. As we grow old together, Lalie and I, we don't have to remind ourselves not to curse the night. We don't begrudge the opportunities of generations unborn. We hold on as long as we can to all those things which make this life unique and richly splendid.

GENERATIONS

Grandfathering and walnut gathering is what I should like to designate last Saturday. It was on that day in 1987 I heard from a two-year-old little boy for the first time the words, "Grandfather David." I suppose I'd thought I'd not live so long. After all, grandfathers are usually remembered like tall, Black Walnut clocks standing in the front hallway, measuring time with long pendulums. Or, they are dimly represented by faded pictures in dusty family albums. Or, they are no more than vague memories of a moment or two distantly past in time, as walnuts were dropping one by one from trees undressing for another deep winter's sleep.

I am young, said I. I live and breathe and love and laugh and upon special occasions I'm very silly. How could I possibly be "Grandfather" David, said I, as the two-year-old, Samuel Stephens Dick III, made a castle in front of the Issac Shelby Crouch house in the bottom land sown with winter wheat. But, now I've come quickly to recognize the warm, quiet, peaceful relationship that exists between newfound grandfathers and their grandsons. Neither expects anything. Neither needs be reprimanded. Yet, the bond is undeniably there, a bond simply not discussed, not evaluated, not challenged, not questioned. Competition is not a factor. And that is good.

The father, who was present and available as needed, must have also felt a wonderment concerning the role he was playing. Sam Dick, the television anchorman at the station "in town" had come out to the country on a Saturday to be the bridge linking three generations on the land where Sam III built his castle and laid claim to his 8th generation prerogatives. Of course, that is a word of no significance to one so small and innocent—but the grandchild's prerogatives were evidenced in the way he worked with smooth authority to construct the castle with the soil wherein his seed had first been sown. Wheat will spring up around the castle, and it will become a place for new adventure with the passing of autumn and winter. And the grandson will come back to take another step in the direction of distant maturity.

Downstream, where Plum Lick Creek empties into Boone Creek at the Plum crossroads there is nothing to empty on this day: it is bone dry. There has not been nearly enough rain to keep water flowing. The bridge over Boone Creek is redundant. There's not one drop of water to be troubled. The creek bed is as dry as black walnut powder.

There he was, a cousin, tracing back to the family from which sprung Great-grandmother Cynthia. Cousin Marvin Hedges was hulling walnuts. Each year—sometimes plentifully as it was two years ago, sometimes sparsely as last year—neighbors gather the falling walnuts and bring them by the pickup truck load to Marvin. From the central collection point, a semi-trailer truck pulls away with 40,000 pounds of freshly hulled walnuts and heads out from Kentucky, across the heartland of America.

The Black Walnut, with its hardness and its intricate patterns so finely conceived, symbolize for me the grandfather heart. If it were possible to seize a hammer and open my grandfather's heart, and if you could open my grandson's heart, you would discover all the connecting patterns. There you would find Joshua, Polly "Jr.," Cynthia, William, Lucile, David, Samuel II and Samuel III, but you would not find the fate and circumstances that gave their lives their variant outcomes, nor would you be able to determine the love and hate relationships, the joyful and the painful experiences. The winds blew differently upon us. Storms blew some of us to the ground. There were lightning bolts that split some of us asunder. Some of us were made into fine furniture, some of us were cut up for firewood and we burned brightly on winters' hearths while some of us simply grew older and finally gave back ourselves to the earth from whence we had come.

As the new grandfather watches as his grandson builds his castles, the elder is not fearful. The patterns are set, only the unpredictable causatives cannot be controlled. Nor should they be. Life then would be too mechanical, would lose its charm and its challenge. It is the inner core that sustains us all in times of trial. As the patterns laid out inside Black Walnuts, we owe our inner strength to the generations that have gone before.

Grandson, I say quietly to myself, I am very glad you spent a part of this Saturday here on this soil where many good things will always grow tall and well. So will you if you be patient and above all, be true to yourself. Keep building your castle. Inside your heart the echoes of the voices of your many grandfathers and grandmothers are cheering you on. Should you fail, they will not grieve. Should you succeed they will smile. Either way, they will all be there, and it will be you who gives their lives their richest meanings.

TO BE IN CASE,
OR NOT TO BE IN CASE

The sound of rain peppered the tin roof over the side porch. Leaves felt it too. The October coolness crept around the corners of the house.

"Tobacco may be in case."

The morning bath and the dressing had an air of hope. Before breakfast, feet moved through the wet grass, the dampness cutting through the sides of the shoes. The sheep shook their fleeces, and lowered their heads against the steady rain.

"Tobacco may be in case," said the farmer again to himself. I smiled inside myself, saying nothing to anyone else, for no one else was present and that was good. Last night, I'd called the strippers to ask them to be ready in case the tobacco were in case. I, the farmer, did not think at the time how strange such a sentence would sound to one unfamiliar with burley tobacco terms—"strippers" and "in case." A lifetime of talking and thinking in this way was all that mattered, as the farmer lowered the tailgate on the pickup truck so that the lamb that had stayed there all night might be free again. Delivery to a customer in Lexington had not worked out.

"Something right ought to be happening today," muttered the farmer as he climbed behind the steering wheel of the pickup truck.

"After all the work it has taken this year, the big day has finally come, the day for starting the last job in the tobacco in 1990."

Had it really been worth it? The transplanting in the greenhouse, the trimming of the tops of the plants to make them stronger, the transplanting to the tobacco patch, the plowing, the side dressing, the topping, the spraying for suckers, the suckering of the suckers that refused to be killed by the spraying, the dropping of sticks, the cutting, the housing, the opening and the closing of the barn doors to insure the curing of the leaf.

What would the price be this year?—that's the question uppermost in tobacco farmers' minds at the beginning of the stripping seasons, a question frequently asked, but never answered with certainty.

"If it's $1.70 a pound, that'll be a few cents more than it was last year. Every penny counts. Yes, every penny counts," said the farmer to the windshield wipers as he drove toward the barn where the first tobacco was housed.

I opened the main doors of the barn and stepped inside. The leaves hung down, as if to say, "Well, here we are. We've done about as much as we're going to do. Today's as good a day as there's going to be."

I reached up and gently squeezed the leaves on one of the stalks.

"In case. Yessir, in case."

I tried a second stalk, and then a third. It was all the same. The brittleness was gone. The leaves could be handled without them breaking. The time had come to do the final job. I closed the barn door, and drove back to the house. I went to the telephone and called the strippers.

"It's in case."

"We thought it would be. We're on our way."

"The string is in the pickup."

"What about the plastic?"

"There's some in the shed."

"What about the bailers?"

"In the stripping room. We'll need bumper jacks.""

"We'll bring ours."

"Bonus if you do a really good job."

"Don't worry. We'll do our best."

The tobacco farmer headed for his job at the university. He thought about the possibility of one day spending all his time on the farm. It was a nice thought.

TOBACCO STICKS THE WAVE OF THE FUTURE?

Communicating with 150 students in Introduction to Journalism last week about "verbal" and non-verbal" communications:

"'Verbal' means communications spoken or written—why do you think that's so?" the professor asked of no one in particular.

"Words are involved," came the reply from out the deep bank of row-on-row 156 students in the Whitehall Classroom Building.

"Fine. Let me give you an example of non-verbal communications. See, here I am in my blue pickup truck, the one with the racks on it that you see parked over there (motioning in the direction of the journalism building), and I'm heading down a little country road. I do something you hardly ever see anybody do here in Lexington. I've got my hands on the steering wheel, and another pickup or car is approaching from the opposite direction.

"I lift one finger, the forefinger on my left hand or my right hand if it's on the steering wheel. The person in the other vehicle does the same thing." We've just communicated. It wasn't necessary for us to do any more than that to know we're potential friends. We are Good Samaritans if called upon. We would do each other a favor if given even half a chance.

"Sometimes, we might raise the whole hand," bending it slightly at the wrist, but only the forefinger is enough. "We wouldn't do this," I say as I make a gesture with my entire arm. "That would confuse the other person."

Later, at the annual faculty retreat, one of my colleagues, Steve Dozier, a photojournalist who moved here from Detroit, talked about

the latest tactics for stealing cars up there. Some robbers have discovered it's easier to steal a car with someone in it, than to have to hassle with breaking into an empty one and risk having to jump start it while the car alarm goes off.

What works in Detroit might not work so well on a country road in Kentucky. There are several folks I know who would look upon this sort of thing as a case of right bad manners:

"Get out of that pickup," says the highway robber to someone who has just finished a long hot day in the tobacco fields.

"How would you like a tobacco stick wrapped around the end of your nose?"

I'd no more mess with a tobacco field worker as the sun was going down, than I would a coal miner on the way home after 10 hours of going without sunlight. Detroit has come to a sorry pass, and so have many other shining examples of modern urban civilization. The recent subway wreck in New York City is another wretched case of "leaving the driving to us." Sometimes, there're things that can be more dangerous than smoking—like driving through Detroit or taking the subway in New York. I wonder why they don't put up "hazardous to your health" signs for those situations?

Maybe their federal funds ought to be cut off. Maybe those God-fearing, law-abiding folks up there ought to arm themselves with tobacco sticks. The government would probably force them to put health warnings on the sticks—"This tobacco stick could be hazardous to your health"—and that would be just fine. If anybody took the time to read it they might avoid a funny-looking nose.

Well, it's time to close down the word processor up here at the University and head for the barn. The weather is turning cooler. There was a cricket in the bathtub early this morning. I got him out before the water hit him. When I left to dress, I made sure I stepped around him. Crickets are cherished at our house. So is human life out there on the road, and nobody has a right to threaten it.

Non-verbal communication being what it is, we who live in the country hope we never lose the quality of our lives, reflected in the time-honored habit of raising the forefinger from the steering wheel when anyone passes our way. It's an honest holdover from the time when we touched the brim of our hats to both men and women. It's a fine substitute for the spoken and the written word. It's a gesture that says, I respect your space, and it would be mighty nice if you would respect mine. Should you need a little help, that's possible too.

What's this tobacco stick on the gun rack? Just an old friend of mine, minding its own business, thank you.

Chubby worked the ground in the bottom land until almost midnight. From my front porch vantage point I wondered some more about wage and hour laws. Chubby's concern was tilling in the seed of the winter cover crop before it rained. Shortly after midnight it did rain. By then, Chubby was at home in bed.

That's what makes farming different from factory work. Down here where the soil is alive and the seeds are straining and the promise of sowing is all around us, we don't punch in and out on clocks. We don't put in for overtime, either, and time and half is another way of saying, work one and a half times as hard. The idea is simple: most farmers work until the job is done. We might have to call it quits for the night when the gas runs low in the tank, or our stomachs might be growling for food to the point that it makes more sense to eat than plow, but farmers who're committed to the profession of agriculture just keep on keeping on.

Another thing or two: farmers look on the bright side—if they didn't they'd go crazy, or give it up and move before their time to town, which is pretty much the same thing. Moving to town for some would be more or less the same feeling a born-free animal has upon waking up one day in the zoo. Oddly, the people who visit the zoo have a tendency to think they're not members of the zoo, too.

Farmers look for ways to lay a little something by. That's because when starvation sets in, it's the city folks who'll be coming out to see the farmers about what went wrong. Where else would they go? Next door? Maybe, but what they would likely find there would be total strangers in the same sinkhole. This reluctance to be friendly is most pronounced in places like New York City. But, it could happen in modern day meccas such as Louisville and Lexington. In many citadels of civilization saying, "Hello," sometimes invites strange stares.

One last time, and then I'll quit and go sit in my rocking chair: not only does farming feed 8-million people day in and day out in New York City, farming has fed a world of cities every single day since man deliberately dropped the first seed in the ground. You'd think we'd get a little respect. But, that's all right. Punching clocks may be all right for some. As for us, we'd as soon work on getting the job done—so we can kick back and enjoy the freedoms farming brings to tillers of the soil.

There have been days when different workers have restored my faith—models of dignity, simplicity and devotion to their work in the finest sense of the word. These were Kentuckians who knew their jobs, loved their jobs, and were determined to do them to the best of their ability.

Lalie and I loaded two lambs into the pickup truck and headed up the road. We drove across Cane Ridge to Paris, and from there proceeded north to Cynthiana, where we'd left the charger and battery for the Super C tractor at Robert Hendrick's repair shop. Terry Whelen had a very satisfied smile on his face, because he'd managed to fix the screw I'd twisted off the starter switch.

"Enough threads for a nut, and then I attached this other screw into that nut, and if you twist this one off it'll mean a new switch." I felt pleasantly guilty. A less decent person might have lorded it over me. Terry didn't.

"How about the battery?"

"Just fine. I put a good charge on it, and if this doesn't start your tractor, load 'er up and bring 'er over here."

"How much do I owe you?"

"Nothing."

"You sure?"

"Yep."

Earlier, I had paid to the little repair shop on Railroad Street in Cynthiana $36 to have the starter fine tuned. "All we do is starters and alternators," Mr. Hendricks had explained.

"Find a niche and fill it, treat your customers fair and the world will beat a path to your doorstep," I said out loud as we drove north on U.S. 62 through Oddville. "Used to play them in basketball," I remembered as we passed the old school.

"Looks like a storage space now," said the lady, who had agreed to play hooky on this glorious summer day. "At Claysville we take KY 19," said the navigator to the pilot.

By now, we were soaking up the views along the North Fork of the Licking River. There were a few manmade eyesores, but they were exceptions rather than the rule. A long swinging footbridge had withstood the floods of the years, a reassurance in times of modern concrete spans. If Robert Frost would be a swinger of birches, we'd be swingers of footbridges. Just inside the city limits of Brooksville appeared the sign: "Don Galloway Drive."

"Must be nice having a street named for you," said one slightly envious farmer, who had attended college with the tall, handsome man, who went to Hollywood and distinguished himself with Raymond Burr on "Ironsides." At the Guignol Theater at UK at mid-century, the farmer had played the dentist in the "Diary of Anne Frank," and Don Galloway had played the storm trooper. The director, Wally Briggs, had squeezed the acting talents of the dentist and the storm trooper until there'd been little left in either.

"Do you know Don Galloway?" I asked the young man at Kern's Meat Processing.

"My father went to high school with him," said the new generation, and the subject was dropped there. The two lambs were left at Kern's to pay their ultimate sacrifice—a fact of life giving all shepherds grave and awkward moments. Yet, it's an act repeated again and again down through the centuries.

"Let's go home by way of Blue Licks," said the pilot to the navigator.

"O.K., we take KY 19 south to KY 165, through Mt. Olivet to Piqua, and that'll put us right at Blue Licks."

The drive across KY 165 provided views rivaling the Blue Ridge Parkway of North Carolina, even the panorama from the mountains overlooking the Bekaa Valley of Lebanon. The vista stretched on one side virtually it seemed to the Ohio River. On the other, sparsely inhabited Bracken and Robertson counties lay like paradises awaiting discovery by new Daniel Boones.

Arriving at the Blue Licks State Park, we parked the pickup before the large, graceful monument to the fallen heroes in the "last battle of the revolution," and we walked up the steps to pay our respects.

"This monument, the gift of a grateful Commonwealth, commemorates the heroic pioneers, who, in defense of Kentucky, here fought and fell in the Battle of Blue Licks, August 19, 1782...So valiantly did one small party fight that, in the memory of those who unfortunately fell in the battle, enough of honor cannot be paid."

Daniel Boone's son, Israel, was a private in his father's force. Israel, too, paid an ultimate sacrifice. More than two centuries later, two Kentuckians returned home, refreshed, and grateful for all men and beasts, who've made the good life possible for others.

THE JOYS OF HOME-GROWN HAM

C rossing over Plum Lick Creek, hearing the November water splashing against Old Blue, then coming up the lane past the corn nearing harvest, an old-timer remembers Thanksgivings past, and thinks of Thanksgivings yet to come. He remembered the pumpkins and the shocks of corn, the crisp air whining in the weather boarding of the meat house where the hams hung as the hour approached for unhooking them and taking them down.

Yep, the old-timer sighs, that's about the size of it. It's all those little things that added up, make the difference, the difference between loneliness and togetherness.

It was there in the way the yearling lambs looked yesterday morning after they were fed and watered. They looked contented. There was trust in their eyes. They didn't know their purpose, but they were satisfied all the same. They can hardly be faulted for their God-given nature.

It was there in Lady's eyes, too, and she almost let the hand that fed her, touch her. Lady knows her purpose. It's to protect the lambs that don't know their purpose. Lady thinks for them. Her reward is the satisfaction of taking care of somebody.

It was there in the eyes of Sunspot and her two kittens, one all sunshine color, the other all cloudy skies. Each had the "feed me" meow going, which is past purring. Cloud, the cantankerous white cat, was probably down around the barn, lying in wait for something juicy. The cat population is in its ascendancy now, and unless hungry coyotes get past Lady to do a little catnapping, there could be a problem for which none of us will give thanks.

With the days dwindling down to Thanksgiving, a decision will have to be made soon about which old ham to take from the meathouse. A plumped-up turkey is fine, but two-year-old home-grown ham is finer by far. You stuff a turkey, but you blanket an old ham. Who would want turkey and dressing for final rites when they could have two-year-old ham and beaten biscuits?

Ah, the joys of taking down the ham from the rafter where it has hung with such stillness for so long! Even the last earthquake made it sway barely if at all. The slow walk to the kitchen is an important part of the ceremony. The ham carries well.

There are many ways to prepare old ham, but one is to cut off and save the hock for soup, trim away the rind and most of the fat. Leaving a little may shorten a life, but what's a life without some old ham fat?

Next, place the masterpiece in the sink at the end of the day, and fill the sink with water. Along about midnight, climb out of your warm bed, add a stick of wood to the bedroom fireplace and go out to the kitchen to admire your work. Drain away the water, turn the ham over and refill the sink to the top. Go back to bed and dream about Thanksgiving morning. You'll have something to wake up for.

First thing in the morning, go back to the kitchen, drain out the second water and move the ham to the center of the kitchen table. Prepare a "dough blanket" using 4 cups all-purpose flour, 1 cup brown sugar, 2 tablespoons each ground cloves, cinnamon and dry mustard and 1 teaspoon black pepper, adding just enough water to make a stiff dough. Roll the dough out on a floured surface—the counter top does fine as long as you promise the missus that you'll clean up— and wrap the dough blanket over the top, around the ends and underneath the ham. Be sure there are no holes or torn places in the garment.

Place the ham on a trivet in a roasting pan and put it into the oven to cook slowly (275 degrees) for about five hours for a 15-pound ham, or about 20 minutes a pound. Tend the fires in the fireplaces, give the cats a bowl of milk, give Lady a bone with some meat on it, put a little sorghum on the lamb's grain and don't worry about anything any more than you absolutely have to.

Praise God and don't forget to send Happy Thanksgiving to all God's creatures.

GETTING READY

he early morning fog, and the hunkering-down stillness of the evenings here on Plum Lick are sending messages. Something tells me it's time to be getting ready for winter.

The midday warmth is deceptive. It can lead to cursing the cold when it inevitably arrives.

Around these parts, winter happens once a year, and it should come as no surprise. Wishful thinking won't change any season, so the best thing to do is to put things in order.

I've taken the bicycle wheels off the garden cart and had them checked. No need for flat tires on a cold December night when the lambs start arriving. The garden cart is handy for a variety of pre-winter jobs, like bringing up baled hay from the stock barn to insulate the faucets on the backside of the big house. Then, there's the water faucet in the stock barn to insulate. No need to be up to your elbows in newborn lambs and have the water supply frozen solid. I'll want to be sure all the light bulbs are working in the lambing barn, and I'll remember to have some spares in case the darkest and coldest night of the year causes burnouts.

The water warmer will need to be in place and working properly. Waiting until the last minute is really silly, and leads to more useless cursing. Worst thing of all is to blame the sheep. Man has no call to classify all sheep as dumb, when man, who ought to know better, is dumber by far.

It's time to call the chimney sweep. Having a clean chimney (without dead trapped birds in it) is a consoling feeling when it's time to build up a really hot fire in February. Clearly, it's not a time for well-done birds. Most chimney fires are caused by accumulated carbon deposits, and if there's anything scarier than a chimney fire, I don't know what it is. A chimney sweep is one of the cheapest insurance policies available on the market today. When they're pretty and come dressed in high hat and tails, it's an even better bargain.

The firewood cradle needs to be handy by the door, and now is the time to fill it. The collection of kindling craves to be in a dry place that's easily accessible, and several boxes of country matches ought to be handy.

Those whistling drafts are saying, "Plug me up, or you'll be sorry in March!" I don't want to get behind on this one, especially the one that cuts from beneath the bathroom window and gets folks off on the wrong foot first thing in the morning. Otherwise, we might just as well turn to the outhouse, and everybody knows that's a terrible idea.

All the vehicles need to be checked: antifreeze; spare tires; air pressure; an emergency source of air pressure; gloves; a dry change of clothes; especially heavy shoes and socks; windshield scrapers; an uncluttered garage in which to put the vehicles to sleep each night; and the road scraper ready to go in case we're snowbound.

The pantry should be filling up in case the world grinds to a halt in the middle of a blizzard. There's nothing so miserable as an empty stomach at the height of an extended snowstorm on Plum Lick, or anywhere else in either the civilized or uncivilized world. Trouble is, civilization has spoiled us rotten, and most of us wouldn't know what to do if we had to rely solely upon ourselves for anything longer than three days.

October is a fine time to start Christmas shopping. The basic stuff should be done before Thanksgiving, I believe, because this allows more time for the simple enjoyment of the richnesses of both holidays. It's when these two traditional days become all glommed up with commercialization that the original meanings of Thanksgiving and Christmas tend to be lost.

I saw a woolly worm the other day, and what I saw was not immediately reassuring. Fact is, it scared me real bad. He was black on both ends with only a little brown in the middle. I said to myself right then and there, "Mr. Wooly, I hear you talking, and I'm going to spread the word: beware the winter of 1989-90."

CYCLES

n the way out to the sheep lot, the shepherd of all God's creatures keeps a sharp eye out for the giant webs around the old apple tree. He doesn't want to destroy even one of these masterpieces of industry and ingenuity. Urban-bound Kentuckians in 1992 may be too busy to take time out to watch the creative process, the intricate spinning and toiling. The works of art are there first thing in the morning, made to order. There's a dual purpose, but as far as the spider is concerned the primary and quite likely only purpose is to build up food stores for the coming of winter.

As a child growing up on a farm in Kentucky, the last thing in the world we'd think about doing would be to take a trip to see leaves changing color. It would never have occurred to us to buy a camera and load it with film to document what we'd seen. We'd stay at home on Mt. Auburn and use the cameras of our minds, our beings, our innermost satisfactions to know intimately the autumn experience.

As another leaf unloosens its bond to the tree and as it floats earthward, I turn to Lalie and say, "I love you," and "Do you remember the time?" and "Look over there, do you see what I see?" This is the time for understanding the miracle of autumn becoming winter, in time to become spring again with the return of fresh new leaves. The likeness of humankind and the families of leaves is a pleasant and satisfying contemplation. We begin our lives with the exuberance of springtime. We are forced from our sleep within the buds borne of generations of leaves to become Wordsworth's "brotherhood of venerable trees."

In summer, combinations of sunlight, water and microorganisms interact to produce food for the trees of life, at the same time expanding the volume of life-giving oxygen for a thirsty atmosphere, a beautifully working process, the manufacturing of food, very much like a commonwealth, whose disparate parts should be working in harmony. The result is not only survival, but the enrichment of all living things. Eternal spring and summer are contrary to our way of life in Kentucky. Autumn and winter are necessary to complete the seasonal cycle making us unique. If we can only come to understand what we are has depended so greatly on all those who've gone before us, and what we do now and in the future will matter immeasurably to those who follow after us.

As we sit here, you and I, watching all these glorious Water Maple leaves descending, we know what our destiny is. We give grateful thanks to those who are sleeping in the earth, and we take solace in the knowledge our own descendants resting in tomorrow's dreams may one day recall we were intimately involved in creation.

THE FLOWER PART OF US

In spring we had rolled down the windows of the car as we rounded the curves at Bunker Hill, so as to let the night air of Kentucky come in. The scent of the locust blossoms filled us with smiles. It was like a spray of sweet perfume in late May. We couldn't remember when the blossoms had ever been so abundant, or so fragrant. Perhaps, it was an omen.

As we made the turn onto the Plum Lick Road, the green and wildly growing fence rows formed the path leading home. As we turned into the main gate of the farm, the Big Dipper hung down low in the direction of Plum crossroads. The other constellations spread themselves across the midnight sky.

Times such as these cause us to rejoice that we did decide to go home again, despite the warning of Thomas Wolfe that such a thing is impossible. Home for us is the peace that comes when wrapped in a profusion of stars with a piece of moon as an anchor.

But, it was this year's locust blossoms that had us speculating that the season ahead would be unusually bountiful. So far the pattern seemed almost perfect. The calving had been regular and normal. There had been a minimum of breech births and other such difficulties. We'd been untroubled by wild dogs and other varmints. The bulls had been reunited with the cows, and procreation for next year's calving had quietly begun. This year's calves romped in the tall bluegrass and fescue while others lounged out of sight, the seed stems blowing softly overhead. It was a time of fullness of heart, a time for hide and seek. To miss this time, for children as well as brute animals, was to be denied the thrill of untested adventure.

Later would come the somber reality that all are destined to depart this world. The fact that there would be no exceptions would increase the incongruity, but with longer life would come a special awareness of natural order.

By definition, to be born is to begin the dying process. And for this there should be acceptance, graceful agreement that by so crossing the earthly threshold we become the sweetest of fragrances blowing across the throbbing countryside. This eternal aspect of our mortal selves becomes, at last, the finest part of us. And yet, it is so difficult for humans to comprehend, and I am no different in this than my brothers and sisters.

To say we don't fear death, I suspect, is rather brave if not cheap talk. Our finely tuned rational minds combined with our fierce instinct for survival cause us to resent perpetual night. We expect the sun to rise each morning and bathe us in its warmth. We automatically reject death as a pleasurable experience.

The animals that lack reason and sagacious remembrance of past encounters do not have the intelligence to fathom the consequences of their birthing. They may see the death of an offspring lying in plain view and still not perceive its meaning. There may be instinctual puzzlement, an anxious unbalancing of brutishness, but there is no longing, no tears to be shed. If the animals understood death as we do they would hold news conferences to make statements about slaughterhouses.

The human tragedy lies so much within our understanding that death is so final and irreversible in terms of bodily existence. The hope of mankind lies in our grasp of immortality, the sweetness of our spirits finally set free, precisely where the matter of living begins to make its most important sense.

We are not unlike the locust blossoms in the latter part of spring. Our trunks—both tall and straight—are cut down to be used for fence posts or burned for warmth on cold winter nights. It is the flower part of us—our love, compassion, unselfishness, helpfulness, kindness of heart for humanity—that sets us apart from all else in this world that faces dissolution.

And it is the fragrance of our blossoms that reaches through time to reunite us with those who've gone before as well as generations still unembodied. Not to stop and savor these spiritual enrichments is to miss the best that life has to offer and was always intended to be.

I want to remember this the next time a loved-one passes away.

SISTER JANE

From the very beginning—even before I was born—Jane had looked upon the prospect of a baby brother as a major nuisance. She vowed to throw me into the furnace. But as the years went by, we became close as little brother and big sister. We loved to talk about the meaning of life and death. Our childhood beliefs matured into the concepts of adulthood, and at last—in her 66th year, my 58th—we had our rendezvous with the moment of truth. It was a time we both had dreaded, that moment when we would say our last goodbye.

During her final days, with her children gathered around her, Jane's voice was barely a whisper. Her breathing was difficult. For me, the brief moments we spent together while she was in the hospital were probably more important than all the other times we had sat for hours at her kitchen table, holding our own summit conferences. The final moments culminated more than half a century of two Kentuckians compromising, commiserating, cajoling, damning, finding favor as well as fault.

We were discovering ourselves, really. We were constantly looking for answers, and we were never afraid to ask the toughest questions: what is alcoholism? does tobacco always cause cancer? is there a God? what was Daddy like? why was Mother so unhappy? why go to church? why is welfare in such a mess? what should be done about misbehaving children? what is misbehavior? is there a Heaven? is there a Hell? is war always justifiable? is divorce an ethical way out? is sex outside marriage ever defensible? what could we have done to have made a difference in our lives?

Jane wanted to live. She struggled to live. She looked death squarely in the eye, and she knew she wanted no part of it. The Crouch blood has not flowed in our veins for naught. Stubborn to the end, Jane did not run to embrace sweet eternity. She had come by her earthiness honestly. She and I grappled with a Heaven with streets paved with gold, and a Hell where the Devil cavorted with a horned head and a forked tail, and we rejected both. We held on passionately to the earth from which we had sprung.

Jane was superior to me in many ways, but in the art of spotting phonies she was especially astute. I had to be careful about that in her presence, because of my tendency to shilly-shally. I had a bad case of the Kentucky political tendency to be a mugwump, a person who sits on the fence with his mug on one side and his wump on the other, a very un-Crouch characteristic, and Jane could see it coming a mile away.

"Don't be a chameleon," she would say whenever I seemed to be changing my colors to benefit a present situation.

"I don't think I'm being a chameleon," I'd replied, lamely.

"Yes, you are. When you were in Dallas you thought that was the greatest place in the world. When you were in Atlanta, same thing. Washington, D.C., New York, and now Plum Lick—you have a way of changing to suit your circumstances."

That hurt. But that's the way it is with truth. Jane had the Crouch tendency to tell it like it is, and I admired her all the more because of it. I took the criticism to heart, because I knew if she didn't love me, she would never have taken the time to talk with me about it. She would have fallen back on the tactic taken by a good many of our forebears—she would have ignored me altogether.

Jane loved laughter. She appreciated the rich joke and the earthier the better. A low-down dirty joke could make her throw her head back, stamp her foot and declare, "Shoot!" Jane's was a rollicking personality without being totally boisterous. She had control. Hardly anything was ever done mindlessly. Jane was as smart as anybody who ever grew up in our part of Bourbon County. She was on the dean's list at Randolph Macon, but she didn't graduate, because she fell in love with Harry. They were married during World War II. Harry Tolson Richart Jr. returned home a hero, but he and Jane were destined for hard times. He died in the Veterans Hospital in Lexington and was buried in the Camp Nelson National Cemetery overlooking the Kentucky River.

Jane was a consummate reader, who could have been a writer. She had an opportunity to try out in Hollywood, but she turned it down. Her last year in High School, Jane had been the heroine in John Fox Jr.'s *Trail of the Lonesome Pine*. Her portrayal of June Tolliver had put a lump in a ten-year-old brother's throat: "She sat at the base of the big tree—her little sunbonnet pushed back, her arms locked about her knees, her bare feet gathered under her crimson gown and her deep eyes fixed on the smoke in the valley below." As far as I was concerned, my sister Jane <u>was</u> John Fox Jr.'s June Tolliver.

As she lay there in her hospital bed in 1988, the oxygen mask pulled aside for a moment, Jane said, "I've been building my coffin all day."

It was impossible to argue with that kind of directness. The quiet determination to meet death on her own terms and in her own way was typical of my sister's strong individualism. It was not arrogance. It was not disrespect. It was God-given, deep-seated strength that courses down genetic pathways, each generation becoming more powerful and courageous than the one preceding. And there was an increase in sweetness as we spoke of love.

"I love you," I said.

"And I love you," she replied in words barely audible. Our lives were now touching as they never had before.

"That's the most important thing of all, isn't it?—love, I mean."

Jane smiled.

As our time together neared the end—the family, Harry III, Ann and Liza, moving softly, speaking in tones more hushed—Jane motioned for me to come closer. She had something she wanted to tell me. She looked directly into my eyes as if to find the depths of my soul. Her last words to her little brother were:

"Pray for me."

"I will. And you pray for me," I said.

"I will," said Jane.

CRICKETS

Plum Lick is my Lake Isle of Innisfree:

"Dropping from the veils
of the
Morning to where the
cricket sings;
There midnight's all
a-glimmer, and moon a-glow,
And evening full
of the linnet's wings." [7]

I find myself, with Yeats, much in tune with the legions of crickets outside my window at this softer and mellower time of the year, late August, as the whole commonwealth drops slowly from the season of summer to the season of autumn. The change is so gradual as to be almost imperceptible, and were it not for the male cricket rubbing his front wings together announcing his territorial imperatives, we might fatalistically conclude there'll never be a timely reprieve from the oppressive heat.

There's something about the cricket that sets it so far apart from other insects—the abominable, yet indomitable cockroach for terrible example. I have absolutely nothing good to say about the aforementioned beast, whose beneficial purpose has yet to be revealed to me by the Great Creator.

On the other hand, the cricket has a manner and style and sense of rhythm suiting my fancy. In fact, the cricket may indeed be not nearly as intelligent as the unspeakable cockroach—I just happen to place some values higher than brain power; heart and song power commend themselves quite nicely. I should like to know more about my soul mate, the cricket, and I pledge myself to study what makes him sing the song he does, the way he does. Somehow, instinctively, I identify him as friend rather than foe, and for that reason I have never knowingly killed one. I have no idea why I believe it would be a case of murder, but I do.

Milton heard the same sound as did I, and that causes still more pleasure as the season stirs softly from summer to autumn:

> "Where glowing embers
> through the room
> Teach light to counterfeit
> a gloom
> Far from all resort
> of mirth
> Save the cricket
> on the hearth." [8]

The Cricket's Song, which has for this moment reconnected me with Milton, is a reminder that when our hearth here on Plum Lick has been warmed both by the logs burning in our bedroom fireplace and the friendly cricket hiding in the crevices of our mantelpiece on the first chilled night of late autumn, I'll have the good sense to take down John Milton and read again, deeply.

Have you been noticing how on certain nights about this transitional time, the spiders have been working overtime on their spinnerets? When I left the house early on a recent morning to drive to my classes at the University of Kentucky, there were three very large, masterfully crafted webs on the yard gate. I asked Lalie to come out and look at them with me as they glistened in the dew and the diffused morning light. Would we have recklessly destroyed these remarkable creations? No more than we would have ground a cricket underfoot.

What was even more memorable about this particular morning were the exhibits of spider webs all along the frontage fence on the Plum Lick Road, as a spider's gallery, it was. And it was as if there were something especially compulsive in the air that was driving both spiders and crickets to be about their appointed rounds in regenerative fervor.

The early morning fog was tucking in the creek banks with a wispy, thin blanket of Kentucky fog as light and delicate as any in Scotland or the Himalayas. The invisible vapor emitted by the leaves of our Water Maples here at the Isaac Shelby Crouch house has cooled us for another summer, but now the photosynthesis is showing the first signs of slowing down. The light from the sun has changed more than we've had the time or inclination to observe. Yet, on the drives from Plum Lick, over Bunker Hill, across Cane Ridge to the UK campus, I've been noticing the diffusion of light. It's this wonderful radiant understatement that tells me the change of the seasons is occurring even though the arbitrary and artificial calendar has not yet confirmed it. There's a softness now, where before there was a harsher glare. There is an indirection, a seasonal shyness, where there had been merely the shortest distance between sun and earth. This subtlety is more priceless than gold or silver. I tell myself to enjoy the miracle while it's here. True, it will come again, but I might not be here next time. Slow down, I remind myself. Do not rush madly through such a beautiful transformation.

As I walk across the almost deserted campus at the time between the summer sessions and the beginning of another fall term, I imagine the arrival of the new class of students. That time, too, is close at hand. The very reason, the only reason in my view for college professors doing what they do is about to evidence itself. From down on the practice field come the first sounds of the trombones, the clarinets, the saxophones, the flutes, the cornets, the French horns, the trumpets, the cymbals and the drums. It is the haunting sweetness of those first notes which signals the renewal of the educational process.

"They've come back!" I tell myself. I feel a resurgence of energy, and there's a smile on my sunbaked face. My mind is beginning to prepare me for the autumn of another year. I've heeded the call of the crickets, I've marvelled at the sight of the spiders' silken webs, I've wandered through banks of early morning fog, I've paid homage to these latter days of the Water Maples' leaves. I realize what is happening in nature is also manifesting itself within me, for I am a part of nature—I'm not apart from it. The extent to which I can truly understand and appreciate this, the better I will be able to go forth with some grace. The students returning to the campus will rescue me from any morbid view of this annual state of affairs. But, I shall resist the temptation to discuss it very much with them, for it is not their time to reflect upon it in the same way that I am finding it so necessary to contemplate the passage of the years. Their time for this sort of diffused musing will come later after their major rashnesses have been expended.

As for me, I will return from the campus each night and begin thinking about the gathering of firewood for the cold nights soon coming. I will be grateful for the old Water Maple, which a summer storm blew down, and I'll take my sledgehammer and steel wedges to begin working up the wood for our hearth. A cricket or two will have made it inside, knowing there will be a friendly fire and no meanness on my part. A spider or two will be at work somewhere in the attic, perhaps, but I'll not go check. The leaves will have all fallen from the trees, but the roots will be lying dormant, awaiting the coming of another spring. The light will have passed from pale yellow to steel-blue cold, and Lalie and I will be settling in for the winter.

THE EARTH SHOOK

Ravy and I returned home to Plum Lick the night of September 6, 1988, a perfectly normal evening in the most peaceful of places. The only thing missing was Lalie, who was working late at the newspaper. Following my retirement from CBS, and Lalie's retirement from Revlon, we've tried our hand at running two weekly newspapers. I've been director of the School of Journalism at the University of Kentucky since 1987, but the fixed foot remains at Plum Lick no matter how frayed the nerves, or how empty the pocketbook.

The dogs were fed and watered, the sheep were bedded down, the cows and calves were at peace with themselves on the hillside, and the 138-year-old two-story frame house we call home felt as secure as the Rock of Gibraltar. After a peanut butter and jelly sandwich and a tall glass of milk for me, a little dessert for Ravy, the odd couple piled up in Grandfather Bill's and Grandmother Laura's bed. Ravy requested and received the Cinderella story, once again reminding her father of witching hours.

We were sound asleep in a dreamland of fairy tales and office intrigues when precisely at 10:28 p.m. the Isaac Shelby Crouch house convulsed as if hit by a jackhammer. The floors seemed pressured up, the walls pressured in, the ceiling punched down. My feet hardly touched the floor from my side of grandfather's bed all the way to the kitchen. My first coherent thought was that a 100-car Louisville and Nashville freight train had jumped the track between Paris and Winchester and was heading straight up the Plum Lick Road.

Next I thought the furnace had turned itself on and was blowing up in slow motion. I turned the knob of the back door, expecting to come face to face with a tornado or a rodeo full of bulls with their cinch rings drawn tight.

Everything outside in the back yard was deathly quiet and motionless. "Why am I standing out here in the back yard? What in the world is going on in the paradise of retirement?" I mumbled to myself. I walked around the side of the house, past the cistern to check the horizon for a fireball marking the crash site of the jumbo jet that must've failed to gain altitude after takeoff from the Greater Cincinnati Airport. There was no fireball.

I looked up at the old, tall stone chimney on the north side of the house, and saw nothing to suggest it might fall down. Confused and disoriented with a peanut butter and jelly sandwich sloshing around in a glass of cold milk within a fraction of an inch from a fully awakened duodenal ulcer, I opened the screen door of the side porch, put one foot on the step, and felt another convulsion.

The dogs howled.

It was then I was sure I wasn't dreaming. It had to have been an earthquake. It couldn't have been anything else. I had just experienced an after-shock. I went inside and found 5-year old Ravy sound asleep.

I decided it was time to call somebody and find out what was officially going on. Call the police, or call the sheriff? I decided to call my son, Joshua's great-great-great-great grandson, Sam II, the anchorman at the CBS affiliate, Channel 27 in Lexington.

The phone was dead.

The dogs were still howling.

I didn't like this at all. I considered loading the gun in case it was a Soviet invasion. If cosmonauts had crash-landed I was not going to take any chances. I tried to pick up some reassurance from radio, but all I could find were music and sports, music and sports. It could be the end of the world, and all we probably would hear would be music and sports. I resigned myself to wait 15 minutes for Sam's 11 o'clock news.

Sam's first words were: "The earth shook."

A retired CBS News correspondent could not have written it better. Way to go, Sam. As it turned out, the epicenter was confirmed to be in Bath County, the other side of Bunker Hill, a hop, skip and shudder from Plum Lick. No injuries and no major damage, but who ever said nothing much ever happens down here?

A REASON FOR PLUM

Old Joshua's great-great-great-grandson (it kind of makes me feel warm to call myself that) wrote an open letter in 1989 to the Official Mapmakers in Frankfort:

Dear Mapmakers:

It has been reported you are considering removing Plum from the maps of the Commonwealth. Before you perform this surgery, without consulting the patient, let's first consider bygone days.

According to Perrin's History (1882), "Plum Lick...has had quite a number of names, and if the world stands still long enough, it'll probably have a few more."

The crossroads of KY 57 and 537 near the juncture of Plum Lick Creek and Boone Creek was probably known first as Pin Hook because the water hooks to the right, especially after heavy rains. Plum Lick Creek gives Boone Creek a kick it had not had up to that point. We think we know the origins of the names of Plum Lick Creek and Boone Creek. Indians on hunting parties probably brought plum fruit into the area, the way we buy Moon Pies at Workman's Grocery to see us on our way to where it is we're going. When the Indians spit out the plum seeds, they took root in the "dark and bloody ground." Wild Plum trees still grow on farms in the neighborhood of Plum, descendants of the original seeds popping from many an Indian hunter's mouth: Catawba, Cherokee, Chickasaw, Creek, Iroquois, Shawnee and Wyandotte.

Daniel Boone's brother was killed by one of these Indians, and Edward's burial spot is marked by the Daughters of the American Revolution beneath a Buckeye tree less than a mile downstream from the crossroads.

L.B. Thomason was the first postmaster at Plum in 1878, when James B. McCreary was completing the first of his two terms as governor. Governor Jim had better sense than to mess with Plum.

"The population of the place is forty souls and as many bodies, and the business is comprised in two stores and a blacksmith shop," wrote Perrin.

Just because Plum no longer has a blacksmith shop, or a post office or two stores in 1989 is no reason to erase the name from the highway maps.

"Lou Ellen, don't you think they ought to keep Plum on the map?"

"Well, yes, I suppose so," Lou Ellen will tell you in a Plum second. She and her husband, Ray, have been operating Workman's Grocery in spite of earthquakes, politicians in general and map changers in particular.

The state mapmakers' rationale for removing 'Plum' is that the community is not incorporated and doesn't have a post office. Who says you have to be incorporated and have a post office in order to keep your name? Having Plum on the map is as important as Peedee in Christian County, Philpot in Daviess County, Pierce in Green County, Pilot Knob in Madison County, Pilot Oak in Graves County, Pomp in Morgan County, Polly in Letcher County, Primrose in Lee County, Putney in Harlan County, Pilgrim in Martin County, Pigeon in Pike County, Pigeonroost in Clay County, Pine Knot in McCreary County, Pippa Passes in Knott County, Pottertown in Calloway County, Prosperity in Edmonson County and Paradise in Muhlenberg County.

If you take to believing everything they say in Frankfort, you might start thinking nothing much happens in Plum and all these other little out-of-the-way places. That's what we're trying to do— stay out of the way. There ought to be a few places like ours that don't look and smell like New York City, Chicago or Los Angeles.

Yours for better maps to
interesting places,
David Dick
Plum, Kentucky
October 1, 1989

PART TWO

J. LARKINS

THE BALONEY SANDWICH

"Hi, Joe."

"Hi, David."

"Where you heading?"

"Going to St. Louis; how about you?"

"Heading back to Washington."

"Have a safe trip."

"You, too."

It would be the last conversation I'd have with Joe Creason. It was the late '60s. The place was Standiford Field in Louisville. I was heading east. Joe was heading west.

Joe died August 14, 1974.

Later, while still a CBS News Correspondent, I would be heading south on KY 11. Just outside Bethel in Bath County I noticed a historical marker on the edge of the roadside cemetery.

"I didn't know Bethel had a historical marker. I'm going to turn around, and go back and look at it," I said to myself. It would be the first time I'd known that Joe Creason, "Kentucky's Man for all Seasons," had died and been laid to rest in the beloved soil of his Commonwealth. A Kentucky Coffee Tree above his grave was putting down its roots in the direction of Joe, the way he would have wanted it.

"Damn it," I'd muttered on that day. "I've been gone too long. Covered too many stories from Washington to San Francisco."

The rest of the trip down to Plum Lick was more solemn than it usually was in that period of time when I returned from wars in Central America to look for peace and sanity on Plum Lick. It had always been the place where I wanted to put down my own Kentucky roots, while there was still time left to enjoy it.

Jessie Stuart called Joe, "...a writer with natural talents if one was ever born, a man who reaches the people through the printed page, a goodwill ambassador with a sense of humor who brings sunshine when the day is cloudy..."

In his 1972 volume, *Joe Creason's Kentucky*, Joe wrote: "I agree that my repeating a funny story involving someone from Harlan or Louisville or Turkey Neck Bend, passing on a fact of history, providing a sample of folklore, or undertaking a ridiculous lost cause won't make the troubles that beset us disappear. But, since there's something therapeutic in laughter, these stories might cause our grave realities to seem less mountainous. I doubt a chuckle will do much to bring peace or cool to a long hot summer, but it might not do any harm either."

Joe Creason was sitting sideways at his desk against the wall on the 4th floor of the Courier-Journal building at the corner of 6th and Broadway in Louisville. It was the early 1960s. The Beatles had arrived in the United States, Harpo Marx and Stan Laurel had died and Cassius Clay had become Muhammad Ali.

I'd come down from the 6th floor, where the WHAS Radio and Television newsroom was located, something like loping from one tiny corner to another in the Bingham animal shelter. Usually, we cowered or postured in our respective places, like distant cousins in the extended Bingham family of employees, mildly distrusting each other, from time to time meeting on one or the other's turf to sniff at each other, pawing the ground and peeing with good affection.

"Joe, I'm going down to Barkley County." (There is no Barkley County in Kentucky. Due to the sensitive nature of this story, names have been changed to protect the guilty.) "I'm doing a documentary on the Angels' Wings hydroelectric dam. Need some contacts down there. Figured you'd know of some."

"Frolic Fain at Caninesville."

I pulled up a chair and sat at Joe Creason's knee. Joe had emerged as the Kentuckian's Kentuckian. He loved his state with a simple, well-stoked passion. It showed with the assurance of his sharp chin, like it was chiseled from a piece of the Palisades. He had a smile that reached far back in his eyes, rolling like a slow breeze across his Marshall County face, coming to rest on thin but firm lips.

Joe's wife, Shella, is a distant cousin of mine on the Bath County Crouch side of the family. While she still provides sweetness among cousins where it's both needed and appreciated, at the same time she's always seemed to possess the Crouch genes that one day would provide her with the strength she'd need to live resolutely after Joe's fatal heart attack when he was only 55 years old.

"Frolic Fain runs a little store at the Caninesville crossroads west of Moonbay," said the lips with a twang that couldn't be mistaken with anything heard north of the Ohio River. "Ask anybody there how to find it. They'll tell you. By the way, be sure to ask Frolic for a baloney sandwich."

"Why?"

"Because they're the best baloney sandwiches you'll ever find anywhere. Tell Frolic how good his baloney sandwich is, and he'll take good care of you."

I thanked Joe for the crucial information. In a few days, I was on my way down to Barkley County. There was no problem at all in finding the Caninesville crossroads. Once locating it there was no question as to the whereabouts of Frolic Fain's grocery store. It guarded the crossroads like General Somoza's pillbox in Managua.

Walking inside Frolic Fain's grocery store (later I would be brought up short by a word expert at CBS, who said it was incorrect to say, "grocery store"—a "grocery" was one thing, and a "store" was another thing, but if you put the two words together you exposed yourself as being a dummy from Kentucky or some other southern redneck state. That was one of the several reasons why I retired from CBS at the earliest possible age—55—in order to return home where people might talk "dumb," but in fact were about as smart as anybody ever produced up there in the great Ivy League centers of learning.

"Grocery store," "speaking of rain," "hollerin' rain," having as many "ideals" as "ideas," being "fair-to-middlin'," "reckonin'" it to be true, eating "dinner" at the middle of the day, "supper" at the end of the day, having one post, and another post, making two "posties," calling your wife "ole lady," calling your husband "son," calling your daughter "girl," saying something was "slicker'n a mole," or "nervous as a cliff rat," or "shakin' like a dog shittin' bones" were dependable fixtures of language in the Plum section of Kentucky, as well as many other nooks and crannies where body English and plain expression always counted more than fancy words.

If there were anything that stood out about Mr. Fain and his grocery store it was the spit-polish shine on his meat cutting machine. Everything on the outside might be going to hell in a hand basket but inside, Mr. Fain's meat cutting machine was clean as a hound's tooth. For miles around there might be unspeakable littering—everything from beer cans to abandoned refrigerators, junk cars to busted bedsprings—inside Frolic Fain's store, the meat cutting machine was enough to have made the poets proud.

Cleanliness is next to Godliness were words surely written for Frolic Fain and his meat cutting machine in Barkley County, Kentucky. The mechanism looked as if it had just come from the factory box. It had a shine on it that would dazzle the sphinx. If you looked at it too long it would make you blink.

The counter where Mr. Fain's customers sat and ate baloney sandwiches was as clean as a dog's front fang, but it couldn't equal the meat cutting machine. There wasn't a speck of dirt on the counter, but there was no chance a body could see a face in it what with its dull linoleum finish. You could part your hair by what you saw in the surface of the meat cutting machine.

"Mr. Fain, I'm from Louisville. Joe Creason said I should look you up."

"Did?"

"Yessir, he did. You see, I'm doing this television documentary on the Angels' Wings dam, and I thought, I mean Joe Creason thought, you could put me in touch with some folks who are for it, and some folks who are against it."

"Maybe."

The reporter shifted ground, operating on the theory that more times than not many male Kentuckians, especially when approached by total strangers, are not immediately pleased by the full-steam-ahead approach. There needs to be some hemming and hawing, a little behind-scratching, some toe-in-the-dust turning, some hitching-up of the pants, a little throat clearing, a rattling of cough and a deliberate spit to nail a fly at four feet. Both sides need a chance to take several deep breaths before undertaking anything that might conceivably lead to hard feelings. Many northerners simply don't understand this, and, of course, there are a good many Kentucky urban dwellers, including a passel of Japanese and other newcomers who've put their more primitive pasts behind them.

"Mr. Fain, I sure would like to have one of your baloney sandwiches."

Mr. Fain said, "How did you know about my baloney sandwiches?" He had that watchful look, revealing his natural Kentucky tendency to want to know what strategy lay behind any such request.

"Joe Creason told me. He said you had the best baloney sandwiches between here and Louisville."

Nothing more needed be said. Mr. Fain turned to the refrigerator, reached inside and took out a long tube of baloney that looked like it'd been made in baloney heaven. He walked to the meat cutting machine and threw the switch. That meat cutting machine hummed like the sweet juice of glory. The blade turned in anticipation that it was about to do what it was meant to do since the coming of the Industrial Revolution.

Frolic Fain's sure hand eased the tube of baloney toward the blade. When they touched, it was divine consummation. "Scrooommed," they touched, and one slice lay over like a ballet dancer touching her toes. "Scrooommed," and the second slice joined the first, a pas de deux to have done Dame Fonteyn proud. Frolic gathered the two slices, married them between two slices of light bread and laid the critter on the counter. He stood back and smiled. I bit into the sandwich and smiled back. Of such encounters do lasting friendships take root and grow with never a backward glance.

A few weeks later, I returned to Barkley County to do some clean-up work on my forgettable, one-man television documentary. I made several of those during my time at WHAS, and none cried out for Pulitzers or Emmys. I wouldn't receive an Emmy for another ten years, when Arthur Bremmer pumped five shots in the direction of Governor George Corley Wallace in the Laurel Maryland Shopping Center. I learned pretty quickly, in the post-Edward R. Murrow years, more careers were made as the result of assassinations or near-assassinations, wars, hurricanes or mayhem, generally, than some of the best, most thoughtful documentaries. None that I know of was ever based on a baloney sandwich.

It was a hot summer day in Caninesville, and when I arrived at the crossroads I was more thirsty for a soft drink than I was hungry for a baloney sandwich. Wouldn't you know it?—Frolic Fain's store was closed. There was a sign on the door, which said, "Back in 30 minutes." There was nothing to do but wait. I looked for some shade on the side of the building, and that's where I came upon a sorry dog, sleeping and snoring as if there were no tomorrow. He was one of the ugliest dogs I'd ever seen in a lifetime of admiring all kinds of dogs.

He was a scroungy dog. His ribs showed. When he breathed, little puffs of dust rose up and settled back down on his crusted nose. He was a Camelot for fleas. He reminded me of an old crumpled throw rug that had spent more time outside the house than in it.

About this time, Frolic Fain drove up in his pickup. At the sound of it, this good-for-nothing dog jumped up like he'd been shot from a cannon. His target was the front door, and by the time Frolic had his hand on the knob, that dog had his crusted old nose snug up to the crack in the doorjamb. His nose quivered, throwing off tiny, fine flecks of dust, shimmering in the sunlight slanting across the tree tops, finding their home on Frolic Fain's doorstep.

When Frolic opened the door, that dog took off running down the front of the counter like he was at the head of the stretch at the West Memphis dog track. He rounded the counter corner, all four legs tangling and untangling. He headed up the backside of the counter like a dog who knew where he was headed. He was going full-tilt until he reached the meat cutting machine. That's when he threw on the brakes. He jumped up, put both scrawny front paws on the edge of the meat cutting machine and licked the whole thing, clean as a whistle.

Frolic Fain smiled and said, "Bet you want another baloney sandwich."

I smiled back and said, "Yep, reckon I do."

"UP THE TREE!"

T here've been many dogs with whom I've crossed paths—Nip and Tuck, Dusty, Mom, Nugget, Moby, Sis, NCAA, Muddy River, Turk, William Stamps, Beauregard, Stonewall Jackson, Heidi, Button, Baby Red, Tar Baby, Booger Red, Ole Miss, Ewedawg, Lambdawg, Lady, Ravy's Marshmallow Cocoa, Pumpkin, Duchess, Zoee's Patricia O'Casey's litter of 15 and many more lost in the murkiness of dog time—but one dog I'll never forget was the one I met while covering a Willie Nelson birthday party when I was working for CBS News.

A reporter at a Willie Nelson birthday party has a dog's work if you want to know the truth about it. The scene is usually one of those masses of humanity kind—once you're into it, you tend to wonder if you'll ever again see the front gate. The sun is usually blistering hot, because it's the 4th of July in Texas and the crowd is packed so tight there's hardly any way to keep from either being stepped on, or stepping on somebody else. The drinking of beer and the smoking of funny cigarettes produce a congenial atmosphere for the most part, although unpleasantries are just as apt to break out as not. Slights are exaggerated along with egos, biceps, tall tales and questionable music appreciation. Frankly, I've never been able to understand why humans are so determined to pack themselves into anything as tight as tuna in a can. Most dogs have better sense.

On this particular occasion, though, an unusual dog demonstrated wisdom and considerable courage.

He rose above the crowd.

I had retreated across the highway south of Austin, across the road from Willie's birthday party, to our helicopter landing site. We'd chartered the chopper so we could have aerial pictures of Willie's bash and to provide for the quickest exit possible. Our strategy was to fly from Austin to San Antonio in order to feed the satellite to New York.

I was standing there talking with the rancher who owned the property when I noticed his two dogs. One was a German shepherd, and the other one was about as strange a looking dog as I'd ever seen up until that time, which was a period of 58 years of being acquainted one way or another with a broad assortment of dogs. He was cata-houla-strange, if you know what I mean: one eye a different color and cant than the other, splotchy colors of fur, one ear up, the other down. As is usually the case with people, appearances among dogs are deceptive.

"What kind of dog is that?" I asked the rancher.

"That's a tree-climbing dog."

"A what?"

"A tree-climbing dog, didn't you ever see a tree-climbing dog?"

"No, I don't believe I have," I said, with my best suspicious Kentucky tone of voice.

"Here, I'll show you," said the rancher, who took one look at the dog and ordered, "Up the tree!"

Folks, that dog acted like he'd been waiting for the sweetest words in the world and needed to wait no longer. He tore up the loose gravel and went through the air like a Lear jet taking off from the Dallas-Fort Worth Airport. He landed about six feet up on the side of the nearest tree, the bark flying like sparks from a sickle that had just touched the grindstone. He didn't stop for anything or anybody. He cleared the main trunk and reached for the stars. He walked around in that tree as if he were a bird. He must've thought he was a bird. I stood on the ground and marvelled.

I'd never before nor since seen a dog walking around in a tree, and he acting as if it were the most fun in the world. He had a pretty good view of Willie's birthday party across the road, but I'm pretty sure he didn't need that mess for inspiration. He seemed to have figured it all out for himself: old dogs can thrive on original tricks. There's no reason in the world only birds should feel at home high in trees.

After a while the dog returned to the ground, and the rancher went inside his house. My New York producer approached, and I said to him, "Come here a minute."

"Yeah?" he replied, like a 57th street cab driver asking a rider to repeat a street address.

"Did you ever see a tree-climbing dog?"

"A what?" he snapped, like the cab driver countering with, "There's nothin' there but a vacant lot."

"Watch."

I looked the dog square in the eye, and said, "Up the tree."

That dog did it all over again. I said, "Jack, we ought to do a story on this dog, because it's better than the one across the road." Jack harrummphed, and went to make another telephone call having nothing to do with the singular importance of my discovery of a tree-climbing dog. Maybe this was one of the last turning points in my final days with CBS. Everybody was coming to understand, one correspondent was losing it.

"BA-ROOOOO, BA-ROOOOO..."

The dogs were barking downstream. You didn't need to be a genius to know we had a potential problem. They were not our Plum Lick dogs. Blue and Muddy River were fastened up and NCAA (she answered to "Neeka") and Turk were close by the house. At the 1850 house in the valley of Plum Lick Creek in Bourbon County, Kentucky, a hundred years after the first logs were slotted into place, a few years after the retirement party at CBS, darkness had fallen, settled in for sure, and I doubted the trespassers were up to any good.

I was just settling into my blessed retirement from covering wars, drought, floods, hurricanes, tornadoes, armadillo races and Willie Nelson birthday parties. There had been several close calls, when I thought for sure I was about to buy the farm: Jonestown; Beirut; Nicaragua; El Salvador; the Laurel, Maryland, Shopping Center. I'd always thought of retirement as a place of peace, where the whupped would prop up feet, take another sip from mint juleps and go quietly into that Great Good Night.

Back at CBS, a "good night" was a technical and legally binding term meaning a worker was officially off the clock. If you called technicians back 30 seconds after giving them a "good night" the union contract automatically imposed a stiff penalty against the company. Back then, most of us lived by our many little good nights. We chose to ignore the final Great Good Night from which there would be no call backs, nothing extra in the paychecks. After "retirement" to the banks of Plum Lick Creek the mint julep trail was frequently interrupted by the yapping of dogs.

I went over to Wayne's house and asked him if he'd come with me to check out the latest barking. Wayne rubbed his eyes, put on his shoes and brought his gun. Wayne, our farm manager, almost always kept his gun handy in case there were anything to shoot. Wayne can shoot as straight and fine as Daniel Boone or his brother, Squire, or any one of the Long Hunters pioneering in the Dark and Bloody Ground before the American Revolution. Wayne is as comfortable with a gun as a foot is to a wool-lined moccasin. He can draw down on a groundhog and have a bullet between his eyes before the creature has time to agonize five seconds as to whether it might be a good idea to head for the safety of his bunker. Whether fighting the American Revolution, the War of 1812, the American Civil War, the Spanish American War, World Wars I, II or, God forbid, III, I would feel better off having a Kentuckian like Wayne in the trenches with me.

We drove down the lane to Plum Lick Creek, and I kept the pickup truck near the bank as we headed on in the direction of the ruckus.

"There they are," said Wayne. I looked, but I couldn't see the dogs. It wouldn't be the first time Wayne had seen something I couldn't. He could spot an uninvited dog across the creek, through the trees and past the rocks, and put a bullet in one ear and out the other like it was made to take that road. The homeless hound would never know what hit him.

"They're coon dogs, and there's the coon up there," said Wayne, pointing to the top of the Water Maple on the creek bank by the spot where there was a place in the creek wide enough to ice skate. I looked, but I couldn't see the coon.

126

"Don't reckon we'll shoot coon dogs will we, Wayne?"

"No, don't wanna kill coon dogs."

By now I could see the two dogs all right, and they were busy "Ba-rooooo, ba-rooooo"ing. The coon was not much more than a woeful shadow high up in the Water Maple. He was holding on with his claws curled around the last limb up there. Wayne called softly to the dogs, "C'mon-c'mon," and they came over to see us and make friends as warm as old cousins. We patted them on their heads and scratched them behind their ears. They were wearing collars, and on them as plain as could be were the name of the owner and his telephone number. Wayne and I decided to go back to the house, so he could find a couple of chains to tie the dogs up, while I went to the telephone in the kitchen to call the number on the dogs' collars.

As it turned out, the telephone number was in Menifee County, a right smart way from where the dogs were presently located in Bourbon County across the road from Montgomery County. A lady on the other end said her husband and son were coon hunting someplace, and probably would be out all night. I told her, if he called in or came back home without his dogs, he knew where he could come and pick them up. She seemed relieved there was no bad news, at least not yet.

About this time, a pickup truck came tearing up the road to the Crouch house, and out came a man looking like he'd just walked out of an L. L. Bean catalog. He had everything on him anybody would ever need in an emergency. He had lights and whistles and more pockets than most dogs have fleas. He was the most serious looking coon hunter I'd seen during my short experience as a retiree from 19 years of hunting for stories for national television from Cincinnati to Commodora Rivadavia in the Argentine Patagonia.

"Who lives here?"

Now when he said that, it didn't come across as mean as it sounded. He was just a Kentuckian who'd parted company with his prize coon dogs. He didn't have time to waste over being polite in any round about sort of way. He was direct, and he wanted to know.

"I do. And I know where your dogs are. We had thought we were going to kill them, because they were in the same field with livestock, but when we realized they were coon dogs, of course, we didn't shoot them."

Wayne, he didn't say anything.

I'd been gone from Kentucky so long I'd turned into a blabber-mouth. On top of everything else, I talked too fast. I hadn't yet learned how to keep my mouth shut and shuffle my feet. L. L. Bean turned white like he might faint. He swallowed hard. His Adam's apple moved up, down and back again before it stabilized in the mid-dle of his throat showing through his red flannel shirt.

"Sure glad you didn't do that." Now, that part of the communica-tion carried the unmistakable message there ought not to be anybody stupid enough to kill coon dogs. Yet, if they had done it, even on somebody's own property, they'd probably have to deal with the man who owned them, no matter if the man were trespassing.

Down deep inside I was right glad we hadn't shot those coon dogs. If we had, we'd probably would have had to pay for it.

It was like the day in Esteli, Nicaragua, when one of General Somo-za's national guardsmen drew down on me. I was quicker and maybe smarter than most groundhogs; I could see the enemy, and I knew he wanted to kill me. I ducked on that day a fraction of a second before the soldier pulled the trigger, and the next thing I heard was the bullet grinding into the stone wall a hair's length above my head. I tore at the concrete sidewalk, using my fingernails like mechanical claws digging into a saucer of butter. I scrambled inside a nunnery and cowered with the sisters and the dead and the dying until the fighting subsided long enough to escape safely.

"If you'll follow us we'll take you to where they are," I said, as color began to return to L. L. Bean's face. Wayne and I climbed back into our pickup truck, and the coon hunter and his son climbed back into theirs and we retraced our tracks back to the big Water Maple. When we arrived, there were no dogs to be found. But, the coon was just as forlorn a shadow as it had ever been in the top of the tree.

"Ha-looooo. Ha-looooo," called the coon hunter, the sound of his voice carrying down Plum Lick Creek, reaching with patient insis-tence toward the abandoned and crumbling house where old Joshua had staked his claim a dozen years or so after Daniel had passed through the trace on his way from Boonesborough to Lower Blue Licks. It was the homestead where Polly Sr., and then Polly Jr. had baked their cornbread, and my great-grandmother Cynthia, Polly Jr.'s daughter, had raised her brood and died before her time. It was the site a hundred years later and a hundred yards away from the house, where there'd been a killing and where there'd been a suicide after the shooting of family pets.

"Ha-looooo. Ha-looooo," floated down the stream and vanished among the groundhog holes, the shaggy Water Maples and the deserted springhouses, where the womenfolk had stored their milk for churning butter, and they'd hung meat against the heat of sultry days and muggy nights.

The coon hunter's outfit included one of those powerful lights positioned close to the chest, so no motion needed wasting with long-handled flashlights, eliminating the chance they might be dropped into water. Of course, L. L. Bean could have fallen in himself but his shiny hip boots would have kept him dry.

The coon hunter shone the light back and forth across the creek bottom, where the corn stubble rustled in the cold, dry breeze, and he kept "Ha-looooo"ing and "Ha-looooo"ing with every once in a while a "Yah, yah, yah." The coon hunter, and his son growing up to be just like him, would listen for a response, but there was none.

It began to occur to me they might think Wayne and I had already shot the dogs and dragged them off to the ditch on the other side of the hill, where most of our dead animals are left for the buzzards when they return from winter vacations.

If the man and the boy believed we'd done that, they didn't offer a hint. It would have been very impolite if they had, and might have made us mad to boot. It was as tense a moment as any I'd experienced in Matagalpa, Nicaragua, or Sensuntepeque, El Salvador.

To tell the truth, I was glad the dogs had moved on, because I didn't want to see the wretched shadow shaken down from the tree in order for there to be a fight there in the middle of the night until something died. Even so, I knew in the pit of my stomach, the coon was going to die, one way or the other. The coon hunter, who had given up "Ha-looooo"ing as a lost cause for the moment, shone the high-powered light up to the top of the Water Maple. It turned the shadow into a round gray mass about the size of a small pillow.

Wayne brought it down with one shot.

The shadow hit the water with a dull splash.

The coon hunter waded out and brought the dead critter up to the bank. About five or six pounds, we estimated. We talked about who would take the coon, and we finally decided Wayne should probably take it home with him to feed his own dogs.

We visited a spell. Tension eased. The coon hunter showed us colored pictures of one of his last trips to Vermont. He had pictures of coons like some fishermen have fish on strings. It was mighty clear, here was a man who took coon hunting to be roughly the equivalent of a crusade, and he fully intended to pass along the tradition to the young boy by his side. Wayne and I said if the coon dogs showed up later we'd tie them up, and the owner could come back and take them. He and his son went off into the night as quickly as they had come. When I returned to the house, and stood there undressing in the bedroom, Lalie's voice came simply and clearly from under the covers.

"Why did you kill the coon?"

I thought I'd have as quick an answer as she had had a question, but I didn't. I slept on the question and dealt with it off and on for two or three days. I never came up with a satisfactory explanation.

It was the hunter and the hunted. The hunter was not at home with his feet propped up, watching professional football. The hunter was not chasing Iranian students down the streets of Dallas or errant congressmen down the halls of Capital Hill. The hunted was trying to stay ahead of the dogs. They had been bred to "Ba-rooooo, ba-rooooo," not to jump up into somebody's lap in a rocking chair and lick somebody's face and wait for a squeeze and a hug. That made sense for about a minute.

Why hadn't I told the coon hunter he had no business turning his dogs loose to roam to Kingdom Come? I answered that one by saying, the next time I might, but when a coon hunter pays $2,000 for one of his dogs there's little chance I'm going to stand there in the middle of the night and lecture him about coons and ethics.

That made sense for about a minute.

Let's say we had not shot the coon. After he had come down he would have become the hunted all over again, and the dogs, somewhere, sometime would have returned, "Ba-rooooo"ing, and "Ba-rooooo"ing, and next time there would have been that awful shaking of the pitiful shadow out of the tree, and the terrible struggle to the finish.

That made sense for about a minute.

It was months before Lalie's words stopped ricocheting in my brain: "Why did you kill the coon? Why did you kill the coon? Why did you kill the coon?"

I never did come up with an answer but, on cold nights down by the Water Maple on the edge of the creek, sometimes I think I can still hear, "Ba-rooooo, ba-rooooo, ba-rooooo..."

COYOTES

The coyotes returned. They massacred the sheep. At least, that's what we thought. Since that day when we were too stunned to cry, too confused to think clearly, I've learned a few things.

I was off teaching at the University, Lalie was working at the newspaper in Mt. Sterling and Wayne and Judy were picking and hauling peppers. It was a sorry crop of peppers, more trouble than they were worth, spindly, gnarled and tasteless to boot—about like some of the stories we were putting into the newspaper. The coyotes struck in broad daylight, we told ourselves from our anti-coyote way of looking at things. We figured we were always right and coyotes were always wrong, sort of in the same way Senator Lloyd Bentsen's father and I had talked about endangered species. Mr. Bentsen stood there outside his home in McAllen, Texas and declared: "If I saw a rattlesnake crawl up in my yard, and I knew it was the last rattlesnake on the face of the earth, I'd kill it."

"What would you do if you saw a coyote coming over the hill?" Jim Loy, the "Known Liberal" had asked back at the CBS News Bureau in Dallas before the retirement and return to Plum Lick.

"I'd shoot it," replied the correspondent, who had concealed his passive conservatism about as long as anybody ever had at the place where liberalism in all its varieties seemed more esteemed than the opposing view on matters of almost any sort. Age also had something to do with it. It's one thing to be ultra-liberal about coyotes when one is young and lean and mean, it's another thing when the days are winding down, and coyotes are yipping in the middle of the night, enough to make the short hairs stand on the back of a wrinkled neck.

"Why would you shoot it?" the "Known Liberal" had wanted to know. He was agitated, but not as much as I.

"Because, damn it, Jim, we won't be running an old folks' home for coyotes, what's why. We won't put out troughs, and fill them up and send out invitations for all the coyotes in the neighborhood to drop by for a meal, that's why. And we won't wait for a coyote and his no-good buddies to kill our sheep before we pass sentence, that's why. We'll just shoot the bloody bastards."

Jim, the gentle "Known Liberal," sighed and turned away. He knew he was arguing with somebody who had made up his crusty old mind, and there wasn't much sense in wasting any more time on lost causes. He might as well have been trying to convince General Somoza to look at the reporter instead of into the television camera. "Excuse me, Mr. President," I said during my last interview with him before he was assassinated in Paraguay, "would you look at me instead of at the camera?"

"You're right," Anastasio Somoza Debayle had said with his bluntest bunker mentality, "I am the president."

Later, after the retirement party in Dallas, and after the return to Kentucky, on that sultry September day there had to have been more than one coyote that came over the hill. It was as if, I thought, they had come to settle old scores. We had started out with 30 ewes and one ram. One ewe had died of heat stroke during the summer, which left us with 29 ewes and one ram. Wayne had been putting the flock up each night, turning them out in the small pastures near the big house. We knew we were running a risk during the daylight hours, but we felt we had no choice but to gamble that much. We can't be shepherds every waking moment, I said, no matter how much we might wish for it.

The first time we turned the flock out to graze they had run to pasture like children on an Easter Egg hunt. Sheep and children have something in common, I wrote in my journal: they are innocents. That's what I believed at the time. Less romantic and more accurate folks would disagree, but I took the position that children and sheep have little awareness of potential danger, making them vulnerable, making varmints like coyotes appear more clever than they actually are.

I'd thought quite some little bit about why God made coyotes in the first place. Without pretending to understand very much about the universal evolutionary scheme of things, at the same time trying to deal as compassionately as possible with life and its inconsistencies, the only thing I could conclude was, God made coyotes to remind us we pay dearly for our innocence. It may make innocence more precious and more needful of protection, all at the same time. Without getting up a crusade and doing an Onward Christian Soldiers on coyotes, I just wanted to help the sheep a little bit. That's sort of what Wayne wanted to do, too, although the shooting part always seemed to please him more, and he was very good at it. When he took aim with the .222 and blew away the first coyote who came visiting this year, we took a picture of it and it appeared on the front page of *The Montgomery Times*. We wanted the public to see the evidence. Wayne had a pleasant smile on his face as he held up the coyote by its tail.

But after all, this coyote had been a mother nursing her young. She had been playing the survival game by all the rules she knew with instincts finely tuned. She'd never bargained for favors, had never wagged her tail or licked a hand to win a soup bone. She had just made it her business to go out and kill where the killing was good, when she needed it in order to survive. One look at her fangs and her claws was enough to tell anybody she'd been engineered to kill. But now she was dead. It only took a month for one of her pups to come back seeking revenge, I rationalized. I was so mad about what was happening I felt like saying it even if it didn't make sense. Revenge is something humans understand, even if coyotes don't, which may be to their everlasting credit. Coyotes are just hungry. If they understood revenge they would by now have gotten up their own army and done an Onward Christian Coyotes on Wayne and me. They wouldn't have gone after the sheep, they would have gone after us, the ultimate human source.

And so, when the first coyote pup came up through the alfalfa in the bottom adjacent to the killing field he was looking for something to eat. Wayne spotted him and managed to get off one shot from the .222 with the telescopic sight. He missed. It was one of those rare times. The target was a smidgen too far away. The coyote turned tail and lit out back down the alfalfa field as fast as his young legs would carry him. Wayne fired again to make a statement more than anything else. Coyotes may not understand revenge, but they do seem to know it when a .222 bullet whistles across the tips of the hairs on their heads. I began thinking, we should have known right then and there it would only be a matter of time until the rest of the litter would come out of the woods in Joshua Meadows and cross over to pay us another call. The innocents on the killing field were too tempting for self-respecting coyotes to ignore, was a thought somehow appearing plausible.

Not once did I suspect some of our own dogs might be thirsty for the taste of blood.

It was more convenient and more conventional to think the coyotes must have bided their time. When they came, it was with lightning fury. By the time I heard the "coyote" attack had taken place I hurried to Wayne's house to tell him I was sorry.

"That's life," he said and reached for his gun. He went with me to do what we thought had to be done. We couldn't be sure whether coyotes had attacked, or whether it might have been our own dogs.

As we drove up to the big house, Chief and NCAA were running in circles out front. They looked like dogs worn out from killing sheep. Blue and Muddy River were penned up. It became their alibi.

Wayne looked at me, and I looked at him. I nodded. He steadied the .222 on the sideview mirror and pulled the trigger. Chief's head popped up 50 yards away. His four legs crumbled. We went to look at him. We checked inside his mouth and ran our fingers around his teeth. They were yellow, but there were no wool strands caught there.

NCAA jumped into the back of the pickup as if we were going somewhere and she were going for a ride. She ignored Chief's body stretched out on the driveway. We called her out of the truck. She came, and we opened up her mouth. There were no wool strands. Wayne and I looked at each other. We didn't shoot her. Wishing Chief were still alive wouldn't bring him back. Something had killed the sheep, but we didn't know for sure what it was.

Nine ewes had been dead long enough in the September sun to begin looking worse than they had when the attack began. Half of one ewe had been eaten altogether. The attackers had slashed and mangled the rest almost as if for sport. Darkness had set in when we drove to the back field to the burying place.

We dropped the carcasses of the sheep, along with Chief's brown body with the blaze of white on his barrel chest, in the ditch fast filling up. As we drove away it was a relief to be gone from it. Wayne and I went to the shed to look at what was left of the flock. A yearling ewe had all four legs broken and part of its face missing. Wayne shot six more ewes and took them to the ditch in the back pasture. Of the

14 ewes surviving, all but one or two were limping.

Some say farmers are to blame for breeding the survival instinct out of sheep. In my emotional state that day I was thinking, that's the same as saying we're responsible for sheep not being as clever or as treacherous as coyotes, or the same as saying children ought to be something they're not. I was also reacting to those who say, "Sheep are dumb." I muttered, "If sheep were real smart they wouldn't be innocent, wouldn't be sheep and there wouldn't have been a need for anybody ever to have said: "Feed my sheep."

Jim, if you're out there listening somewhere, I'd just like you to know I think I understand coyotes better now. I know they only eat when they're hungry, and even then they pick out the weakest and dine with precision. They're not the bloodthirsty maniacs so many people think they are. It's not a matter of innocence or revenge. It's survival.

HOG KILLING TIME

For a while it seemed God was on the side of the hogs. He would let them off the hook, so to speak. But, the King boys and I stuck with it and by late that awful rainy night in January of 1988 we all went home with enough fresh pork to see us and all our dogs through the winter.

You would have thought scalding boxes had gone out of style. Fact is, they've just about gone out of sight. There're a few sitting around in tobacco barns, collecting junk and wearing holes through their metal bottoms, but most modern folks wouldn't know a scalding box if it ran down the hill and bit them on the leg.

Naturally, it's only fit and proper we searched Bath County as far as Bethel for what we needed to scald the hogs. Over on Flat Creek Road we ran into an acquaintance in a pickup truck who was willing to let us borrow his box, provided we returned it the next morning. That's a right neighborly thing to do. Not everybody will let you do as much. There're still a few old-timers who're downright fussy about their scalding boxes.

All we wanted to do was to scald two hogs. But you'd think the hog god had something else in mind. We built a fire until we were just about blue in the face. No matter how hard we tried, we couldn't get the water in the box anything like scalding hot. It can't be lukewarm. It can't be boiling. Somewhere in the happy middle is scalding. They've stopped teaching this sort of important stuff in school.

The two hogs—the overweight sow that wouldn't breed, and the not-much-to-write-about boar—kept rooting around in the stock barn as if to say, "Ya'll ain't smart enough to get that water scalding hot."

Well, as my mother, Lucile, a Crouch if there ever was one, used to say, "Let me tell you something." When Mother used to say that, it was time to listen, because the fat was on the edge of being in the fire, and what a hog didn't know could get it worked up into bacon.

We dug another trench and built another fire straight from scratch. As darkness settled in on us, the next fire took off like it was made for television. Steam rolled out of the box like a bathhouse in Hot Springs, Arkansas. Bath County, Kentucky, was about to be made proud. When Wayne was asked if he thought the two bullets he'd brought with him would be enough, he replied: "Two hogs, two bullets."

I knew by the sound of that we were in business. The first .22 found its home between the eyes of the big sow, which weighed 500 pounds if she weighed an ounce. The boom on the back of the David Brown tractor wouldn't reach high enough to raise the sow entirely clear of the ground, but we moved her gently and maneuvered her, slick as a mole, into the scalding box.

The trick is to leave the hog just long enough in water hot enough to loosen the bristles, but not so hot or so cool as to cause them to "set." Hog bristles that have "set" are about as hard to remove as steel reinforcement rods from concrete.

The next trick is to get the scalded hog out of the box. Not everybody is cut out for this line of work. Make a mistake, and you get scalded along with the hog. You have to have chains fore and aft, and you have to know how to use them in order to move the critter up onto the nearby scraping board. If everything has gone just right, you should be able to remove all the bristles, much as you would remove the feathers of a chicken after it has taken the final bath.

My grandmother, Laura (everybody called her "Lala"), who grew up on Plum Lick, used to be real good at taking a chicken's head off.

You just don't see lady folk performing this basic job as you once did. It always seemed to make this little wisp of a Plum Lick woman right pleased. She'd clamp her right hand tight on a chicken's head and squeeze until its eyes closed. Then she'd wind up like an Argentine bola champion and rotate the chicken over her head about three times at arm's length. She followed up with a snapping wrist action befitting an All-Star pitcher, slinging the chicken's body, which is to say all of it but the eyes-closed head about 20 yards down and away from the side of the house.

While the body flopped around like chickens always do in these situations, Lala would toss the head aside, wipe her hands on her apron, and wait until the flopping stopped so she could go pick up the chicken and march off with it to a pot of boiling water.

Well, that was the effect the evening's work had on me and the King boys—Wayne and Darrell—in slaughtering two hogs. We were right satisfied to be there at the source, so to speak, instead of having our wives go to the supermarket and pick out bacon, sausage, pork chops and pork tenderloin at the meat counter as if it had never been parts of critters in the first place.

The best part of all were the hams, which would be cured and hung in the meathouse for the next two years. "Dodo" Baldwin of Paris, who'd just as soon cure a fine ham as he would argue a court case, helped me put up my two hams and a shoulder. As far as I'm concerned a two-year-old ham is every bit twice as good as a one-year-old ham. Be patient for two years, take it down, soak it overnight, wrap it in the dough blanket described earlier in "The Joys of Homegrown Ham," take it out of the stove, peel off the dough blanket and throw it away, draw a sharp knife across the glorious top of the ham to slice off that first aromatic morsel, lay it between a hot buttered beaten biscuit, and if that don't make you jump up and slap your pappy, I don't know what will. As "Dodo" says, "it might even make you want to reach out and hug your mammy."

THE OUTHOUSE

T here's no place like home and there's nothing so humbling as a trip to the outhouse at midnight, when there're two inches of snow on the ground, the temperature flirting with zero. There's nothing so satisfying as when that divine institution—the Noble Outhouse—rising majestically from its often ridiculed, often neglected, seldom heralded past provides a much needed haven and solution of problems for troubled spirits and tortured bodies. There's nothing so mortifying as the realization that those givens, which we've come to take for granted—running water and indoor plumbing—have been shut down tighter'n a well digger's igloo in the Klondike.

In the first days of January, 1988, we lost what never had been when the Crouch house was built around 1850. Later, the cause of our crisis would be diagnosed simply as "pressure," which blew a valve at the wellhead down by Plum Lick Creek. For two days, we'd know a little of what it was like back in the days of Joshua and John Houston.

We'd come home that night to another kind of Siberian Express, planning to take hot baths, as well as attending to other necessary matters as those occasions demanded. We felt a sudden numbness when the faucets produced not so much as a drop of water to brush our teeth. You can let hot baths go, and you can let your teeth go, but when you've got to GO, you've got to GO. That's precisely the moment the noble outhouse offers itself to huddled masses yearning to be free.

The first thing to recognize is there are few choices in the matter. The sooner this reality is addressed, the better it will be all the way around, which is to say, the shortest distance between point "A," the warmth of the bedroom, and point "B," the outhouse is a very straight and narrow path, unmarked, uncharted and unknown.

Set aside your underwear briefs and reach for the long johns, top as well as bottom—you'll be very glad you did. They may not be Fruit of the Loom but that's all right, because nobody goes fancy on a midnight mission to gloryland. Next, sit down calmly and put on your long socks. One of your few options is whether to put the socks over the legs of the long johns, or let the legs find their own way on the outside of the socks. Personally, I favor pulling the socks up over the long johns, because it not only seals off the ground-hugging, razor sharp air, it looks kind of pretty having a little color on the bottom part of your legs.

Next comes the red, plaid all-wool shirt, lending additional color to the top part of the body, as well as adding another important layer for warmth. Now, you're ready for the selection of pants. It's no idle choice. Your best bet is battlefield khaki with an insulated liner. Don't be foolish and try to cut a corner here, because you may not live to regret it. Then, reach for the 100-percent wool-lined coat, which you had the good fortune to buy in Uruguay, when you were on your way to a Patagonian winter assignment at the time of Argentina's suicidal invasion of the Falkland Islands. The coat worked wonders when doing television standups on the cold, windswept hill overlooking Commodora Rivadavia on the coast of the godforsaken South Atlantic. It would be just what the doctor ordered on a midnight invasion of the outhouse back home on Plum Lick.

Shoes, of course: city slippers won't do on the night of the brogans. I hope you've given yourself enough time to lace them up properly, because this is certainly no occasion to be tripping over untied shoe laces, landing nose first in crusted snow. Hat and gloves: I know you haven't been accustomed to going nattily attired in hat and gloves on your regular trips to your usual throne room, but on a mission such as the one I'm describing, you're best advised to leave nothing to chance. You're probably just as well off to forego a scarf mask to ward off the wind. It might tend to confuse strangers in the night, who would suspect you were intending to burglarize your own house. Likewise, it might spook your dogs, causing them to bite you on both ankles.

A sturdy flashlight is recommended, even on nights of the full moon. It comes in handy when determining where the bulls are. It's not a good idea to have the outhouse situated in the bull lot, but then it's an imperfect world. On my pilgrimage of '88, a 1,500 pound Hereford bull stood squarely in the middle of the straight line I had drawn to connect Point "A" with Point "B." The outhouse has a way of regenerating courage. I gave the bull a cold-hearted stare, calmly stepped around his puzzled expression and proceeded on my way. Loose shoelaces at a time like this, along with a faint heart and a lack of commitment could have had the net effect of canceling entirely the trip to the outhouse. I had done my homework, and I was ready.

During the brief moments I spent inside the humble throne room, a three-seater, I resisted the temptation to fantasize about the lingerie pages of old Sears Roebuck catalogs and speculated only for an instant about the possibility of decorating the inside walls with Playboy centerfolds. It was cold inside and outside. First things, first, as Eric Hoffer said.

Something suddenly struck me. I wondered why it had never occurred to me before. The trip to the outhouse had definitely turned on a light. I discovered the solution to all my problems. I knew in a flash how I'd pay off the mortgage on the farm. I would not have to die in Beirut, Nicaragua or the Laurel, Maryland, shopping center.

A question lit up my brain: where and how in the year 2000 will the estimated 6.2 billion people in the world be using the bathroom? The divine revelation in the outhouse at midnight on Plum Lick with two inches of snow on the ground and the temperature flirting with zero was that the best investment in the next century is toilet futures!— porcelain bowls, creative seats, floats, fuzzy covers to conceal the truth, scented cleansers, assorted paper, innovative toilet paper dispensers and other amenities to make the inevitable more enjoyable, plumbers' colleges, how-to-fix-it books, water saving devices, foot warmers, back scratchers, book shelves—and bidets for all mankind!

I DO HEREBY RESOLVE...

I f some 1993 New Year's resolutions resemble 1992's, it's only because some things take a while. Samuel Butler, the 17th century English satirist, son of a small farmer, knew how weak-willed we tend to be on making and keeping promises. Therefore, no apologies for the following lofty objectives for the first year in Kentucky's tricentennial:

To distill the essence of every tick of the clock...to observe more sunrises and sunsets...to allow the rain to refresh the face of the human and earthly condition...to welcome the snow when it flies ...to build a snowman when there's enough material at hand...to take a child on a sleigh ride...to draw a picture on the breath blown on a bedroom window...to gather firewood more carefully...to build fires in the bedroom and living room fireplaces more thoughtfully...

to count blessings daily...to give thanks without fail...to choose more wisely...to relinquish the benefit of the doubt...to try to understand others' points of view...to smile more often...to compliment more generously...to forgive more readily...to look for the good in everything...to remain optimistic no matter how grim the circumstances...to avoid pessimism as if it were leprosy...to remember lepers deserve help too...to avoid prideful tendencies...to avoid gossiping...to remember every individual has a right to stand center stage in the best possible light...

to anticipate the return of spring...to read a good seed catalog...to place orders early for seed...to draw a blueprint for the vegetable garden...to disregard the blueprint as desire dictates...to replace the broken window in the workshop...to put a small space heater in the shop and sit on a high stool and look through the new window while drawing the blueprint for the vegetable garden...to look for a warm spell to repair the water spigot on the garden's edge...to assemble the garden tools from about four or five different hiding places and to take inventory to see how rich the gardener is...

to realign the books on the shelves throughout the house...to throw away some bookkeeping records which will do nothing but confuse those who will follow during the time of the Great House-cleaning...to make it easier for descendants during the time of the Great Housecleaning...to make it easier for descendants to come to a better conclusion as to what the old feller was really all about...to have a go at the closets and give Goodwill enough stuff to clothe an

army division...to re-hang pictures slithering off into dusty corners in the attic...to re-store to some appropriate wall space the stuffed Golden Amber-jack caught while fishing with Cor-nelia Wallace off the coast of Mi-ami Beach...to give assurances as necessary that the catching of that fish was on a totally innocent occasion...

to spend more time ensconced in the leather Brazilian beanbag with a book whose pages have so far gone unread...to sit at the writing desk and share a thought or two with those who've for so long have gone without hearing so much as a word from one who used to be counted friend...to meditate...to be silent, too...

to eat earlier and therefore have more pleasant dreams...to rest well without using sleep as a drug...to avoid sleeping the better part of one's life away...to stay up all night reading a good book...or working on a problem needing immediate attention...to put all sleep dreams where they rightfully belong—on yesterday's scrap heap...to replace all last night's sleep dreams with tomorrow's waking dreams...

to exercise by walking and running...to lose 50 pounds of plump, lumpish, potbellied fat....to cause envious acquaintances to utter words of discouragement and defense—"don't you think you've lost ENOUGH?"...to recapture the feeling of thinness, slim and divinely svelte...to remember to encourage all others by saying, "How nice you look" no matter how fat or thin they are....

EWEDAWG

wedawg peeked out of the portable kennel. She seemed ready to accept us at face value. She didn't know her name was Ewedawg. Even after we called her "Ewedawg" several times it didn't matter. She was at that stage of five-week puppy life when any name would do.

We took turns holding Ewedawg to our faces on the theory it's not every day you have a chance to be so close to so much fluff. There was a trace of grey on each floppy ear. The rest of Ewedawg was a furry clump of big feet, barrel chest, broad back and long, curved tail. She would grow up, we said, to become 100 pounds of Great Pyrenees watchdog for our flock of ewes. But, at that precise moment on the edge of the Kentucky State Fairgrounds in Louisville, Ewedawg was cute and we kind of wished she wouldn't grow up at all.

Dr. Robert McCrory, who lives down in Benton in Joe Creason's home town in the far western paw of Kentucky, had come to the Fairgrounds for an Angus show. We'd made arrangements to meet him there to pick up one of his litter of Great Pyrenees pups. We'd first met Dr. McCrory in Louisville more than a year before, when I'd spoken to the association of veterinarians. He'd heard me talk about the "coyote" attack on our sheep. He figured he quite possibly had the solution.

There's hardly anything, I told myself, more disconcerting to a coyote, wild dog or any other living creature to come messing around in a flock of sheep only to discover one of the "sheep" isn't a sheep, but a dog in sheep's clothing. Instead of a "Maa" there's a bellow making the bark of a Border Collie sound like the echo of a little rock in a five-gallon can.

Sheep don't "Baa"—they "Maa." Maybe one day they'll learn to sound more like humans, but I hope not. They cough like humans, and sneeze like humans but the day they start talking like humans is the day I hang up my shepherd's crook.

When a Great Pyrenees barks, it tends to get a coyote's attention. Coyotes are too smart for it, but if they were dumb enough to ignore a

Great Pyrenees bark, any kind of a coyote could just about kiss his behind goodbye. The Great Pyrenness has the idea of guarding sheep bred into the genes, one of those holdover crusade things. The only reward is the dog satisfaction of knowing a job well done. The only medals are a piece of coyote or other dog hide hanging out of the corner of the mouth, much as a Cheshire cat gloats with a canary feather in the same place.

We paid the good doctor for Ewedawg and headed back east to Plum Lick. Ravy wanted to stop along the way and buy toys for Ewedawg. We tried to explain that wouldn't be the thing to do. It's pretty hard to argue with a five-year-old child and a five-week-old Great Pyrenees all at the same time, sort of like trying to catch lightning bugs with a sock with holes in it. We tried to explain Ewedawg would not be coming into the house, not even as a puppy. She would be going directly to the sheep barn. The only time any of us would have to love on Ewedawg was now on the way home from Louisville. "Resist the temptation to make a pet" of this animal had been one of Dr. McCrory's last pieces of advice. The dog should know who you are, and she shouldn't consider you a threat. Beyond that she has a job to do and being a pet is not one of them. "If she comes around the house, give her a whack on the hind end and send her back to the barn."

Selective breeding is hard for some pet lovers and animal rights folks to accept. When the animal is the most cuddly thing this side of a national teddy bear convention, it's all the worse. Two sensitive but searching eyes fastened on us as if to say, better play with me now, because as soon as we get to Plum Lick, please take me to the barn so I can get a head start on taking care of your sheep problem. Dr. McCrory had explained the necessity of having some place for Ewedawg to hide in the barn to be able to get away from the sheep, which at this time could kill her if they cornered her. We rigged up a wooden gate, and hoped that would serve the purpose.

When we arrived home we went straight to the barn. We set Ewedawg down in the middle of the main sheep pen, and we turned and walked away. On the one hand, it seemed the most natural thing in the world to do—cooperating with the natural order—yet, at the same time there was something disturbing about it. Depositing a beautiful ball of fluff in the midst of manure and flies and dried up dead rats and the steamy smell of sheep somehow seemed contrary to more civilized behavior. But we were following doctor's orders. Doubtless, Ewedawg's genes would take control.

Two days later, I returned from a long night of off-the-farm work. I went down to the barn to see how Ewedawg was getting along. I looked everywhere. I called. I whistled. I pleaded. I coaxed. I cajoled.

No Ewedawg.

No beautiful armful of fluff.

Damn the natural order. Damn the genes.

Damn the sheep, and damn the coyotes.

Ewedawg was gone.

The shepherd walked in great dejection to the house. The world was heavy on his shoulders. He was practicing his "Ewedawg-is-lost" alibis for the five-year-old. From over his shoulder he heard Blue and NCAA putting up their usual fuss from their kennels. They had their most cantankerous and half-hearted barks going full tilt. They carried on like that whenever their tight little world might be threatened by a newcomer.

In fact, they knew something the shepherd didn't. A different sound was coming from somewhere down around the sheep. Wasn't that a baby bellow of a bark? Had to be!

I jumped back into the pickup and returned to the barn. The baby-barking stopped. I took a step and listened. Another tiny bark. Then nothing again. I took another step, and listened. There it was again: another small sound that one day would become the roar heard 'round the sheep lot! For now, it was nothing more than a small piece of a larger puzzle—Ewedawg, the Great Pyrenees puppy, was hiding under the feed room floor, just as her genes were telling her to do.

Outside, where the night air was cooling from the heat of the day, the sheep were in their pasture, the stars were in their heavens. The Big Dipper and the Little Dipper were poised over Plum Lick. The Great Hunter was on station and two shining eyes and a black button nose were peeking out from beneath the feed room floor.

Ewedawg grew so fast during the first four months of her life, the shepherd figured it was time to take her out to see if she had any desire to work with the flock. Dr. McCrory, who had guaranteed she'd work as a guard dog else she'd be destroyed and replaced, had said these pups usually start working when they're about four months old.

For a Great Pyrenees, work means adopting the sheep and living with them as if the dog were a sheep. The dog knows instinctively it's not reasonable to expect a sheep to be anything other than a sheep. So, knowing sheep won't come to the dog, the dog must go to the sheep. All of this is most disconcerting to a predator when it comes sneaking up on a juicy meal—only to have it bark. This ability cannot be taught. It's either in the genes, or it isn't. Ewedawg had been penned with three 50-pound lambs for 30 days. They'd been sharing a fenced-in corner of the stock barn shed. To look at the four of them you'd think they were all cut from the same cloth. The only difference was one of them had a long tail.

I went down to the barn to take the one with the long tail out to the pasture to see what she would do when confronted with the older ewes and rams, especially the Dorset ram, who flat-out hates everything and everybody, including himself. I don't know why the Dorset ram is so sour on the world. He's so mean, he can be slap in the middle of 17 ewes falling all over themselves around him, and if he should spot the Hampshire ram on the opposite hill being halfway nice to some beautiful little lady lamb, the Dorset will walk over there and knock the living stuffings out of the Hamp who over time became downright paranoid and could hardly be blamed for it. Life never has been fair, and apparently the Dorset had long ago dedicated himself to keeping it that way.

Our Dorset is a reminder of the schoolyard bully, who's never really satisfied unless he's punching somebody on the end of the nose. The Dorset acts as if he got up on the wrong side of the bed every morning of his life. He's a miserable, disagreeable son of a cuss, is what he is. One thing I discovered at CBS, where there were numerous bad-acting Dorset rams and several super-bitch Dorset ewes, the really bad actors eventually "got theirs." Sometimes, it took longer than it should have. Occasionally the put-upon sought and obtained revenge with lightning speed. There was the legendary CBS employee who was fired, went across the street to "The Slate," became unconsciously drunk, returned after midnight to the CBS newsroom, dropped his pants and his underwear, climbed atop the copy machine, squatted and photocopied the part of his anatomy he believed his superiors to be, and routed copies to each one of them.

Meanwhile, in the land of retirement the shepherd put a piece of twine around Ewedawg's neck. What possible good he thought that would do was anybody's bad guess. Ewedawg was about as suited to a leash as a hummingbird is to a coat and tie. We went walking toward the first stone fence, and Ewedawg probably viewed it as a likely place to be hanged by about six feet of twine. She put down her big, fluffy white paws as if to say, "If you want me to go over this stone fence with you, you're going to have to do something about this worthless piece of twine."

Realizing the dog's superior intelligence, the twine was removed to better enable Ewedawg to be her own self, in her own space, in her own way. Ewedawg and the shepherd walked together out to the pasture where the flock of 60 ewes, two rams and two lambs were busy minding their own business, the business of discovering new shoots of grass in order to nip them level with the ground, the same business sheep have been fully engaged in since the early days of civilization. The first thing to notice was that Ewedawg didn't run around barking. In fact, she never barked once. She seemed to have a firm grip on the notion that barking was like yelling wolf in a crowded flock.

The Great Pyrenees genes were working, but the sheep's genes were sending messages, too. With a strange dog and the two-legged critter, who was never up to much good, appeared in their midst, they sensed real danger and responded by getting out of Dodge. This didn't seem to hurt Ewedawg's feelings. She tagged along and acted as if getting out of Dodge made all the sense in the world. The flock would slow down, Ewedawg would slow down. Somebody wanted to play, Ewedawg would play. The flock would spook again and head for a corner of the field, Ewedawg would look at the shepherd, then look again at the sheep as if to say, "These folks need all the help they can get."

The Dorset ram decided it was time to reassert his authority. He lowered his head and started walking slow and straight at Ewedawg, who promptly sat down and stared back. Dorset and Great Pyrenees met nose-to-nose, toes-to-toes. Ewedawg made the first move. She was meeting the Dorset more than halfway. She rose up on her haunches, placed one fluffy white paw on one side of the Dorset's shoulders, one paw on the other and planted a big kiss right between his eyes.

Not long after the kissing, we began to see we had a problem. We feared something bad would eventually happen, but we hoped it wouldn't. When Wayne came up to the house to tell us about it there was a look on his face that only came when there was unusual trouble, the kind causing us to search our souls for answers.

"Ewedawg killed a lamb."

"Are you sure?"

"No doubt about it."

"How do you know?"

"She was still with the lamb when I came up on her."

"Damn."

Wayne and I had what-should-we-do looks on our faces. There was nothing much that could be said. Usually, any dog caught in the act of killing a lamb is put down immediately, but since we had not actually seen what had happened there was sufficient doubt to put us into a quandary.

"Let's think about it. I'll call the man who sold her to us."

Ewedawg was put on a chain—one end attached to her, the other end to a truck tire. That slowed her down considerably, and kept her from roaming off the farm. Of course, we would be glad when the huge dog was under control, but at that moment Ewedawg's idea of territorial borders was as broad and as deep as her Great Pyrenees heritage. She did not understand small enclosures, just as Dr. Mc-Crory had said she wouldn't. Deed descriptions on the pages at Betty Jo Denton Heick's county clerk's office at the Bourbon County Court-house didn't mean a thing to Ewedawg, whose horizons stretched far beyond human concern.

The first thing to be understood was, Ewedawg was not a pet. She was a working dog. That's what she was bred for, and that's what was expected of her. Maybe some folks believe selective animal breeding just happens without careful elimination of undesirable individuals.

The only way to improve the breed is to propagate and nurture the best genetics. The bad seed must be halted, dead in its tracks.

I contacted Dr. McCrory and told him what had happened. In a few days a letter arrived. It said, "If she attacked and killed the lamb, destroy her. If she mauled the lamb like a toy and it died that's not as bad. Keep baby lambs up until they are able to get away better. Whip her severely if you see chasing or contact with sheep. If she is staying with sheep and you feel she has some benefit, give her time. If she was raised with working dogs they would clobber her. Also take her off puppy chow and put on cheaper maintenance. She will have less energy to burn. If all fails, destroy her...The main thing is we do not want to perpetuate the wrong kind."

There were two deep sighs in the big house. I folded the letter and Lalie stirred the pot on the stove. There was just a twinge of human emotion that would not be denied. Maybe there was a longing for a different kind of world in which nothing ever died, a world in which there were no lamb chops—mint jelly, maybe, but no chops—a world in which all dogs have constitutional rights to be as muddy as they please.

"Wayne, since we didn't actually see what happened, let's give Ewedawg another chance."

"O.K."

A few nights later, I went down to the barn. Ewedawg had the truck tire pulled up close enough to allow her to be inside with the sheep. There were no dead lambs. Ewedawg looked as if she were in the right place at the right time doing the right thing. The genes were humming. There was peace all around. Over in the nursery, the big Suffolk ewe had delivered twin lambs. I went back to the house to bring down the family to enjoy the sight. The child walked slowly to one of the drowsy lambs, picked it up and held it close. The Suffolk didn't seem to mind. Lalie went over to spend some time with Ewedawg. Lalie held Ewedawg's face in her hands, and I knew right then and there that it was not Ewedawg who was in trouble. It was I. I stuck my hands deeper into my winter coat, and I said a little prayer Ewedawg would never have to be destroyed. As we walked back up to the big house, I looked up at the stars hanging over Plum Lick, and I repeated the short prayer: "Oh, God, help Ewedawg."

149

We knew something was not right when we came home late, and Ewedawg boomed one of her great barks down by the gate at the head of the lane leading to Plum Lick Creek. She usually was closer to the barn where the sheep seek shelter, and the lambs drop from their watery beginnings.

"Why is she down there?" Lalie wanted to know.

"Hi, Ewedawg," said Ravy into the darkness by the cattle holding pen.

"I don't know why she's there," said I, knowing full well it was not a good sign. We went to the house, and went to bed because we were very tired. I decided I would check in the morning to see why Ewedawg was so far removed from her usual place. At sunrise, I walked down to the head of the lane where Ewedawg had wrapped her chain around the gate, snugging her in tight, preventing her from going either way. I removed her collar, and she waited patiently while I untangled the chain. I replaced the collar and felt the great, white dog jump up on me. I smoothed back her thick coat, and wondered again what had happened to cause her to be where she had not been before. As we drove away, Ewedawg plodded up the embankment toward the house. The truck tire was hardly holding her back. That was the last we saw of Ewedawg until we arrived home that evening.

She was not by the gate. She was not in the barn. She was not out with the sheep. I kept thinking the flashlight would find her somewhere in the darkness, but she was not there. The young lambs jumped back and forth across the wet weather runoff, the ewes congregated around a roll of hay and the Dorset ram glared back into the bright light, annoyed by the disturbance. I went to the house, explained why I'd be late for supper and drove over to Wayne's house.

"Have you seen Ewedawg?"

"She's in my back yard."

"Did she kill another lamb?"

"Yes."

"How many?"

"One."

"Damn it."

We went around to the back yard, where Ewedawg was giving a cat the idea it probably made a great deal of sense to move on down the road. Ewedawg did not threaten Wayne or me.

"I whipped her good."

"For now, I'd like for you to fasten her up in the vicinity of the barn, so she can't possibly get to the lambs. I'll call the man who guaranteed her, and we'll go on from there."

Supper went as well as anyone had a right to expect. I slept with a clear mind, but a heavy heart. I cautioned myself about allowing my heart to stampede my mind, influence it maybe, gentle it perhaps, but not run away with it altogether. It was a call I had to make. It was my mind, not my heart directing my hand to the telephone. The voice from western Kentucky spoke, evenly and compassionately:

"You'll be doing her a favor."

"What if we had her spayed and found her a home, wouldn't that be all right?"

"You shouldn't do that. She's not socialized. She's done it twice now, she'll do it again the first chance she gets. She'll kill something. The next time it may be somebody's chickens, or somebody else's sheep. It could even be somebody's child. She could wind up in a dog pound. She's not going to fit in. A disturbed dog that messes up once will mess up again. You can't change that."

I wrote about Ewedawg in the local newspaper and people I didn't know began coming up to me, asking about Ewedawg. There were letters. I told friends I had thought about writing a children's book called Ewedawg—there'd be a fluffy beginning, a crisis in the middle but then a happy ending. Now I knew if there were to be such a book I would be hard pressed to know how to write the real ending so a child would understand it, and not be harmed by it.

"Sure, I think you should write the Ewedawg story," said the voice from western Kentucky.

"And it does have to have an honest ending, doesn't it?"

"Yes."

"Thank you for your help."

Then, said the kind but firm voice on the other end of the line: "There'll be a new litter in February."

Ewedawg was in my dreams, in my waking thoughts and in my heart as well as my mind. She wouldn't go away. I knew something had to be done in a hurry. As Dr. McCrory said, she had messed up, and she'd probably mess up again. "You can't change a disturbed dog," kept ringing in my ears.

I knew I wouldn't take Ewedawg in to the vet and have her "put to sleep." I remembered a report I had done a decade before for CBS in Houston, Texas. It was the story of thousands of dogs facing senseless death every year in the county's dog pound. Many of man's best friends had been simply neglected, allowed to run wild over an area as large as Los Angeles. Many others had fallen out of favor with their masters, had been abandoned in a family's move to greener pastures or had become old, no longer wanted, less tolerated than they'd been when they had been adorable puppies.

The doctor at the dog pound had no respect for dog owners who expected him to do their dirty work for them. The fact that these unwitting, confused animals would eventually become cheap, protein-rich fish food did not make the executioner feel any better. The scene was one repeated over and over throughout Kentucky and most other states. A hand gives the dog a last soft pat on the head, the needle is inserted in the lower leg and in seconds the dog sinks into oblivion, the carcass stacked on top of all the others in a nearby cart. Some still quiver too long after the moment of truth. Other dogs are gassed—a hideous but necessary remedy, given how so many people are about the dogs in their lives.

I had come to the knowledge that responsibility for a dog's life begins at or very near birth and continues without interruption to that final moment of truth. I knew taking a dog to the vet to be put down had become an accepted practice in the United States, as it had in many other parts of the "civilized" world, but I now viewed it as a cop-out, especially when handling working dogs on the farm. They are animals in the same way cattle, hogs and sheep are animals. Working dogs have a function to perform, and they are bred for that one thing. An Australian Shepherd or a Great Pyrenees snoring away in front of a living room fire becomes a sad sight.

When the time comes to put the dog down, you just have to take that last walk over the hill, said the veterinarian at the dog pound in Houston—shoot the dog and then sit down and feel bad about it for as long as it takes. Then, you get up and walk back across the hill and spend your days working with other dogs.

I knew I wasn't going to ask Wayne to shoot Ewedawg. This would be my decision and my execution. I remembered the sight of Lalie that night down at the sheep barn with Ewedawg's Great Pyrenees face in her hands, and on foggy nights I'd hear Ewedawg's rich, deep bark echoing along the creek bottom. Whenever these thoughts occurred, I knew I'd have a hard time walking over the hill with Ewedawg.

There had been a call from Dr. McCrory, telling me there was a another two-year-old Great Pyrenees bitch with a litter of pups. I could have the mamma dog, and with Ewedawg put down there would be a credit toward the purchase of the older dog. "She's already a working dog, and she'll know what to do."

I thought about it. I dreamed about it. I agonized about it. I prayed to the great dog god about it. Then, it finally came to me. I had the solution.

"You're probably not going to like this, but hear me out."

"O.K." There was a knowing smile in the "O.K." that came across in the telephone conversation from Benton to Plum Lick. Dr. McCrory knew very well I lacked the courage to walk over the hill with Ewedawg.

I went on: "First thing we do is we spay Ewedawg. No more little Ewedawgs to grow up and go bad."

"O.K."

We buy the mamma dog and bring her and her litter here to the farm. We get credit for Ewedawg, and we try to sell the pups. Whatever we make on the pups we send to you."

"O.K. That's all right. If the pups sell, they're mine. If they die, they're mine."

"I'll come to get the mamma and her pups as soon as possible. I think it'll be good to have them here right away, because I'm hoping Ewedawg will see how a sheep guard dog is supposed to behave."

"It may work."

"Do you know what I'm going to name the mamma dog?"

"What?"

"Lambdawg."

LAMBDAWG

L ambdawg stood her ground outside Benton, Kentucky. She wasn't about to let the vet or me come into her lamb lot, not without a ruckus. Her three Great Pyrenees pups, marvels of white fluff, were scampering around as if to say, "'Aw gee, Mom, what's the problem?"

King, the daddy of the pups, was chained. He looked and sounded as if he believed the vet and the person with him would make a nice supper. He was as regal as Lambdawg was raggedy. She was shedding because of the ready-to-be weaned puppies. I had driven 300 miles from Bourbon County to Marshall County on the western side of the Land Between the Lakes just to pick up Lambdawg and bring her back to Plum Lick. The idea still was for Lambdawg to help rehabilitate Ewedawg, who had broken all the rules of the Great Pyrenees code, when she killed and ate the two lambs she was supposed to be guarding from predators.

While Ewedawg had gotten off on the wrong paw, her older half-sister, Lambdawg, had never laid one of her massive, white-furred paws on the loves of her life, the defenseless sheep, young or old. In fact, her owner said, when a lamb recently died of natural causes, and the frail little body was tossed to the other side of the fence, Lambdawg went over there, lay down, curled her body around the lifeless form and tried to comfort it as if it were her own.

The owner coaxed Lambdawg into holding still while the vet attached a leash to her collar. That's about when all hell broke loose. Lambdawg balked like a maverick. She stiff-legged it all the way across the lamb lot. Her pups, soon to be sold locally, were confused. They retreated in the direction of the barn. The daddy acted as if he could care less.

Maneuvering Lambdawg into a two-door Plymouth was a little like trying to put a billy goat into a lunch bucket. One side of the car was all vet and Great Pyrenees. But sooner than I ever thought possible, Lambdawg was in the back of the car, her hind legs and rear end folded on the seat like a crowded sack of potatoes, her front legs and soulful face hugging the vet's shoulder like a long-lost friend.

We returned to the doctor's office for shots and tattooing. It took a major whammy to reduce the beast to a manageable shag rug. After a few painless moments, Lambdawg was sporting my telephone number in her ear, and her former name inside her lip. Dr. McCrory is a firm believer in properly identified dogs. When Lambdawg woke up she received all her shots and was checked for heart worms. Sedated with a tranquilizer, she was ready for the six-hour trip back to Plum Lick. It was to be the longest and most harrowing six hours of her new owner's life, with the possible exception of the drives between Beirut and the Israeli-Lebanese border in 1982.

Even sedated, Lambdawg was determined to drive the Plymouth. My shoulder became hers to nuzzle on. I made a move toward a kiss along about Central City on the Western Kentucky Parkway, but Lambdawg would have no part of it.

In the vicinity of Leitchfield there was a clear and present danger. Lambdawg knocked the automatic shift on the floorboard from drive to neutral. The Plymouth roared like a wounded Banshee. With one elbow on the cold nose of the Great Pyrenees, the surprised driver was trying to be sure the car shift landed in the right place. If the shift had been knocked into reverse, there would have been one dead Plymouth, one Great Pyrenees wandering around on the Western Kentucky Parkway and one shepherd making lame explanations to a state trooper who only thought he'd seen everything.

With the crisis behind us, and disaster averted, Lambdawg decided to give me a little kiss as we skirted Elizabethtown, which was a nice thing for her to have done. It was not one of those shameless, lustful canine kisses—it was a little dainty buss on the cheek. It meant everything in the world to me. It occurred to me then how gentle such a giant dog can be when the situation seems to call for understanding. As soon as we arrived home on Plum Lick, I brought Lambdawg to the back door so Lalie and Ravy could make acquaintance. It was a fine and quiet time. After a while, we all went down to the barn together.

Ewedawg was still at the vet's office in town; the decision had been to spare her, but spay her. In a few days she'd be back on the farm. When she returned, she'd have Lambdawg as her probation officer. We had no guarantee it was going to work, but we figured it would be worth a try.

Lambdawg, it's all up to you.   Please be firm, but gentle.

Even though "Princess" was the name tattooed inside her right lip, her name was now Lambdawg, and we were trying to make it stick. If there's anything harder than trying to teach an old dog new tricks, it's trying to change a dog's name after it has had it a couple of years. Never mind all that, Lambdawg was now on Plum Lick to teach Ewedawg a thing or two.

"Lambdawg, this is Ewedawg. Ewedawg, this is Lambdawg."

A whole lot of Great Pyrenees white fur stood immediately on end. Ewedawg was on one side of a gate in the sheep barn, and she must've thought her bowl of food was actually hers. Both sides of her mouth drew up, exposing her fangs. She clawed the middle of the barn floor with her immense paws, and she lunged at the gate like the Siberian Express on the coldest night of the year.

Lambdawg was not impressed. She may have thought, do you mean you've brought me all the way up here to Bourbon County to put up with this? Other than tensing from the tip of her nose to the end of her tail, she didn't feel it was necessary to expend any energy growling, barking or carrying on in general. She may have thought, it's just a real good thing there's a gate separating me from this ill-tempered person.

Wayne and I agreed it was time our bad-acting Ewedawg had had her first lesson. Wayne put Lambdawg on the other side of the gate. The scene can be best described as two Siberian locomotives hitting head-on at midnight. It was not a pretty sight. Ewedawg went after Lambdawg with all the fury she possessed in her body. It might have been enough to slaughter a lamb, as we believed she had done on those two other occasions, but a lamb is one thing, a Lambdawg is another.

The two locomotives rose in the air, their glistening wheels flashing. Primordial roars rushed together like Texas panhandle thunder. The usually optimistic community of rats and mice in the sheep barn scurried for a cover they hoped would somehow save them from certain disaster.

The sheep blinked.

The lambs stared in disbelief.

It seemed as if days were passing before all our eyes, as if the heat of the collision were supercharged in slow motion. Actually, the whole thing required about three seconds, and for 10 seconds more there was raw deflation of Ewedawg's ego. Lambdawg stood over Ewedawg in the corner by the sheep gate. Ewedawg knew she had met her conqueror. Lambdawg's terms were unconditional surrender. Lambdawg sat down, as if to say, now, Ewedawg, Darling, or whatever your stupid name is, this is how it's going to be.

If Ewedawg so much as looked as if she might move one of the hairs on her head, Lambdawg would calmly place her right paw on Ewedawg's shoulder and press down firmly with 83 pounds of Great Pyrenees authority. To rub it in, Lambdawg took her own sweet time eating Ewedawg's supper.

Ewedawg moved off to lick her wounds and lose herself among the befuddled sheep. Lambdawg was on her again like white on Pyrenees rice. As someone has said, cleaning a clock once is not nearly as effective as cleaning it twice—the first time was to obtain attention, the second to make it clear the first time was not a fluke.

While the first lesson took less than 15 seconds, the second one required fewer than five. Ewedawg cowered in the corner like somebody who until this day had considered herself rather beautiful, a top dog as well as top sheep. This time, Lambdawg marched Ewedawg out of the sheep barn. Whenever Ewedawg stopped, Lambdawg followed and put her right paw on Ewedawg's ground-hugging shoulder. It was clear to Wayne and me Lambdawg's idea of unconditional surrender included take-no-prisoners and scorched earth, too, if that's what she believed was required to restore peace and quiet to the sheep. We decided to put Ewedawg back on the chain in the hope that would meet with Lambdawg's approval. It worked for about three days, until we turned Ewedawg loose again.

In the middle of the night we received a call from a neighbor.

"There's this dog over here in our basement. We let her in, because she wouldn't leave our yard."

Apparently, Lambdawg had driven Ewedawg more than a mile from home. I went over and brought her back. I put her on the chain again.

157

Months before there had been every reason to believe Ewedawg would grow up and adopt the flock of sheep on Plum Lick. She would protect them from predators no matter how clever they might be. Real shepherds know better than live by their fantasies. They must live by the realities of lambs born with birth defects, ewes that won't accept their newborn, rams that will break the shepherd's legs if given the opportunity, predators that rip and slash and lap up blood and guard dogs that sometimes turn on the animals they are bred to protect.

Ewedawg had gone bad. She had killed two lambs, or so we thought. Even though I'd been advised to put her down, I didn't have the heart, or the nerve. I had her spayed, as I said I would, to make sure her genes went no farther, and I brought in Lambdawg, the two-year-old Great Pyrenees. The new fantasy was that Lambdawg would take charge, would be a model for Ewedawg to follow in her footsteps. Together, they'd be a formidable team of guard dogs.

Lambdawg took charge the instant she laid eyes on Ewedawg, but the message was as clear as a sharp bark on a 40-below zero night. "Get out of town. Don't come back. Ever."

Ewedawg whimpered.

Head down, long white tail between her legs, she disappeared over the hill. It didn't seem right for me to go with her. She wanted to be alone. Mainly, she wanted to be gone from the fangs of Lambdawg. I couldn't stand it any longer. I went looking for Ewedawg. I found her at a house on the Rock Ridge Road, and I made the mistake of bringing her home one more time.

Lambdawg whipped her again, and this time personally escorted the beaten, unwanted "cur" off the farm. We haven't seen Ewedawg since.

After Lambdawg had the whole show to herself, <u>she</u> began to roam. No matter what was tried, she couldn't be kept anywhere near home. She was tied to tires, and she dragged the tires to Kingdom Come. She was tied to fence posts, and she broke free. Any street smart shepherd should have remembered what he'd been told: it's almost impossible to imprison a Great Pyrenees. And, anyway, who would want to do that? Their concept of territory does not necessarily conform to a human's. Boundaries become relative. They are impossible to enforce.

On an especially hot day, Lambdawg had been tied to a corner post in the back lot. Upon the return home, it was easy to tell from as far away as the barn, there was something wrong.

Maybe she was asleep.

She was not asleep.

She was dead.

She'd become ensnared in the fence. She had hanged herself.

The hand of the sorrowful shepherd reached down to unfasten the leather collar. Lambdawg's fine head fell softly to the ground. There was nothing to do but to return to the house and come back with the pickup truck. It was backed close to Lambdawg's long, limp body. The shepherd said nothing. He wrestled Lambdawg onto the tailgate. He closed the gate, so she wouldn't fall out.

They went over the hill together.

He parked the truck near a grove of locust trees. He turned the ignition off, and went to the rear of the truck. He opened the tailgate and rolled Lambdawg over the end of it. He dragged her inside the grove, then turned and walked away.

LADY

Ben Ardery heard about our unprotected flock of sheep. He lives in a restored early Kentucky house in the western part of Bourbon County. Ben offered a Shar Planinetz (also spelled, Charplaninatz) guard dog, a Yugoslavian breed.

The first thing Lady did after she arrived on Plum Lick was to run away and hide. It appeared the third time with sheep guard dogs would not be charm. Lady avoided the shepherd as if he had the plague. She could not be tricked with food. She was a loner with absolutely no desire to socialize with any human. Lady was never scolded. But, all the coaxing in the world wouldn't work. She was written off as a failure. She disappeared for days.

"Ben, she just disappeared." The words, when practiced, sounded hollow.

Finally, one morning, looking north up across the bottomland, I saw something that looked like Lady. I went out there, and called her to come to me. Slowly, and cautiously she advanced toward me, her V-shaped ears and black nose angled toward the ground. She actually permitted me to touch her face. Then, as suddenly as she had come, she was gone again.

Days went by. I left food in several locations. Sometimes it was eaten, sometimes is wasn't. I said, to heck with it. It seemed, sheep guard dogs and I were just not meant for each other. I dreaded the day I would run into Ben, and he'd ask me, how's the dog? "Ben she just disappeared." It didn't sound any less hollow.

But, finally, there was to be a dog story with a happy ending. I looked out to the sheep lot on a cold November morning, and there was a sheep that didn't quite look like a sheep. The nose was blunted, the body more slender, the movements possessed more grace. Lady had not only come back, she had taken charge. She had cast her lot with the flock. I took her food to her, and she closed the gap between us, but this time she stopped short of my touch. I set the food bowl on the ground and turned back to the house. I didn't look back.

Two years later, nothing has changed. Lady still won't let me touch her. Most of the time, I've resisted the temptation to try. She's doing her job, and I'm doing mine. We don't have time for petting, I also try to remember. There's a wildness about Lady that will not be tamed. When she sees me coming, she sometimes barks and moves to one side or the other. She knows nothing about the submissive behavior of most dogs. Her genes carry more of the characteristics of the wolf and the fox.

Lady has been seen chasing coyotes over the hill. One time, two coyotes showed up as a team, one seeming to act as a decoy for the other to move in for the kill. Lady would not be fooled. She saw two predators and made a decision on which would receive her undivided attention. It was the one closest to the sheep. If six coyotes had showed up, it probably wouldn't have made any difference. She would have stood her ground.

Sometimes, Lady rounds up the sheep and brings them back to the house, as if carrying out a tactical maneuver she knows exactly how and when to employ. Usually, the sheep ignore their guardian angel, but when she sends out the word, it's time to "move it," they move it.

It put the shepherd to reading up on old dog breeds. The Charplaninatz has been around since before the fall of the Roman Empire, although relatively little known today in the United States. The breed has been predominant in the ancient region of Illyria on the Northwest Balkan Peninsula on the coast of the Adriatic Sea. The characteristics of Lady include an expression of the eyes that is fearless, but no matter how determined she may seem to be, she has never attacked a human.

There are numerous sheep guard dog breeds at work in the United States near the end of the 20th century: the Great Pyrenees, Komondor, Akbash, Anatolian, Maramma, Kuvasz and Shar. There is no perfect breed, and as is the case with livestock, there are as many differences within a breed as there are between them. There are also hybrids that defy categorizing.

Lady is in a class all by herself. Since her arrival on Plum Lick, we've not lost a single sheep to a predator. She has never hurt a sheep or a human. There's only one problem: she needs shots for heart worms and rabies. We can't catch her. She'll have to be tranquilized before she can be taken to town. I don't look forward to that day, be-cause Lady wouldn't understand the vet's office. She has won her own liberation despite all odds against her.

I deeply miss Ewedawg and Lambdawg, but all the fantasizing in the world won't ever bring them back.

Blue, NCAA, Turk, Pat, Heidi, Beauregard, William Stamps, Dusty, Nugget, Nip and Tuck have all gone over their hills. I remember each one with special affection. Each in her or his own way made an important difference in my life.

MAX

Quinn and Max arrived on Plum Lick after a long drive from Pennsylvania through West Virginia. A sheep shearer's life is like that. Quinn Bosworth's been at it for more than 10 years, and his sheepherder's dog, Max, has been holding up his end of the bargain for the better part of that time. Quinn, with blacksmith's arms and hands as soft as a summer breeze, set up for business as usual in the stock barn. He sheared 15,000 sheep last year, including 5,000 angora goats.

Max, he lay low.

"That dog hates unemployment worse than any animal I ever saw," said Quinn as he laid out his shearing platform. He set up the iron brace that holds the motor that drives the shears, attached a horseshoe on one end of the linkage for balance and a trailer-hitch ball on the other. Quinn's more efficient than he is fancy.

Max, he lay low.

He settled down the 60 ewes and two rams with a stare that could keep a cobra inside a bottle until the exact moment of his choosing, then coax it out and make it dance for its supper.

"Max has got a real good hard eye," said Quinn with his Michigan accent, not at all the way we talk with our soft drawls on Plum Lick. When he says a word like "eye," it comes out very pure as a midwestern northerner would pronounce "aye." Of course, if God had wanted everybody to speak like somebody from Iowa—pronouncing it "aye-oh-wha"—he would have us all been born there, and we wouldn't be saying, "ah-wa."

Max he lay low.

When a sheep came too close to Max he'd snap a little piece of nose. The sheep appeared to understand Max real good. They seemed to know what he was talking about. If more folks, especially children, were snapped on the end of the nose every once in a while it might be an entirely different world. One thing I've come to notice is how many misbehaving children belong to experts in children's behavior. You ever notice that? There's a lot of child abuse going on, no doubt about it, but sometimes it gets to be where there's a lot of adult abuse perpetrated by little criminals passing themselves off as innocent children.

Max, he lay low.

"Max, what's one plus one?" asked Quinn as he set up the iron frame that holds the wool sacks, as smooth as tying his shoestrings blindfolded.

Max barked two times. "Max, what's one plus two?" Max barked three times.

Quinn smiled, and asked for the first sheep.

Wearing his sheepshearer's moccasins, and a leather glove on his left holding hand, Quinn wielded the cutting tool like the conductor of a philharmonic orchestra. His motions were fluid and even. Down the belly, over the insides of the hind legs, across the rump, along one side, across the top of the head, then up the belly and under the neck, across the back in sweeps befitting a bass player: the fleece came off in one piece, looking fine enough almost to throw over your shoulders as if it were a finished greatcoat.

Quinn smiled, and asked for the second sheep. I had timed him at two minutes and 30 seconds. "I would have worked faster if I had known you were timing me," said Quinn.

Quinn has studied with the best of the sheepshearers in New Zealand, while in the same lifetime pursuing journalism at Michigan State University. There may be a connection between the two professions. Richard Nixon probably felt sheared by Woodward and Bernstein. Spiro Agnew possibly noticed the nicks of the nattering nabobs of negativism. But, once all the wool was off, they had to feel cooler in the heat of a summer day.

It's understandable that most sheep don't want to be sheared, but after the job is done they often look as well as feel better about it, although they'd never let on, especially to the shearer.

While some have argued that an expert shearer like Dan Rather should not have engaged in a wrestling match with presidential candidate George Bush, sometimes that's the only way to remove the wool.

Walter Cronkite was generally perceived to be a good shearer, because he avoided the second cut problem. Cronkite's fleeces came off in one smooth piece, ready to be tied and bagged, making everybody involved feel as if—that's the way it is.

Max, he lay low, as if to say, so much for strong backs and weak minds. When Quinn said, "Way-to-me," Max moved to the right. When Quinn said, "Go-bye," Max moved to the left. When the shearer said, "Down," and "Watch'em," Max hugged the barn floor and put the evil eye on the sheep. Some of Quinn's journalism had rubbed off on Max, especially the "watch'em" command.

"What's two plus two?" said Quinn to Max.

Max barked four times.

"Good <u>boy</u>," said Quinn, as he tallied the last of the 60 ewes and two rams.

JONATHAN HEARNE

One look at Jonathan Hearne was enough to convey trust: soft-spoken, full-flowing beard, easy smile, gentle hands, smooth as he stood by the car.

"You the sheepshearer?"

"Yes, I'm the sheepshearer," replied Jonathan Hearne.

While Jonathan went to the barn to set up his equipment, I drove over to Joshua Meadows to negotiate for one of the tobacco housers to come over and help bag wool. Joe was the designated bagger. He seemed relieved to be out of the hot tobacco barn, where the crew from Magoffin County was handing off from the wagons to the stretched legs and reaching arms among the tier rails.

"You ever bag wool, Joe?"

"Never seen sheep sheared."

When we arrived back at the sheep barn, Jonathan had set up his rig. He put a large fan in one of the openings on the south side of the shed.

"When you've got your arms around a sheep with the body heat at 110 degrees, it's kind of nice to have a little breeze stirring."

I caught the first ewe, and felt strong as I used my right hand to pull up and back on her head, while at the same time grabbing wool over her tail and using my knees to walk her in the direction of Jonathan. If he was impressed he didn't say so, which probably meant he wasn't.

Joe, crouching in the corner, seemed hypnotized by Jonathan's clean sweeps with the shearing blade down the ewe's underside, up one flank, around the head and down the other side, completing the circle. Nobody said much of anything as the shearing continued throughout the morning. As each fleece came off, Joe took it to a small container, and when that was full, he emptied it into the large wool sack hung up on a hoop outside the barn door. Joe stood in the sack and packed the wool in tight.

The behavior of the sheep was no different from what it had been 1,989 years ago: they bunched together, believing in safety in numbers, which of course was hardly any safety at all. They moved in a tight orbit, dreading the possibility of being cut off from the rest of the flock. In that way, they were no different from people in New York City. Once they were manipulated to a spot next to the shearer the sheep were as quiet and as poised as on-deck baseball players at Yankee Stadium. It  took practically no force to hold them there, as long as one hand was cupped beneath the lower jaw, while the other hand applied pressure at the top of the shoulders.

Midday came. The three of us, Jonathan, Joe and myself, went up to the house for cheese and baloney sandwiches. We drank sun tea. We talked about Hurricane Hugo a little bit, but mostly we fell into talking about being kind to animals. We went at it from the sheep-shearer's perspective, the veterinarian's point of view and people in general. We agreed handling animals gently was the proper way. We saw no reason to do otherwise. Meanness to dogs was another issue receiving our careful attention. By the time we walked back to the barn we had decided, also in this regard, animals and people were critters of a kind.

Joe was needed back at the tobacco barn, because they were filling the center. Without him they wouldn't be able to hand the sticks all the way to the top. I knew what that meant. The sheep catcher was about to become the wool bagger too, and after about an hour, I thought I'd faint in my tracks.

"He retired from being a combat correspondent to return to his home in Kentucky where he dropped dead while catching sheep and bagging wool." I didn't like the sound of the obituary.

"Jonathan, I'll pay you extra to catch a few and bag some."

"Want some water?" said Jonathan.

I nodded.

"Try it with a little vinegar. Now, if you taste this and don't like it, you can spit it out and it won't make me mad."

I tried it. It tasted like lemonade with an extra sharp edge. Jonathan said it was something he had learned from a feller in New England.

"Helps me get through the hottest part of the day."

As for me, I think it saved my life. From now on, I'm adding a spoonful of vinegar to my water. I may even patent it and pay off the mortgage on the farm. I'll call it: "Jonathan Hearne."

NCAA AND THE FINAL FOUR

Court Days in Mt. Sterling have included a dog here and there traded for pocket knives, hunting guns and old ham sandwiches. Actually, there are many reasons for dog trafficking, none of which should be entered into lightly. Sometimes, the dog is better off traded, sent to a better home or a kinder or smaller master.

One of my favorite dogs was NCAA (pronounced, Nee-ka.) Nee-ka's formal name was spelled NCAA because she was picked up as a stray in the vicinity of Rupp Arena during the Final Four tournament in Lexington. Len Press, who retired in 1991 as the founder and first Executive Director of the Kentucky Education Television network, and his wife, Lil, who set up the Governor's Scholars program, and their son, Lowell, were taken over by NCAA. Nee-ka was like that. On a dog sense scale of ten, she was probably a 9.99, a Border Collie, exact parentage unknown, bright-eyed, tail high, entirely committed to the proposition there was no wall that could not be climbed, no fence that could not be jumped, no lock that could not be jimmied, no rope that could not be chewed clean through, no chain that could not be worried loose, no door that could not be opened, and hardly any other dog that could not be intimidated (Nee-ka was smart enough to know a Pit Bull and a few other fierce folks when she saw them, and when she did she could execute an exquisite, strategic withdrawal, so that it did not appear to be anything other than good common dog sense.)

The Press family hated parting with Nee-ka, but they had to do it because even Lexington can only stand so many NCAA's at any one time. They asked if there might be a permanent home for NCAA on Plum Lick. Of course, we were honored because as far as we know there hasn't been a county tournament down here, much less a Final Four. Our Final Four in 1987 were: NCAA, Blue, Muddy River and Turkey.

Blue was a rather strange-looking, strong-as-a-mule, sweet and not the brightest half-breed dog in the world. She was half Blue Heeler, half common-as-dirt mongrel with a generous touch of Beagle. Her daddy was an Amburgey Blue Heeler from Mt. Sterling, and her mother was an assorted Beagle who wandered in from somewhere and fell head over dewclaws for the uptown Blue Heeler, who fell victim to a heavy dose of tobacco spray. After Blue's aristocratic daddy died ignominiously as a result of the chemical poisoning, Blue's mamma was left holding the litter, which is always the way it is, of course, in dog world as well as human world. Mamma and children moved into what used to be Bill's Garage on Queen Street in Mt. Sterling. Everything was fine until Bill, who a few years later passed on, figured he had no humane choice but to call the dog pound folks.

Blue may not have been half as smart as NCAA, but something must have spoken rather directly to her from the dog god, informing her there was nothing good headed in her direction. The dog pound folks showed up, and carried off Blue's mamma and brothers and sisters and, so far as I know, gave them all one-way tickets to that great dog heaven in the sky. Who would want to take them and give them homes on earth? Nobody, of course, stepped forth immediately. Blue, on the other hand, could not be found anywhere when the dog pound authorities showed up, but the next day after they'd gone back to do their dogs-in-heaven business, Blue showed up again as regular as clockwork. That probably was the smartest move Blue ever made in her entire life. It so impressed Bill he didn't call the dog pounders to come back and finish the job. One day, I was having my car repaired at Bill's Garage, and when I saw Blue, I knew right away the dog god had meant for the two of us to be friends until the final buzzer, so to speak.

So, Blue came home with me, and right from the start when we would ride in the pickup truck, the two of us would howl together. Until you've taken up howling with a dog like Blue—who should have been designated a Blue Howler instead of a Blue Heeler—you've not had a full life. The two of us could have done the Star Spangled Banner at opening day in Riverfront Stadium in Cincinnati. Word about Blue and me must've never gotten up that far, because we never were invited. Too bad. We could've put a lump in the throat of the entire baseball world. We could have made Pete Rose give up gambling. We could've saved him before he went too far and finally got caught. We could have given the Reds winning seasons every year.

The third dog in the Final Four on Plum Lick in 1987 was Muddy River. She was an Australian Shepherd, and she had some fairly distinguished lineage. Her grandfather was Booger Red from Wilkinson County, Mississippi, and her grandmother was Tar Baby from the same neck of the woods. Their master was Mr. John Hewes of Horseshoe Hill plantation. He ran a dog operation down there like there was no tomorrow.

Mr. John's dogs were always in one of three places—in their pens, in the back of the pickup truck or out in the field setting Simbrah cattle on dimes. When Mr. John said, "Get'nthetruck," his dogs jumped on like the train was leaving the station. When Mr. John said, "Bring'emon," the dogs were off the truck like it was The City of New Orleans passenger train heading over a cliff into Buffalo Bayou. For time out of mind, Booger Red, Tar Baby and their cousins would round up a hundred head of big, brusing Simbrahs like they were 100 pussy cats about to be stuffed into a sack and dropped into the Homochitto River. The dogs always had the good sense to go after the farthest cow first, and I've discovered this to be a cardinal rule in teaching at the college level: bring in the strays first. If you don't, it messes up the entire process, because it tends to scatter the main herd.

Mr. John never had to leave his pickup truck. He was like Leonard Bernstein giving the woodwinds their cues—"Go-Bye" for clockwise movements, "Way-to-me" for counter-clockwise, "Eeeeesy" for the voce sotto and "Down" for the final notes. Booger Red and Tar Baby lived for the day when a cow would turn, lower her head and charge, the unspoken cue to bite the cow on the end of the nose. There's hardly anything in this world a cow hates worse. One bite on the end of the nose conveys a message with such impact there's never a need to do it twice. The dogs would put the cows wherever Mr. John wanted them. It was their life's work. It and he were their reason for being.

Mr. John bred Booger Red to Tar Baby, and from that litter came Baby Red, which Mr. John gave us to bring back to Kentucky. We in turn gave Baby Red to Bill and Lena Gilvin on Bunker Hill, and they used her to bring in their cattle. Baby Red was mated to Honest Abe of Mt. Sterling, and from that litter came Muddy River. With a background like that, how could a dog possibly go wrong?

Muddy River lost the whole ballgame right after opening ceremonies. She didn't roll over and present her belly when NCAA told her it was time to do that. NCAA put so many tooth marks in Muddy River's head she looked like a tin can with holes punched in it with tenpenny nails. From that day on, NCAA never again felt it was necessary to have the least thing to do with Muddy River, and the feeling was entirely mutual.

On the other hand, NCAA loved Blue, although in a sort of perverse way. It was written in the NCAA rule book that NCAA was commissioned by the dog god to keep Blue under absolute control at all times, total submission, actually. Blue came to understand this reality rather quickly. It appeared to me Blue didn't love NCAA, but came to accept her as the final authority and that was that. If a number of University of Kentucky basketball coaches, players and alumni had come to terms with their own NCAA as quickly as Blue had hers, there wouldn't have been all that fuss and the Lexington Herald-Leader could have spent its time winning a Pulitzer Prize for something else.

In Blue's case, how could you possibly love it if your lover was constantly biting you on the nose, nipping at your ankles and pulling on your ears? Blue knew to fight back was to make her head look like Muddy River's—a tin can with holes punched in it. On the other hand, Blue was fearless when it came to breaking up a bull fight. It was enough to have made a Bear Bryant proud. Blue would go tearing into a bull's face and make his nose feel like an old rubber ball with little pieces out of it. Blue would light out after a cow, and if a flying hoof caught Blue full in the face she'd go right back after the cow as if nothing at all had happened. Blue wasn't a half-breed Blue Heeler for nothing. If Bill Curry had 11 Blue Heelers he would win the Southeastern Conference in a cake walk.

Muddy River was pretty good at herding cows, but her problem was a lack of discipline she doubtless acquired from her master. I broke her to the choke collar too soon, and it ruined her. I decided to keep her in the hope that one day she would provide us with the genes of Booger Red and Tar Baby, and one time we thought we had her bred, but it was not to be. The best part of Muddy River was her name. Other than that, she was a total failure, and we finally gave her to a Bath County fellow who took a shine to her. For our part, she was good riddance.

Then there was Turkey.

To talk about Turkey is to cry. He was a rich-blooded Dachshund I bought from a lady in Lexington. I presented Turkey to Lalie and Ravy as a first Thanksgiving Day present on Plum Lick. Turkey was all love. We began calling him, "Turk," but that didn't stick. It was Turkey from the moment he arrived on Plum Lick to the sorrowful and hot summer day when he died. The basket in which he slept was at the head of our bed. He curled up in it like sausage in a bun. When he jumped up on the side of the bed, or on our knees when he sat in our rocking chairs before the fireplace, he would put his head between his paws as if he were praying. He had a soulful look in his eyes that should have melted the most vengeful dog god.

Turkey, of course, did not herd cattle. He didn't chase cats. He loved. With his long ears flapping with the effort, he would run to meet our car when we drove up to the house from the Plum Lick Road. He was the official greeter. One day he didn't show up. After many days went by, and much searching, we knew he wasn't coming back. A week later, Wayne found Turkey in the livestock trough on top of one of the back hills. There had been a drought that year, and Turkey, who loved to roam the farm with NCAA, wanted a drink of water. Somehow he managed to jump into the trough, but he couldn't jump out. When you lose a dog like Turkey, you lose a part of yourself. It's the pain that goes with loving a dog.

The Final Four dogs are all gone. Turkey, the most loved, Muddy River, the least wanted, and Blue and NCAA. We needed a guard dog for our flock of sheep, and Blue and NCAA were both disqualified. We found homes for them in Bath County, and I haven't seen them for years. Recalling them in *The View from Plum Lick*, has caused me to want to see them again. I think I'll do that. I'll stand on the edge of their territory, and see if they remember me. My guess is, they'll come running, and I'll have an armful of half-breed Blue Heeler and Border Collie fighting for my attention. But, then, I could be wrong.

Maybe they can't forgive me for giving them away. I couldn't blame them for that. We'll see. There's one important thing to know about a dog. They don't have to forgive, because unlike humans, loyalty comes first.

MOM AND NUGGET

I t was one of those early morning moments calculated to throw the rest of the day into total darkness. I had meant well when I had temporarily given a home to two more dogs, Mom and Nugget, two splendid Golden Retrievers, bringing our dog population in 1988 to six. That was back in the glory time of Blue, Muddy River, NCAA, Turk, and then, Mom and Nugget, as diverse and impossible a crowd as ever one assembled.

Due to a couple of cold wet nights I'd put Mom and Nugget in the shop where they'd at least be dry, since their outdoor kennel didn't have a shelter. This left Muddy River looking pretty much like a muddy river in her enclosure, and Blue and NCAA more brown and bedraggled than blue and white. Only Turk received royal treatment, snug as a bug in his rug-lined basket inside the human house. When one reaches the level of six dogs, one crosses the line of diminishing returns: more mud and you-know-what than you ever want to believe. Just feeding the mongrels is bad business, especially at the end of a long, hard day at the office.

After the rain slacked off and the sun began to shine again, I knew it was time to rearrange the dogs. The problem is I didn't dress for it. I should have gone about it in an old camouflage suit. Instead, I dressed for regular work at the office. There I was in my gray slacks, blue wool jacket, white shirt, power-red tie and network television correspondent's coat. I was ready to meet the Queen of England, if necessary. As soon as I went into the shop to put the leashes on Mom and Nugget I began to get the idea I might be in a little trouble.

Wrestling with two cooped-up golden retrievers while dressed fit to meet the Queen of England is a contradiction in terms. Mom hung a toenail on the side of my face. If I hadn't drawn back as quickly as I did I might have needed stitches. Nugget, meantime, was determined to present me with his tennis ball, an act so important to him it precluded taking "no" for an answer. Trying to walk down a slippery slope with two Golden Retrievers on leashes is roughly the equivalent of coming off Mt. Everest on broken skis. Only a miracle kept Mom, Nugget and me from winding up in the gurgling water that churns down from the farm behind us whenever there've been several days of rain. Naturally, Mom and Nugget were not overly enthused about trading a warm shop for a wet outside kennel, and getting them to cooperate was like trying to thread a needle with knotted strands.

"Blankety-blank Mom and blankety-blank Nugget, get into the blankety-blank kennel before I read the blankety-blank riot act on you."

If it had not been for the fact golden retrievers are basically sweet-hearts they doubtless would have read the blankety-blank riot act on me. The fact they were dry as kindling after two nights in the shop was definitely in my favor. Otherwise, I would have been a mess sooner than the dog gods had in store for me. The innocent as well as the ignorant tend to become careless, but after taking one look at Muddy River, Blue and NCAA I decided every dog deserves her or his day. They were up to their shinbones in mud. It was time to let them out, even if only for a few dry minutes. I would do this doga-mantarian thing very, very carefully.

I would remember to stand out of the way as they came charging out, and I would resist any and all attempts to jump up on me and lick my face. But as I ever so gingerly unfastened the first kennel, NCAA jumped up on the wire door like a semi going down the interstate on a 6% downhill grade after a thunderstorm with no runaway truck ramp within ten miles.

Four paws and a wagging border collie's tail later I looked like I'd just lost the first round in a mud wrestling contest. My fresh white shirt had suddenly become a white and brown shirt, and my power-red tie had lost its spark. My network correspondent's coat looked like I'd just crossed the Rhine with Patton. My gray slacks had a touch of glory too. At a time like this, anger is not the answer. Reaching down into my deep bag of philosophical tricks I came up with the rationalization that indeed every dog deserves her or his day, that this was theirs and it was something mortal man ought not try to change.

Muddy River, Blue and NCAA had their romp outside, and then with that wonderful predisposition rooted firmly in dogdom, they re-turned to their allotted space on earth and looked at me with their eyes of innocence, as if to say, "Don't you look fine too."

What they saw and what I didn't know was I had broken out with a royal case of freckles. If fact, I looked like I'd flunked out of mud wrestling school and gone on to glory as a mud track driver. But this was not fully apparent to me until I stopped at the J and M Market at the Judy crossroads to buy a couple of sausage biscuits and a cup of coffee. John Baker took one look at me and said, "What happened?"

"The dogs got me," was about the only thing that could be said for it.

Without uttering another word, John dampened a paper towel, dabbed away at my face, then handed me another dry paper towel and said, "You can dry off with this one." There aren't many food market owners who'll go so far out of their way to help a feller who has gone so obviously to the dogs. I thanked John and went on down the road to the University of Kentucky like I had good sense.

BUTTON

Somebody threw away a button, and we picked it up. It wasn't much of a button, but it seemed to have possible value. We found it among the weeds by the side of Plum Lick road not far from the entrance to our farm. You wouldn't think we would have spotted it, because it was so small. It had some color, but not much—gray here and there, with some spotches of brown. It had some energy left in it, but not much. It moved just enough to catch our attention, nothing more. We might easily have missed, along with the discovery of the button, the unfolding of a gentler side of our character, a demonstration of a desire to be generous.

"Please stop the car."

The car eased to a stop on the narrow Plum Lick Road, where it was lined with gnarled trees, vines and weeds too stubborn to die.

"C'mere, you," said the Good Samaritan as she reached into the thicket of growth beginning to yellow faintly with the coming of autumn, the time of the year when buttons bestir themselves a little more anxiously, knowing as they do, after September comes October and after October comes November. Conditions along the roadside change quickly and unpredictably, so everything looks to itself for protection from the arrival of cold and windy nights.

The theory of the Survival of the Fittest does not exclude buttons. It applies most especially to the smallest creations, from the crickets beginning to enter the old house sitting in the valley of Plum Lick, to the spiders stocking year's end webs with sluggish flies. The difference lies in what the human heart and hand are willing to do to improve the chances of the survival of the weaker elements in the environment, those struggling against rather large biological odds. If warmhearted efforts were not exercised, we'd be no better than a crowd of buttons, crickets, spiders and flies, all competing for space and little if any affection.

"Come here, you," said the Good Samaritan again, as she picked up the button, holding the smallness of it in the palm of her hand, her long, slender fingers moving carefully over the grays and the browns engrained on the sides, the top and the bottom of the object tossed aside. Or, had it strayed from an old sewing basket, perhaps? There would be no easy way of finding out.

"You know what I'm going to do? I'm going to put it back where I found it, and if it's here when we come home, we'll stop and pick it up." She gently set the button back where it had lain, patted it softly, and without saying a word she returned to the car, took her seat and looked straight ahead as we moved on up the hill.

We heard a racket. It sounded as if something were all around us making a terrible sound. We looked through the rearview mirrors, and what we saw caused us to stop immediately. The button had bounced back onto the road and was bounding in our direction in one last act of desperation, as if pleading, "Wait for me!"

"Go get it," I said. The Good Samaritan did not need to be told. She scooped up the tiny object and brought it with her to the car. She held the button in her lap, and we talked about the gray and the brown colors. It was as if we'd been tested, at first found willing, then lacking, then willing again. We felt pleased with ourselves we'd found time to do something that might make a difference, if not throughout the world, then at least in the taming of our own insensitivities. The button was virtually defenseless. It was losing odds in the Survival of the Fittest, but, however slightly, we might be providing an edge. We wondered how it came to be that an object so small and unwanted, yet so remarkably designed, had almost ended on a scrap heap of helplessness.

Sometimes, words are not necessary to measure the depths of feelings. There are moments when quiet contemplation involving a husband and his wife are sufficient.

A puppy mutt had become a matter of the heart. It was a castaway mongrel, a cur without a home, two ears destined to be floppy, a tail most likely to curl up or down, it didn't matter which. It was a bad case of mange, some work for the veterinarian in town, where we were headed. It was something to be treated, as well as neutered in time. It was a little girl dog that didn't need anything more than to be given a chance to have a life.

"What will you name it?" he wondered aloud, at last.

Her reply was simply: "Button."

CHIEF

Chief, the Rottweiller, joined us on Plum Lick. Even at eight weeks he had a manner and a presence strongly suggesting respect. His daddy over on Cream Alley Road in Montgomery County had that look that said, "Bud, I don't know who you are, and I'm pretty sure it doesn't matter one way or the other." His mamma, over near Jeffersonville, had a more unequivocal attitude. It was more on the order of "There's only so much territory to go around, I've got mine, and the best thing for the two of us is that you go find yours."

When I went to pick out the pup (having the pick of the litter is one of the many underrated joys of life) I knelt down to see which ball of black and tan would seek me out. The one that did was the biggest and most aggressive. A little pink tongue went to work on my hand, letting me know right off it did matter one way or the other. Moreover, his territory would always be my territory. I took that to mean my territory would always be his territory too, and so long as everybody else's passports were in order they might pass through immigration.

As I walked away with Chief's cold nose buried in my retired foreign correspondent's coat, the mamma dog was lunging against the chain that held her, thank the Lord. I made a mental note to myself, if at all possible, Chief would not be chained. There's something about a chained dog that goes against the grain. I've been a party to it at times in the past, especially with Ewedawg and Lambdawg but I've never liked myself very much for having done it. Kennelling a dog over an extended period is bad enough, but the chain has about the same effect as it does on humans: makes them mean, creates a deep-seated desire to get even. When Chief took his last look at his daddy it seemed to be a matter of relief. There's a world of difference separating the adult, full-grown Rottweiler and the eight-week-old version of the same thing, a little like a bowling ball at the foot of the Rock of Gibraltar. The Rottweiler's ancient ancestor is believed to be the Tibetan Mastiff. That's a lot of dog.

I stopped at the Levee (the Montgomery County Levee) and picked up some puppy chow for Chief. I also laid in treats for Blue, NCAA and Ewedawg in the hope they would feel a little bit better about it when I showed up with the stranger in the night. They have to put up with a lot as it is, and a modern-day version of the Tibetan Mastiff was considerably more than they'd ever bargained for in the worst kind of nightmares. Time would tell how a half-blood Blue Heeler, a Border Collie, a Great Pyrenees and a Rottweiler would carve up their territorial imperatives, but if each would concentrate on his or her mission in life, it would probably work out about as well as it sometimes does in the academic community—Blue to work cattle, NCAA to work sheep, Ewedawg to guard sheep and Chief to guard everybody.

Chief cried the first night, of course, out there in the mud room, but it was a cry filled with character, very purposeful and dedicated. I mean there wasn't anything pitiful about it. It seemed to be saying, I know I'm a little feller at the present time, and I understand puppies are supposed to carry on right smart the first night away from the litter, but I'm here to tell you this baby business won't last long. The rest of the family took turns holding Chief, and everybody seemed to understand the time for doing this was now while it was possible. Chief enjoyed the attention immensely. As soon as he spotted Cloud, the new, solid white cat, the Tibetan Mastiff from the time of the Romans crossing the Alps lowered its cold stare, sending unmistakable messages in multiple languages, and it didn't matter which one.

Cloud managed one sputtering hiss, and moved on down the hallway.

The special relationship between dogs and humans is one of the miracles of life. A certain dependency, an unqualified affection, an unwavering loyalty—gifts which cannot be bought or bargained. They're either there, or they're not. Perhaps, there's an unfinished nature in both man and dog, and the only chance of completing it lies in the two sharing a common bond, naturally and without question. The truth is, the dog gives far more than it ever gets. Often, it gives without ever getting. The human on the other hand need do nothing more than stand still and be loved. The sad part is many humans are too busy for this sort of nonsense. Yet, most all dogs seem to comprehend this entirely and go on about their business of fulfilling the simplest of commands: it is better to give than it is to receive.

PART THREE

J. LARKINS

THE ORPHAN LAMB

he lambing season has begun. It's earlier than usual, because we're still climbing out of last year's "coyote" attack. As we try to play catch-up, the rams have been left with the flock without regard for any specified breeding period. The breeding harness and the marking crayons to identify which ewe has been bred have been stored away in a drawer on the back porch.

There've been several out-of-season lambs, and we've been grateful for each one of them. Especially at a time like this, every lamb is precious to look at and crucial to the profit picture. We had become suppliers for Science Hill Inn in Shelbyville and Beaumont Inn in Harrodsburg, two premier establishments. Our goal is to be a consistent source of quality meat for the finest restaurants in the area, as well as individuals who desire lamb chops for their freezers.

That was what I was telling myself early on a Sunday morning as I walked through the flock congregated in the lot behind the stock barn. I wanted to be sure everybody was all right. Ewedawg had walked with me that morning, when the air was sharp, providing a fine feeling to be out and away from the stuffiness of the house. It was a good time to consider nature, the cycling patterns of God's creatures and the relationship they share with the predators. A program on Kentucky Educational Television had been helpful in understanding that sheep, just as the wildebeest, have their heat periods at approximately the same time, meaning the predators have one major banquet a year. Otherwise, there would be lambs throughout the year, assuring the predators a steady and predictable diet. Efforts to persuade sheep to procreate in the heat of summer is a most difficult assignment. It requires pampering, which I'm convinced is contrary to nature.

When I spotted a ewe on the other side of the wet weather runoff, by her side was a wrinkled and befuddled, tiny creature resembling a lamb. It was mostly all legs. There were yellow flecks of newborn color on the miniature animal, and there was a glazed cast to its eyes. Dazed, the lamb was willing to claim Ewedawg or me as its mother, it was no time to be particular. The mamma ewe, meantime, stamped her feet as the best bluff she could contrive. Ewedawg paid no attention to it, except to be quietly respectful. Meanwhile, I reached down and picked up the lamb, lifting it about a foot off the ground. The newborn heart was beating as rhythmically as a well-wound Swiss watch. The body was warm. Despite the cold morning, all systems were on line, everything "go" as they said at the Johnson and Kennedy space centers.

The plan was to walk a few steps in the direction of the stock barn, let the lamb bleat and lure the mamma ewe into following. After several bleats and responding answers I was about halfway home. At this point, the mamma ewe decided she'd had enough of Ewedawg and me, and she turned back to join the flock. To Ewedawg's credit, she allowed the lamb to claim her as the mamma. The lamb snuggled up under Ewedawg's white, thick coat, and it looked for all the world as if the lamb might try to nurse the dog, like Romulous and Remus nursing the wolf.

There's only so much Roman mythology a self-respecting Christian mamma sheep can endure. She came flying at Ewedawg and caught her mid-ribcage, sending her sprawling teacups over saucers. I had to give Ewedawg full credit. On that day, at that precise moment, she seemed to understand why the mamma ewe was upset. Ewedawg didn't complain, didn't bite, didn't bark. As far as I was concerned, there was nothing to do but to break up an unbalanced situation. I took Ewedawg to the barn, where she'd be out of the way. Then I returned to the lamb, once again united with its mother. The ewe stamped her feet at me, but she didn't follow through as she had with Ewedawg. All the same, I kept an eye on her, because even a threatened sheep can sometimes break a leg for you. As a shepherd becomes older, he begins to worry more and more about broken legs.

I scooped up the lamb and walked in the direction of the barn. When the tired little creature couldn't muster a bleat, I sent out one of my own—"Maaaaa, maaaaa." It must not have sounded too bad, because the mamma ewe followed us into the barn. For a few moments, I rationalized whether to tend my flock and not go to church, or go to church and then tend my flock. Church won out, and that was good because it led to a conversation with Norton Clay, a farmer who's a member of St. Peter's Episcopal Church in Paris, the county seat of

Bourbon. He said I had about 24 hours to get "first milk" into the lamb's stomach. "That's where all the nutrients and antibiotics are," said Norton with confidence born of the experience I lacked.

I hurried home, milked the ewe a little bit (Norton said it would be handy to have frozen and ready for emergency purposes), and then I helped the lamb nurse. There's only so much helping Mother Nature. The lamb simply was not coming out of the shock of its birth. Wayne took the little feller to his house and put him on a bottle. After a day and a night, the lamb was coming around. But when Wayne took the lamb back to its mamma, she must have decided she'd had enough of all the carryings on. She refused to accept the lamb. The delicate bond between the birther and the birthed was broken. Not all the scholarship, computers, modems, guard dogs, shepherds or church folk could change that.

That's how it came to pass, we had our first orphan lamb.

J.L. ARKINS

THE CHRISTMAS LAMB

T he lambs weren't supposed to arrive before the middle of January. It was planned that way. Sometimes, human plans are nothing more than that—just plans. There was a touch of ego in the arithmetic. Put in the rams. Wait five months. That's all there was to it. No time for miracles.

Take the little orange cat, for instance. Somebody or something took it. It's not here anymore. Probably it fell victim to the big orange cat. He's the stranger in the night, who always shows up when the moon is full. It was he who mated with the calico cat, producing the little orange cat and the little grey cat. Now, we guess the little orange cat cramped the style of the big orange cat, so the big guy destroyed the miracle that was the little guy. The little grey cat is o.k. Probably the big orange cat who returns with the regularity of the moon cycle, sees no threat in the little grey cat. The calico cat does not make the connection. She just does what the big orange cat says. No human plan can withstand the miracle that arrives with the big orange cat. He loves them and leaves them, and while it's easy to hate him for that, there is probably method in his madness. Otherwise, we'd be overrun with cats. We'd have to do what the big orange cat does for us without us asking.

Take the sheep dog, Lady. Her miracle is her devotion to the flock. Yet, we can't be sure her watchfulness is so unplanned. She may be driven by internal miracles unmatched by the best Swiss watches. You can almost see the tickings of her brain as she moves among the ewes—her one goal in life, to give helpless sheep a better chance to live.

Take the coyotes. They're out there, mainly over the hill. But, sometimes, a family of young'uns comes up along the creek with their mamma, on the off chance the bad old sheep dog has gone to sleep, too tired to wake up.

Usually, about two o'clock in the morning, when the night sounds are keenest, the coyote young'uns put up such a fuss it's enough to raise the dead. No wonder they can't get an edge on the bad old sheep dog. If they'd be a little more quiet about it all they might have a tasty supper. But I doubt it, because Lady's miracle is to KNOW when the enemy is present.

Take the mice and the rat families down at the corn crib. It's full now. All they have to do is walk in as if the gates of Fort Knox had been opened up to the down and out. Their ship has come in. Bread is falling from heaven. Streets are paved with gold. Stomachs are full at last.

Take the cows and the calves beginning to bulge their mamma's sides. Most human attempts to synchronize the miracles of birth are flawed with error. When the time comes for the cows to deliver, they usually go to a far corner of the field, and there they cooperate with the ticking of the clocks that say the hour has come.

"Come take a walk with me."

"What is it?"

"You'll see. Just put on your boots and come on down to the barn."

"The Christmas lamb has come, I just know it."

He would say nothing more. She followed. The child did, too. They helped each other cross over the wet weather runoff. It was slippery in the mud and on the small rocks.

The Big Dipper tilted down along the horizon to the Northeast. The Great Hunter swaggered in the East, his knife glistening above the treetops.

The man, the woman and the child peered over the wooden fence. With a flashlight they caught sight of the miracle by the side of the ewe, warbling her maternal sounds.

The lamb of Christmas had arrived—while all around, the barn lot was still, as if all God's creatures waited to be sure that the miracle was completed.

MORE MIRACLES ON PLUM LICK

T he hymn sung by the choir in St. Peter's Church in the season of Advent of 1989, caused one of its members, the shepherd's wife, to be tearful. "Lo! the lamb, so long expected," were words too miraculous to be easily voiced. Unknown to the shepherd and his wife attending church, another ewe confined back home at the lambing barn was in her last stages of labor. The past day or two, she'd been choosy about her hay and ground corn. Her sides, especially the right side, had been bulging.

The shepherd's wife practiced Christmas hymns with the choir for an hour following church, while the shepherd paced. Had he known what was happening in the lambing pen he would have hurried there. The shepherd's wife would have too, but neither she nor he had such clear vision. They drove home as if knowing that which had for so long been expected must surely happen soon. They changed clothes, put the child to sleep for a nap and hurried to the lambing barn.

The ewe—number 89—was standing in the middle of her pen. She was straining hard. It was the beginning of another birth of the new season—in its own way an advent. The shepherd and his wife quietly moved to the other side of the barn to leave the ewe alone, to give nature a chance to work out its own difficulties. It was a good afternoon to look after the other ewes, to vaccinate for diseases and give nature a little extra margin of safety.

The flock was bunched together for ease of handling: fill the syringe, hold the ewe, inject the solution, mark the ewe, repeat the process.

"Did you hear that?"

"Sounded like a lamb."

"Let's go look."

The large lamb was expelled. The ewe was mothering it. The shepherd and his wife watched the miracle continuing.

"I think she's got another lamb." The ewe was cleaning her firstborn, while the contractions for the twin began.

"There it is!"

The shiny white feet protruded for a time, and then in one quick contraction, the second lamb fell to the ground. It looked dead. The ewe was ignoring it. The shepherd climbed into the pen and removed the membrane from the second lamb's nose and mouth. It took its first small gasp of air. Again, the ewe was left alone to do what nature commanded she should—take care of her young with no promise of reward except for the instinctive pleasure derived from each caring act. When the rest of the flock were completely vaccinated and turned outside for exercise, the watch resumed by the little pen where the ewe was busy encouraging the lambs to nurse for the first time.

"Does the little one have a clubbed foot?"

Both front hooves seemed clubbed. They would straighten out if forced, but when the pressure was withdrawn they would revert to their abnormality.

"Maybe they'll straighten out, maybe not."

The shepherd in the winter of 1989 was sometimes invited to parties of the Christmas season, so he hurried to join his wife for the drive to the country club, where there were laughter, a generous table and a time to meet old friends to wish them "Merry Christmas!"

Back at the sheep barn, the second-born lamb was falling into the water tub. It was something nature had not put into the pen. Nature is a great deal smarter than that. Fortunately, the shepherd and his wife did not party all night. Once again, they were pulled homeward by their compass, not because they knew anything was amiss, but because they anticipated the simple possibility of being needed. When the shepherd fished the second newborn lamb out of the cold water tub, it did not look good at all. A burlap sack and, later, a towel from the house were used to rub warmth back into the lamb. There was concern the ewe might suddenly disown a warm and clean lamb. Efforts to get colostrum—first milk—into the water-logged lamb were failing. The shepherd's wife came down from the house and held the ewe while a half-inch of first milk was squeezed, tiny squirt by tiny squirt into a baby bottle. The lamb's mouth was forced open, and the artificial nipple was inserted.

The lamb swallowed.

The next morning when the shepherd went to the barn, he found two lambs nursing. One was large, strong and healthy. The other was small and had clubbed feet.

On Sunday, the shepherd was standing in the hallway of St. Peter's. In his arms, the lamb whose front hooves were so weak at birth they curled over as if clubbed, was snuggled against the warmth of humanity. The lamb, born on the previous Sabbath, buried his one-week-old nose in the reassuring softness of an all-wool scarf, the strands of which had originated somewhere along generations of the lamb's great uncles and aunts.

Arthur Hancock, breeder of Kentucky Derby winner Sunday Silence, walked by.

"That's a lamb."

"Yes, we're waiting for our cue."

Alone again, the shepherd reflected on his own Sunday silence sleeping in his arms.

"They're ready for the lamb," said the mother of the child, who would present her own offering at the creche near the foot of the altar. Without protest, the lamb traded one piece of humanity for another. There was a proud and confident smile on the child's face as the Reverend Cliff Pike announced there was a special visitor on this next to last Sunday before Christmas. The six-year-old child with the one-week-old lamb in her arms walked to the front of the church. Father Pike took the lamb into his own arms. There instantly was a sign unto all, especially the children in the congregation, this was a moment for sharing the warmth of one of God's creatures immortalized by Blake 200 years before.

> "Little Lamb, who made thee?
> Dost thou know who made thee?
> Gave thee life, and bid thee feed,
> By the stream and o'er the mead;
> Gave thee clothing of delight,
> Softest clothing, woolly, bright;
> Gave thee such a tender voice,
> Making all the vales rejoice?
>
> Little Lamb, who made thee?
> Little Lamb, I'll tell thee,
> Little Lamb, I'll tell thee:
> He is called by thy name,

> For He calls Himself a Lamb,
> He is meek, and He is mild;
> He became a little child.
> I a child, and thou a lamb,
> We are called by his name.
> Little Lamb, God bless thee!
> Little Lamb, God bless thee! [9]

The children crowded around the lamb. It never made a sound. The children touched the lamb. They did not know about the problem with the clubbed feet. Nobody noticed. All attention was focused on the lamb's face, his eyes and his pink nose. Soon, the Advent service was over. The miniature statues of the shepherds remained in the creche, the wise men, too, and Mary and Joseph, and Baby Jesus. All the carved animals, the camels and the sheep, were fixed in place for the Sunday before Christmas.

It was time to go home and return the real lamb to its mother. Perhaps, she would reject it after all the fuss made over it, all the perfume worn by the adults in church. Possibly the warmth of St. Peter's would cause the little lamb to be colder than ever before as the temperatures kept falling to zero and lower. More than anything else, would the clubbed feet remain?

The mother ewe accepted her child that had gone to church and been the center of such lavish attention. The change in temperatures did not appear to matter. The lamb's bigger twin brother seemed pleased the sibling had come home to the manger in the stock barn on Plum Lick.

Yet, what of the clubbed feet?

The shepherd watched. The lamb went to nurse. There were no minister, no creche, no children and no perfumed adults. There were no sounds from the great organ. There were no voices joining in song. There were no prayers, no anthems, no psalms.

There was no singing of the words, "Lo! the lamb, so long expected." There was just a little lamb—and for the first time, the front hooves did not curl over.

The "clubbed" feet were gone.

189

THEY ARE MEEK AND
THEY ARE MILD

o matter how we look at life, it has no meaning unless death is accepted as part of it. The great difficulty for many are the suddenness and the inexplicable circumstances accompanying the event, which only seems so anti-life.

First, there was the death of the first orphan lamb. Apparently, it had arrived in the world with only enough strength to live a few days. Everybody at Plum Lick Farms was praying for the tiny animal, but it was not to be. From that we learned something more about the uncertainties of entering an earthly life, which after all is only a small room in a larger mansion. Conception itself was chancy. There would be so many possibilities, millions upon millions of them, so many variations that nature in its wisdom would provide to insure even greater positive numbers to offset the inevitable losses. In this way, the onrush of life would be assured. Never mind that we would feel the pain of the loss of the one lamb, the heartache would become an important aspect of the lesson to be learned.

There was the passing away of a neighbor, a respected farmer. Edwin Soper had reached his biblical three score and ten, and yet he was a strong and vigorous man, who had worked hard all his life to be a fine steward of the land, where he and his family lived—their fixt foot on the Cane Ridge Road in Bourbon County. One only needed to drive past his place to know he was devoted to the care of his animals and his crops. The loss of such a man of the soil is impossible to comprehend, much less calculate.

The Rev. Perry reminded the living, this was the final resting place of rich and poor, exalted and unassuming: lawyers, merchants, politicians, educators and farmers. The passing of a man of the stature of an Edwin Soper would become a landmark for his children, grandchildren and neighbors, and it would be a time for remembering how mortal humans are, an occasion for drawing upon the collective strengths gathered to pay last respects.

About the time the funeral party was leaving the cemetery in Kentucky, Pan Am Flight 103 disappeared from a radar screen: an air

controller was monitoring the air space over the little town of Lockerbie, Scotland, where more than 250 men, women and children were
lost in a gigantic, mid-air explosion aboard the jumbo jet. As many as
30 residents of Lockerbie, many of whom probably had never ridden
aboard an airplane, some of them possibly the relatives of shepherds
died in the flaming ruins of at least 40 homes. Christmas gifts aboard
the jet and in the homes littered the blackened ground.

A college professor and a shepherd, walking as one to the lambing
barn in Kentucky, gave silent thanks that the students aboard Pan Am
flight 103 were not from the University of Kentucky, or any other
school in the Commonwealth. He said a prayer for the Syracuse University students, who lost their lives in the disaster in Scotland.

There was absolutely nothing to be done for the orphan lamb, Mr.
Soper or the victims of the plane crash. A Kentuckian went into the
lambing barn to think awhile, the silence broken only by the rustle of
the ewes in their bedding. An occasional bleat caught a bubble of air,
and floated and fell, and was heard no more. A pregnant ewe looked
into the eyes of the human. He returned the contemplation. It was a
searching time for answers. None came.

Then, something happened.
Seven lambs stole through the
gaps in the metal gate confin-
ing their mothers. They
romped with stiff-legged
abandon, as if fitted with
pogo sticks. The lambs, representing life and the living,
raced for the open door through which streamed sunlight. They sniffed
the air. They whirled and ran back as if the future held too much promise
to bear in one blinding instant. But then, the seven lambs turned again
toward the golden moment, bolting for the door once more, as if finding
the new possibilities irresistible. Some of the baby lambs jumped straight
up in the air and pranced when they retouched the ground. Others cavorted sideways, heads down in warm milk delight.

Would they go through the door? Or, would they stay forever in the
security of the one small room of the larger, universal mansion? They did
what they must.

They went outside.

MORE ORPHANS

A s soon as the barn door was opened there was the sound of the distressed, the lost, the unwanted. The sound was coming from the pen where the three older market-ready lambs were squabbling over the last sprigs of alfalfa thrown their way before midnight. It was obvious the newcomer didn't belong there. The nearby ewe with the single lamb was making a deep, warbling mothering sound, as if she had waited two days to deliver a twin. Unlikely as that was, the pitifully lost lamb was placed in the pen from where the interest was indicated. The ewe sniffed the new lamb, sniffed the older lamb and promptly sent the new lamb sprawling.

The mothering instincts of sheep are precisely managed by sight, sound and scent—the new lamb failed on all counts. A walk through the large pen of expecting mothers turned up nothing. For every forlorn bleat there was an equally useless stare. A closer visual inspection turned up no telltale traces of afterbirth.

The unclaimed lamb was officially pronounced "orphan," and the orphan was hungry. More importantly, the little girl lamb had missed her colostrum. A shepherd of the 1990's often has competing responsibilities, so the orphan would have to wait until errands had been completed in Paris, Frankfort and Lexington. Milk was purchased along the way. Finally, after an anxious return home, the orphan was fed. At first, the artificial nipple and the cow's milk were resisted but hunger won out. With a half of a baby's bottle of milk in its belly, the orphan lay down and went to sleep.

Ravy, who was six years old now, was very excited when I brought her home from school.

"Really?!? An orphan lamb?"

"Yes, and you must take good care of it."

"I will," said Ravy with the conviction of someone older.

"You'll have to feed the baby twice a day. That will mean getting up earlier, you know."

"I will,"

Lalie arrived home just in time to help hold one of the ewes, so at least some natural milk could be given to the orphan. It wasn't colostrum, but it was the next best thing. Then, Ravy sat on a bale of hay in the center of the barn, cradled the orphan lamb in her arms and fed it another half of a baby's bottle of cow's milk. Another lamb, about a week older, came over and, for a lack of something better to do, butted the orphan.

"Get away from here," said Ravy with authority.

"I think we should take the lamb to the kitchen and let it sleep there in a box tonight. That way, it won't get hurt," I said. Lalie agreed, and of course, Ravy was beaming.

"Time to feed the lamb," said the shepherd early next morning.

Ravy bounded from bed with a newfound purpose.

"I'll feel better when more lambs are born," said the shepherd to bales of hay and the trough of shelled corn. But, there were no new lambs: none Saturday night, none Sunday morning, none Sunday afternoon.

The Dorset and the Hampshire rams butted heads in the barn lot. A banded tail fell from a December lamb. Lady paced the premises, sending signals to distant predators that if they had designs on the flock, they'd have to deal with her first. Four maturing ewe lambs were put outside the barn to make more room and conserve feed. The full moon had passed its prime and moved toward its descent. Tobacco sticks were counted and placed in bundles of 50. Another hymn was sung in church that mentioned a lamb. Another prayer was offered that lambs would be born healthy, that there would be as few orphans as possible.

About 10:30 Sunday night, Lady began barking. It woke up the shepherd. He lay there wishing the barking would stop, but it didn't.

"Wonder why Lady is barking?"

"I don't know," came the drowsy reply.

"I'm going to see."

"If you need help, I'll come, too."

The walk from the kitchen, down the hill, across the stream to the barn had become a well-worn path. Lady was quiet—as if she'd accomplished her purpose by getting somebody out of bed.

When the barn door was opened there was the unmistakable bleat of the newborn. One of the ewes in the small pens had a fine, sturdy new lamb standing beside her. Everything seemed normal. Then, there was the sound of another tiny bleat out in the large enclosure. The shepherd went there and found another lamb.

"This one's not going to be an orphan."

But, no ewe in the large pen came forward. A slow walk through the flock made no difference. Patience. Patience. Take your time. Don't hurry. Finally, it worked. The first ewe with what had seemed to be a single birth, raised her head and acknowledged the second bleat. When both lambs were in the pen, there were two tails twirling to the sweet taste of first milk. The shepherd stood and watched the twins for a long time.

Then he turned out the light. It was almost midnight when he walked back up the hill. The moon that had been hidden behind clouds reflected a clearing sky.

The horses and mule stalls on one side of the lambing barn had been taken out to make room for individual four-by-four lambing pens. The area that used to be the shed became the largest area section where the mothers-in-waiting put up with a former CBS News correspondent walking among them to slip a cold hand beneath their udders better to judge who was next.

On the other side of the pens, in the center of the large stock barn, became the place where ewes and lambs went after they had spent the first several crucial days in the small pens. No matter how it was divided up, things were becoming crowded. After the first old ewe aborted, the next day there were twins, and for a month I was averaging a 144% lamb crop. Nine ewes produced 13 lambs—not too bad for a new shepherd.

There had been two orphans. The first one had died, but we were determined that the second one would live. Thank goodness, I told myself, the second orphan is female and won't have to go to the slaughter house. That would be a tough one to explain to the six-year-old girl who bottle fed the orphan first thing every morning and last thing every night. The whole business of raising precious little lambs for the slaughterhouse has to be troubling for even the most hardbitten shepherd. But there are cute little pigs, rabbits, ducks, chickens, and calves—the pain for the animal husbandman is to see them grow up to become products for sale and eventual destruction.

The orphan had rather quickly turned into a pest. Any pant leg on a human was as warm and comforting as a mother's breast. The sound of the little animal was so plaintive it resembled a human child. As soon as the shepherd entered the barn, the tiny, forlorn bleat was heard. For a time it appeared the orphan was on her way to survival with all the other lambs, but one cold morning she was doubled up with her hind legs drawn tightly beneath her—eyes closed, the small, exquisite head barely raised above the straw. The bottle feeding with cow's milk had finally resulted in scours.

The shepherd trapped one of the ewes with a single lamb in the pen, and attempted to force the orphan to nurse. It wouldn't work. The orphan's mouth was becoming cold. There was nothing to do but to return the lamb to the kitchen. In an act of desperation, a liquid vitamin was added to the milk. The shepherd sat in the old cane-bottomed chair and began to force the artificial nipple into the orphan's mouth.

The child came into the kitchen.

"I told my friend at school that we could find a nice place to bury the lamb."

There's not much to be said to something like that.

"The school yard would be a very nice place."

The lamb was beginning to take the milk very slowly at first, and little by little the nourishment was entering the small body, which weighed six pounds at birth, but had fallen lower since then. There was no reason to make predictions, no reason to reach for unrealistic possibilities, no justification for giving up, either. The child turned with her mother to leave for school, and the shepherd placed the orphan back into the cardboard box on the kitchen floor.

"This is going to be a tough one," he said to the kitchen walls. "There's only so much anybody can do."

Coming home to Plum Lick each night from the University where knowledge is bound in volumes on shelves stacked high upon shelves, the compassion of the animal husbandman cries out for more understanding. The closeness of creatures—a man, his wife, a child and an orphan lamb—draws tighter. A prayer is sent heavenward. The twin compasses are welded at the center. The fixt foot will not move.

"Little orphan lamb, be alive when I return. Don't be afraid. I'll be back as soon as possible."

The shepherd put on his professor's clothes and drove to the University. He wandered through the shelves of books, met with students to advise them about careers, met with faculty to discuss budgets, curriculum, travel requests, research, publishing, equipment purchases, grants, building space, workshops, sabbaticals, retreats, conferences and grievances. Yet, he was a shepherd in professor's clothing. Plum Lick was calling, and at the end of the day he hurried to it.

The professor's clothes landed in a heap in the bedroom where generations before him had taken their first breaths, and breathed their last. The shepherd's clothes felt snug and warm. As quickly as he could, he returned to the kitchen. He picked up the lamb from the cardboard box on the floor by the stove.

It was plain to see from the position of the head and neck of the tiny creature, life was drifting away. Sheep, he thought, seem to embrace eternity with warmth and acceptance, as if it were entirely natural, a condition welcomed. They reach a point of surrender, beyond which it becomes unseemly to struggle. They become those borrowers of the great goodnight.

The man was relieved that his wife and child had not yet come home from school. Although he knew it was useless, still he tried to force milk into the lamb's cold mouth. He was too inexperienced to know about the importance of tube feeding. The milk trickled down the crinkled neck. It ran onto the man's hand. He wiped it against his shepherd's overalls.

He felt the heartbeat. It was irregular.

Then, it stopped.

There had been that talk about a burial.

"The school yard would be a very nice place," the child had said, when she sensed as well as anyone else, time was running out for the orphan lamb. Of course, though, the authorities would never have permitted such a ceremony. It was one of those precious thoughts lodged in one's heart—not in cold, hard reality. The shepherd wrapped the lamb in a sack. He dug a small grave on a miniature knoll above the wet weather runoff between the house and the barn. He layed the lamb in its final resting place, placing the form into the earth from whence it had come. He covered it over.

He walked away.

TRIPLETS

On the eve of the start of the land war against Iraq, the retired correspondent went down to the lambing barn on Plum Lick. He found ewe #87 in the center aisle. She was stretched on her side. She was straining hard. Her uterus had prolapsed again. It had happened before, but this time it was obvious she was trying to lamb. After witnessing sorrow and tragedy from El Salvador and Nicaragua to Argentina and Beirut, it was no different looking down at one helpless ewe in her moment of agony. I considered going to the house, returning with a pistol and ending the ewe's misery. But, on the way to the house, I thought:

"There has to be hope. I have to try. I have to do something else."

"Dr. Brown, this is David Dick. How are you?"

"I'm fine," said Dr. Frank Brown of Montgomery County, who at 10:00 in the evening knew the call had a lot more to do with it than just inquiring as to how he was.

"It's the ewe with the prolapse again. This time she's ready to lamb. I thought about shooting her, but I decided to call you."

"She's probably not dilated. It'll be very difficult."

"Well, if you're willing to come, I'd appreciate it."

"I'll be there."

"Thanks."

The shepherd returned to the side of the ewe. He lifted her head, and whispered to her.

"He's on his way. Hang in there."

When Dr. Brown arrived, he and the shepherd carried the ewe to the side shed, where there was better light. The doctor administered an anesthetic, and made an incision in the prolapsed uterus. He maneuvered through the entry point and located two feet. A few minutes later Dr. Brown brought out the lamb. It was alive.

"I think I'll leave the umbilical cord attached for a while. The lamb looks to be about a week to 10 days early. Ewe has no milk. Doesn't look good."

Dr. Brown went back to work. He worked his fingers and then his hand into the uterus. He removed the second lamb. It had life too.

"I think you should go to the house for towels for something to dry and warm the lambs. It'll help a lot."

When the shepherd returned, he rubbed the lambs. They responded with gasps for breath.

"I wonder if there's anything else in there," said Dr. Brown as he entered the uterus the third time.

He found two more feet.

The triplet was the largest lamb of all.

Dr. Brown sewed up the uterus. As he drove away, the shepherd walked up the hill. There were three wet, cold, premature orphan lambs in his arms. At midnight, on the eve of the start of the groundwar in the Persian Gulf, the shepherd and his wife were feeding the triplet lambs in the kitchen of the old house on Plum Lick in Kentucky.

While all hell broke loose in the war with Iraq, there were bleats scudding throughout the night on Plum Lick, especially coming up the hallway from the cardboard box on the kitchen floor. The family slept through it. Probably they should have been up every one or two hours with the orphan triplet lambs, but fatigue took its prisoners. At sunrise, two of the three premature creatures, perfectly formed on the outside, but not completely developed internally, had closed their eyes. Their hearts had stopped.

The third lamb was alive. She was hungry. A bottle of warm milk seemed to fix that. The two lambs that had not survived the night were taken outside. The hope invested in the three was now focused entirely on the one. The family—mother, father and daughter—knew chances were very slim. But surely this lamb would make it. So it seemed for two days.

"The lamb is yours," said the father to the daughter.

"Her name will be 'Nibbles,' " said Ravy, who was now seven years old.

Nibbles became an instant star. Her stomach full of milk, she basked in the sunlight streaming through the child's bedroom window. Nibbles brought back memories of "Hawkins," an orphan lamb that had entered, and almost as quickly had exited the life of the father when he was seven years old. It was Hawkins in the child's wagon, Hawkins out of the child's wagon, much as it was Nibbles in the box, Nibbles out of the box.

The day Hawkins died landed like a thud in the pit of the boy's stomach.

The morning Nibbles died was almost the same.

There was a silence that stunned the family. No words were spoken. The members of the family knew livestock are animals, and they should not be pets. It only leads to hurt. But every now and again, a Nibbles or a Hawkins slips through the usual impersonal human-creature relationship. A kiss lands on the side of the creature's face. A warm hug closes the gap. The closeness probably means more to the human than to the creature, yet humans can't be too sure. If the creature had the power to reason, it might say, "Why has it taken so long for you to understand the importance of what you're doing?" But, the creature neither reasons nor speaks, and the human is left with incomplete knowledge.

The human family, it seems, is brought closer by the simple act of kindness shown animals. When the animal turns to go in a direction that has no turning back, it leaves humans with miniature but powerful feelings of helplessness—nothing less than a death in the family. There is, of course, nothing here to compare with death on the battlefield. Yet, the loss of any life carries with it moments of meaning, irreplaceable. As Donne, we are involved in Mankind—any death diminishes us.

PASTORALE

I called up my friend, Steve Spears.

"I'd like to do something nice for my sheep, Steve."

I could feel his soft, knowing smile through the telephone.

"Might be able to help you."

"I was thinking about a little something for a treat."

"We could probably fix you up some sweet feed."

"Everybody ought to be nice to their sheep."

Another soft, knowing smile came through the telephone.

"I'll have it ready for you when you come by."

Anthropomorphizing is one of those $200 academic words. The first time I heard it, I looked it up: "To ascribe human characteristics to...animals," as in "Mary had a little lamb, its fleece was white as snow, and everywhere that Mary went, the lamb was sure to go" ..."Baa, baa black sheep, have you any wool? Yessir, yessir, three bags full."

We generally don't use words like "anthropomorphizing" on Plum Lick. We might call it "playing around." It's what all children love to do, and I never consider the day complete without engaging in at least a little childlike behavior.

I picked up the sweet feed and took it home to Plum Lick. Two days went by before I could find time to give the sheep the treat, time enough for a Mickey Mouse to cut a hole in the side of the sack and be the first to enjoy a taste.

On the morning I decided I'd spare a few moments from what would surely become another hectic, nerve frayed day at the University, I dressed up in my new tweed jacket, donned my cute little tweed cap, and went out to impress the sheep with my all-Kentucky look. I scooped up a generous amount of sweet feed in a pan, and headed for the sheep lot behind the stock barn. I did a reasonable amount of slipping and sliding out there where the pasture was damp and well-decorated with sheep doo. I prided myself on having good balance. The Director of the School of Journalism would not want to wind up in Dean Douglas Boyd's office in the College of Communications with evidences of sheep doo from the bottom of the shoes to the top of the dandy little tweed cap.

The sheep were in the barn, where all sheep with tolerable grade point averages should be at that hour of the morning. I called out, "Heeeee-be, heeeee-be." Ewe number 15, who along with the Dorset ram have taken over leadersheep duties for the flock, stuck her head outside. She sniffed the air and immediately broke into "Oh, what a beautiful morning."

Donna Reed had sung no more sweetly in "State Fair." I pulled down on my tweed cap, and sprinkled a little sweet feed upon the ground. "Heeeee-be, heeeee-be." The flock came out of the barn as if Farley Granger had arrived in town.

Lady, the guard dog, was not about to be had so easily. She lurked over by the wet weather runoff, probably wondering how sheep could be so dumb to fall for such silliness. "Heeeee-be, heeeee-be" was about as repulsive as "Here, Fido."

The Dorset Ram followed ewe #15 up the slope. The Dorset, with his well-earned reputation for butting, looked Farley Granger in the eye as if too disgusted to comment. Farley worked around in a large circle, sprinkling little piles of sweet feed for his darlings, calling all the while,

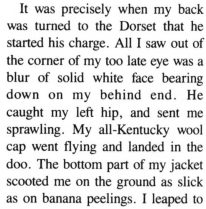

J. LARKINS

"Heeeee-be, heeeee-be."

It was precisely when my back was turned to the Dorset that he started his charge. All I saw out of the corner of my too late eye was a blur of solid white face bearing down on my behind end. He caught my left hip, and sent me sprawling. My all-Kentucky wool cap went flying and landed in the doo. The bottom part of my jacket scooted me on the ground as slick as on banana peelings. I leaped to my feet, fracturing Beethoven's "Pastorale" with curses too numerous and too awful to retell. What's worse, the bad language was disordered and strangely out of sequence. In other words, I sputtered horribly. I grabbed the pan that had been knocked from my hand and I threw it at the Dorset with every ounce I could muster from my mortified body.

The pan caught him squarely between the eyes, and turned him in the other direction, but it wasn't much of a victory. The Dorset had clearly carried the day, and I—no wiser, and sorely wounded—limped off to the institution of higher learning.

RAM SPEED

I told the Dorset ram how friendly everyone was in Minneapolis during a recent meeting of journalism educators. "Why can't you be friendly like that?" I asked.

The Dorset ram's ears went back and quivered in that position that said, "Take one more step in my direction, continue your silly prattle, then turn your back and watch me put some sucker wool on the seat of your pants."

"I'm serious. You do remember me breaking that tree limb across your face, don't you?"

The Dorset ram snorted. He flinched. His eyes blinked a couple of times.

"It just doesn't have to be like this," I said, knowing what George Bush must feel like whenever he has to deal with Saddam Hussein. The trouble, basically, is that President Bush doesn't have the option of breaking a tree limb across Saddam Hussein's face. And yet, the old "two-by-four" approach has been known to produce wonders in some parts of the animal world. Economic sanctions never seemed to have any effect on the Dorset ram. Feed him, or don't feed him, the result is pretty much the same. He prefers to butt people when their backsides are turned. The Dorset ram doesn't take hostages.

About this time of year the old boy is thinking about two things: staying cool in August, and waiting for pleasantly sexy September evenings. If only President Bush could figure out a way to scratch Saddam Hussein behind the ears. It has worked absolute miracles with the Dorset ram. He craves it.

It was just last night I went down to the lane where the rams spend the dog days of summer. I brought along a little salt as a peace offering. I put my arm around the Dorset ram's neck and placed my face against his. Then I scratched him behind the ears. I think the Dorset would trade all the oil in the world for some good scratching behind the ears. Lordy, he loves it.

For the first time it occurred to me to take a ride on the Dorset. I think it surprised him as much as it did me. In fact, he seemed to think it was perfectly normal, and I got to thinking in terms of sheep saddles and bridles.

"You won't believe this," I said later, leaning against the kitchen counter.

"Won't believe what?" replied the skeptical person who was washing dishes.

"I just rode the Dorset ram."

"Yeah, and I've just been offered a chance to do the Playboy centerfold...why don't you come in and rest awhile? I think the heat is getting to you," said the worn-out shepherd's wife.

THE DOG DAYS OF SUMMER

"Hi. I'm the Dorset ram. The boss said I could tell this story. Actually, some of us animals let him think he's the boss.

"There I was, minding my own business. It was a Saturday, and the boss had just come back from Morehead State University. He had five more ewes with him, and frankly I could have cared less. I mean, me and the 18 Rambouillet ewes—excuse me, the boss would want me to say, the 18 Rambouillet ewes and I—had sort of taken the day off from regular reproductive activities, if you catch my drift.

"I was resting against the cool side of the concrete watering trough, the family jewels protected as well as if they'd been placed in a numbered Swiss bank account, when here came the boss down the lane. He acted like he had something important on his mind.

"I watched him round up the women folk to take them to the shed, and I says to myself, 'Now wait a dern minute. There's no need in this.' Sure, I heard him talking about wanting to trim their feet, but a muggy September Saturday should not be made worse by having your women folks' feet trimmed. Give 'em a break. Give me a break.

"Well, the poor befuddled dears, you know how they are (the boss says, he can't talk like that up there at the University what with all the fuss about gender equality, but there's nothing to keep me from telling it like I see it down here on Plum Lick). It's a clear case of the ewes doing whatever the rest of the ewes are doing, you know, doing whatever the flock does. I just never have cottoned to that sort of thing—wooled, maybe, but never cottoned (the boss's wife will probably enjoy that more than him (he?), because she's always been the punny one around the house.)

"To tell you the ram's truth, I just put my hoof down. I stood right there at the gate, and I said to myself, this is enough of this foolishness. The last time I took a run at the boss, he broke that tree limb across my face. I'll never forget it as long as I live. But, what the boss didn't know was he just thought that was a run. Until now, he didn't know what a real run was.

"Remember that guy who played for the Chicago Bears, the Refrigerator I think they called him? Well, let's just say the boss was Joe Montana and he was standing there looking for a pass receiver. I, the Refrigerator, came at Joe like an L&N freight train looking for a roundhouse. It caught the boss totally by surprise.

"I made his britches whistle.

"The boss fell down, and if he had just left it at that I wouldn't have done another blessed thing. But the boss, you know how petty he can be; he jumped up and came at me with a tobacco stick headed for my nose. He missed, and that made him madder. I saw him go for a wood plank, and I made his britches whistle again. Down he went in the mud.

"Well, I figured the ball game was over, and I headed pretty as you please back down the lane with the girls. Would you believe it? Here comes the boss with an old, rusted, iron chain he uses whenever his pickup truck gets stuck in the mud. The same one. Well, that just flat did it. I mean, I lost control. You've heard of ram speed? I backed up a good ten yards, purchased a full head of steam and then I came at that sorry, overweight, ugly, good-for-nothing thing passing himself off as boss, Director of the UK School of Journalism, University Orator and shepherd to boot. You should have seen the whites of his eyes.

"I put the fear of God Almighty into him like it had never been put there before. Instead of whistling his britches, I caught him in the inside of the right leg and spun him around like a top. If he hadn't moved at the last second, about the way he told me he did down there in Nicaragua when that national guardsman took aim on him, I would have broken his leg. In fact, if I could have figured a way to break both his legs I'd have done it. If I could have cleaned out his Swiss bank account, I would have done that too. It would more than have made up for all the little rubber bands he acts like he loves to put on the boy lambs. Come to think of it I should thank him for that, because it cuts (as it were) the competition.

"He got the message. He headed for the house. Lord knows, he may have been thinking about going for the shotgun. Since I had little to lose, I decided to hurry him on his way. I came charging up the lane with the spirit of Casey Jones at the throttle. The boss looked back and saw me, and he climbed the fence. To make my point, I let him climb down, and then I came at him again. This time, he went over the fence and cleared the barbed wire with inches to spare. He headed up through the field, cussin' something awful.

"If I could have talked, I would have yelled at him: 'Yours for better buttin'!' "

"O.K., the boss, he decided to let me tell the next to the last part of the story too. I don't know what possessed him to pass up the chance to gloat over getting even with me for giving him such a fright about ten days ago. After I had whistled his britches twice, put him in the mud once, twirled him like a top once, sent him up the fence twice and finally put him over the fence, I thought he had gotten the message. The boss is kinda strange about not getting messages if you want to know the unvarnished truth about the matter.

"In plain Sheeplish, I did not want my girlfriends' feet trimmed, damn it, no matter how much they may have needed it. Frankly, I'm not interested in their feet. I certainly did not appreciate him not asking me about it in advance.

"How does he expect me to do my job, to pace myself, if, with not so much as an 'excuse me,' or a 'Do you mind, Old Boy?' or a 'Do you think this is a good time, Old Top?' Nosir, he just comes down the lane like he owns the world, and begins hollarin' at my girlfriends, and talkin' about how they'll all feel better after they'd had their feet trimmed.

" 'First things, first,' the boss likes to say.

"Of course, I was relieved he didn't go to the house, get the shotgun and come back and blow my brains out. With us independent-thinking Dorset rams, there's always a possibility with stubborn, misguided shepherds being what they sometimes are. It goes with the territory, as they say.

"Frankly, I knew he wasn't going to blow my brains out, because even he knows how much I'm needed. He was so worried about me buttin' the stuffins out of the Hampshire ram every time he even looked at one of my girlfriends, thinking, I suppose, that if I was always doing that I wouldn't have time to do anything else. But when the lambs started coming, even the boss could count Dorset faces. No ram, no lamb, as we say.

"However, I had not counted on the boss tricking me with the one-two combination of open gate and heavy linked tractor chain. As soon as I saw him open the gate, I'll be rammed if I didn't fall for it. I should have known better, but on the outside chance that he was going to let me into greener pastures, I came trotting up the lane and through the open gate into the corral.

"I came over to the fence and said to myself, 'What's up, boss?'"

"He was muttering stuff not fit for printing in books. Next thing I know, he's tricking me again by sticking his hand through the fence and scratching me behind my ears. The whole world knows what a sucker I am for that. But then he takes this piece of electrical wire, loops it around my neck, and then ties it to the fence. That didn't bother me so much, because I could see he couldn't give me a charge even if he wanted to, which he probably did, if he'd been smart enough to think of it. The really insulting part was throwing that heavy chain around my middle twice and then hooking it to the post. You talk about being chained to the mast. I knew he wasn't going to do cat-o'-nine tails on me, because the boss knows full well he can beat me 'til my dying breath (or his). I can take it. He would just get tired in the process. Or, worse yet for him, have a heart attack.

"No sir, after he chains me to the post and snugs my neck in close to the fence, he marches back down the lane and rounds up my girlfriends. Of course, they'll do anything he says. Here they all come, and the way the boss gets even is to humiliate me by parading every last member of my harem past me on the way to getting their feet trimmed.

"Oh, I heard them snicker: 'Gotcha this time, maa, maa, maa,' and 'How come you chained to the post like that? Maa, maa, maa,' and 'See you later when you're not all tied up, maaaaaaa, maaaaaaa, maaaaaaa.'

"Well, of all the things the boss could have done to me that was just about the lowest down dirty trick of all. Would you believe, when the feet trimming was over he marched the dears right past me again? More ridicule. Who was that feller who said, he never got no (any) respect?

"That's me, the Dorset ram. Or, as the boss would rather I say, "That's I, the Dorset ram."

This is the boss talking. There comes a time to cash in the chips and get out of town. There comes a time when you've had it up to here, and there's no sense in butting your brains out. I tried to tell all this to the Dorset ram, but he only looked at me with his best distrustful eye.

"Old Podner," I said to the evil eye, "Your time has come. Nobody wants you, least of all I know I don't, so what we're going to do is load you up and take you to the stockyards."

"Hello, Paris Stockyards? I've got this Dorset ram I want to bring in."

"Fine."

"How much do you think he might bring?"

"About 10 cents to 20 cents a pound."

That was a long way down from the $350 paid for the old boy in the first place. But, there'd been lambs as well as lamentations. Now, there was no turning back. The Dorset and his running buddy, the Hampshire ram, were maneuvered into the last small holding pen before the short walk up the loading chute ramp. They cooled their heels there for a day. The pickup truck was backed to the opening. There was a part of the shepherd that hated the thought of turning such a fine specimen of ramhood into muttonhood. Visions of the moment of truth caused regret. There ought to be a more dignified end to a distinguished career, even if it included the day the Dorset almost broke the shepherd's legs.

"Last meal, so enjoy it," said the shepherd as he tossed a few ears of corn into the holding pen. The Dorset ate while the Hamp waited. Even on death row, the Dorset was as cool as if he were resting under a shade tree, with the family jewels tucked up snugly out of harm's way. When the warden climbed over the fence to move the old rams up the chute and into the truck, he realized again what a stubborn, arrogant no-good the Dorset was, and would forever be as long as he drew a breath of air. When the Dorset took two short steps back it was time for rational humans to be up on the fence again rather than flat-footed in the pen. From the higher vantage point, the shepherd's crook could reach the beasts too smart to be driven, but beating the Dorset over the head, in the behind and along the side was like striking the Rock of Gibraltar with a #2 pencil.

A perfectly good galvanized water bucket thrown at the Dorset striking him between the eyes looked like a cocked hat when it bounced back and rolled around on the ground. Whenever he saw the opportunity, the Dorset took out his frustrations on the punch-drunk Hamp, who probably figured the slaughterhouse had to be a relief after this. After more than an hour of up-the-fence, down-the-fence, up-the-fence, down-the-fence, the warden was becoming mighty tired. He reminded himself, while he might die of a heart attack, the Dorset would probably still be out there butting heads and breeding ewes whenever he found them.

It wouldn't matter if an army of wardens took railroad ties and wrapped them around the Dorset's head, he would take it and say, if God had given him the ability to speak: "You can whip me until hell freezes over, I ain't getting in that pickup truck." It finally occurred to the warden to go to the barn and bring back a small wooden gate. He would use it as a shield and a prod. Inch by inch, tired breath by tired breath, aching muscle by aching muscle, by nightfall he would take the better part of another hour to move the rams up the chute and into the pickup truck.

"Now then, tomorrow we'll be on our way to the slaughterhouse," said the warden, almost too worn out to talk.

Later that night, a phone call came from Catlettsburg:

"I understand you have a Dorset ram for sale."

"Yes?"

"How much?"

"You probably should know, this ram is trouble."

"How much?"

"You'll regret it."

"How much?"

"Fifty dollars. And the Hampshire with the bad left front foot is thrown in for free."

"Where do we meet?"

"I'll meet you half-way, in Morehead."

"Sounds great."

"You'll be sorry."

The Dorset had won again. All the way from Plum Lick to Morehead, he had a smile on his face.

But, I had a smile on mine, too.

MORE DOG DAYS

The dogs have been howling more than usual. They permit no other dogs to trespass. Lady makes the rounds of the perimeter to assure every ram, ewe and lamb a better chance for survival. Lady asks for no reward other than safety for the flock. She tolerates no pat on the head, nor a nuzzling by the shepherd.

The rams have their breeding harnesses in place. Yellow is the color of the first marking, to be followed in 17 days by increasingly darker colors of crayon. This is supposed to tell the shepherd when to expect lambs. The earliest any can arrive is January 16, 1991. The 18 Rambouillet ewes had arrived from Morehead State University on Friday, August 24, 1990. It had been a pleasant and relaxing ride over and back—solitude, some country music on the radio, a chance to meet new friends and think ahead for the approaching autumn and winter.

One of the major jobs is putting seven acres of burley tobacco in the barns. It's a huge job, but the time has come to do it. The ritual is well-known to generations, who've been involved in the growing of an agricultural product that has become the object of almost as much scorn and criticism as drugs. Even alcohol is viewed by many to be more socially and pathologically acceptable than tobacco. It seems to a good many of us here on Plum Lick that the use of tobacco is not a moral issue for all, but a health issue for individuals. Some of us smoked when we were young, but gave it up when we grew older. Some of us consumed alcohol earlier in our lives, but reduced the amount later in our years. Some of us have never smoked tobacco or consumed alcohol, but at the same time, many of us have refrained from being judgmental about other's freedom to choose.

One view from Plum Lick is that tobacco, alcohol and many other legal pleasures don't kill. People do. This argument will never convince the anti-tobacco advocates. Our response is: when it's illegal, we won't grow it. We're a law-abiding people. From time to time, helicopters fly over the farm at night, searchlights playing on pastures and woodlots where marijuana might be growing. That's O.K. We don't know of any. We just hope the bright lights and noise won't frighten the sheep, cattle, cats and dogs.

In fact, some of us in Bourbon and many other Kentucky counties grew hemp, from which hashish is derived, when we were 4-H Club members back in the 1940s. It was legal. Kentucky farmers had been growing it long before statehood. Funny part is, most of us never thought about smoking it. While the hemp was converted into rope during World War II, we entertained ourselves by smoking corn silks. When we tired of that we felt very fancy and put on airs as we puffed "Indian cigars" taken from Catalpa trees. A good supply of cured corn silks and well-seasoned "Indian cigars" were viewed as assets more meaningful than money moldering somewhere in unexciting bank accounts.

The reality is that 50 years later, seven acres of burley is yellowing in one small corner of the fields of Kentucky, and families will go out with their glistening, razor-sharp knives and spears, and the stalks will make the sound of "shissssh" on the sticks, which then must be loaded onto wagons. The ride to the barn is a short reprieve, for the job of raising each stick with six stalks to the top of the barn is as difficult and hot as it is working beneath the broiling sun.

Tending sheep at the end of another day is welcome respite from housing tobacco. It makes one feel less inclined to ask the flock to jump through hoops. It becomes a time to lean against the fence a while, quietly observing the rams and ewes as they browse for morsels of weeds. The market lambs need watering and some feed to see them through the night. The sun has set, followed by the crescent moon descending. The fog gathers its moisture, and the spiders' webs shimmer in the pale light of another early evening.

A SHEPHERD'S WORK IS NEVER DONE

At the end of November, I've started putting the flock up each evening. The procedure is simple. Simplicity and sheep naturally travel the same paths. With the non-shepherding world becoming more complex, more tense, more psychopathic, actually, tending a small flock of sheep is therapeutic. I close the barn doors to keep the leadersheep (#15) from coming in before she's supposed to. Keeping the flock as calm as possible just makes good sense. Anytime you yell at a flock of sheep, about all you get for it are blank stares. Of course, I still yell at the Dorset ram in my dreams, but that's a different thing.

I put ground corn in the trough alongside the wall of the shed, and have it all done before the doors are opened. Then I go out to the bottom of winter wheat and slowly walk the flock of 55 ewes toward the barn. Lady barks at me and then slinks away. I'm the only human with whom she even remotely identifies, and that's not saying very much.

About one-third of the flock goes through the barn door on the first pass. I tell myself how nice it would be to have a trained border collie to help me, but I know they're expensive. One of the things about being a shepherd is being prudent. The other two-thirds of the flock goes to the other side of the barn. I close the door, and move the sheep inside to a smaller area where they can't get out when I re-open the door. When sheep are in a panic they are almost impossible to handle. That's why a fine border collie with "good" eyes is so effective. They have a mesmerizing effect on the sheep, and can set them on a dime, so to speak. Working by myself, it usually takes two and sometimes three more passes before all the sheep are in the barn. Patience pays. It's a good, warm feeling to have the flock inside. I feed them more ground corn, and let them have a little hay to see them through the night.

The trip to the loft is part of the enjoyment. A barn full of hay is about as reassuring a thing as there is anywhere to be found. While it's pure hell getting the hay into the loft, it's nothing short of heaven to drop the bales one at a time through the opening in the middle of the floor. Again, the important thing is not to hurry. Most of us hurry so much throughout the day, we've just about forgotten how to slow down and savor the moment.

I took time to move seven late lambs to a pen of their own. They didn't like it when I caught them, but after the job was finished they seemed to appreciate their new pampered status. They have their own hay, their own feed and their own water. They don't have to fight for it the way they do when they're competing with the entire flock. Likewise, I split off two old ewes and put them with the lambs. Maybe they'll do better. One thing about sheep, they typically reach the point where they give up and accept fate without fighting. It's a characteristic making these animals all the more interesting, makes a shepherd want to help them, if he or she can (A couple of my friends, Dorothy Haddix and Annie Brown of Montgomery County, are lady shepherds, and Kathy Meyer ran the sheep project at Morehead State University—the program was disbanded in 1992.)

After the sheep are fed and bedded down for the night, there's no call to go running back to the house to watch television. No need either to be in a hurry to eat supper. I like to stand there very quietly and watch the flock move back and forth, back and forth. There's nothing else needed for contentment. In a few weeks the first of the next crop of lambs will arrive, and that'll be a special joy, as well as heartaches for the many that won't survive.

The important thing is not to hurry nature, nor to curse nature. The lambs will be here when they're due, usually on the coldest night of the year. Why it's that way, I don't know, but I'll try to be ready for it. Some will live and some will die. I will want to remember to give

J. LARKINS

every ewe a chance to have her lamb or lambs with as little interference as possible. The temptation to play midwife will be stubbornly resisted.

Two of the summer lambs have been designated as participants on the Christmas parade float in our county seat. I know they'll be glad when it's over. There's nothing like bright lights and a noisy crowd to ruin a lamb's day. But maybe those along the parade route will understand shepherding didn't die 2,000 years ago.

"MAAAAA, MAAAA..."

The birds were singing. The breeze was blowing. Everything was right in the world. It was an early Sunday morning in the spring of 1991. The shepherd and his wife were warm together. They were slowly, sensuously emerging from deep sleep to the ever-changing discovery of each other. A touch, a kiss, a tender embrace were the omens of Sunday morning bliss unfolding. Heaven could wait—church, too.

Suddenly, a "Maaaaa" and then another "Maaaaa" followed by no fewer that three rapid-fire "Maaa," "Maaa," "Maaa's" cut the air across the front porch, sliced through the open bedroom window, ricocheting off the eardrums of the unsuspecting lovers. Instantly, the shepherd knew his Heaven had turned to Hell.

The damn sheep were in the yard.

Sheep in the yard means one thing and one thing only. It means they're feasting on flowers. The sheep's passion and consummation are not just for any flowers. They love most of all the flowers on which the lady of the house has spent her Christmas money, her Thanksgiving money and her birthday money, flowers for which she has almost bartered her soul: the roses, the lilacs, the delphinium, the caladium, the tiger lilies, the non-stop begonias—all the flowers with a rich history, family traditions bridging generations of women, spending their lives trying to make the home place look like something other than tobacco sticks and tools and tractor tires and assorted manure of every kind.

The dead and wounded included the hostas, the plantain lilies from Kathleen O'Fallon's Pleasant Valley Plantation on Buffalo Bayou and the banks of the Mississippi, wisteria from the huge arbor over Mamma's driveway in Woodville, Mississippi, iris from sister Jane's corner in North Middletown and the coreopsis, the feverfew, and the Silver King artemisia from Sarah Hagen's flower garden just down the street from Jane's. The columbines, the buttercups, the sweet William and the yarrow from Joshua Meadows, just around the bend of Plum Lick Creek, the Margaret Windley roses left for us by Margaret and Hilton when they moved from Plum Lick to Ohio—flowers with connections upon which human hands had labored, visions savored through the seasons.

J. LARKINS

It was almost as if—but, no, it couldn't be true—the sheep had convened a council of war, had voted to invade the butcher's territory, where it might possibly hurt the most. First, they would hit him while he was lying with his wife, in order to assure him that nothing is sacred. Then they would complete the settling of old scores by giving a southern belle from Mississippi a taste of what it was like when Grant conquered Vicksburg. While Grant took 31,600 prisoners at Vicksburg on July 4, 1863, the sheep on Plum Lick in 1991 would not be so generous.

The same month Grant was winning his spurs to the west, William Tecumseh Sherman was practicing on Jackson, Mississippi what he would prosecute to the fullest the following year when he torched Atlanta and began his march to the sea. The sheep, too, would scorch the earth, deflowering everything standing between them and Savannah.

The shepherd sprang from his bed like Lee at Appomattox. He went down the hallway from the bedroom to the kitchen as fast as he did the last time an earthquake shook Plum Lick. His bare feet hardly made contact with the floor. He skimmed the surface like the Hovercraft crossing the English Channel from Calais to Dover.

When he went out the back door and rounded the corner of the house it was of no special consequence he was wearing only his underwear, one of the luxuries of living in remote areas such as Plum Lick. City folks can only fantasize running in their underwear through wet, early morning grass on sheep dung-adorned lawns.

The first thing he saw was long-legged lambs stretching their necks to nibble Dogwood leaves. As soon as they saw a human in his underwear it was enough to stop a war dead in its tracks. They executed an orderly retreat, rounded the front of the house again and headed for the open gate through which they had entered. The troops had accomplished their mission. Reconstruction would be somebody else's business.

The shepherd returned inside the bedroom and made the grievous error of laughing. The shepherd's wife didn't think it was funny. Dressed only in her nightgown, tears flowing as hot and bitter as Scarlett's when she returned to Tara, she went out to survey the carnage. About the only things the sheep did not touch were the mint (which usually goes so well with lamb) and the little fuzzy-leafed stachys byzantina—better known as Lamb's Ears.

There was something fiercely determined on Scarlett's face, when later after church she told the shepherd she had prayed God would forgive her—and the lambs.

215

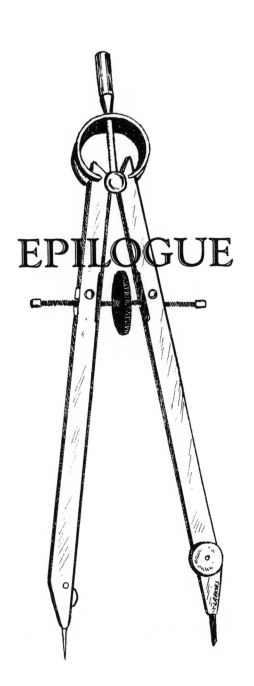

EPILOGUE

WHAT POWERS HAVE I?

"The world is too much with us;
   late and soon
Getting and spending,
   we lay waste our powers
Little we see in Nature that is ours." [10]

The problem is much deeper than wars and other acts of violence in the Middle East, much more profound than that alone. Standing atop one of our hills here on Plum Lick, seeing the fog heavy in the valley, witnessing a barn on the highest point over there looking as if it were a freighter at anchor on the harbor's edge, I raise my outstretched arms upward to the sky to thank God for the wonder of another late winter's morning.

"Here would be a good place for Cathy and Rusty to build a house to carry them and their new child through the early 21st century," I say to myself of my middle daughter, her husband and the 8th and newest generation who'll breathe the rejuvenating air of Plum Lick.

"Yes, I'll 'retire' again to celebrate the year 2,000," I hum to myself on the descent to the house hidden at the bottom of the fog. Only nine more years of "getting and spending and laying waste of my powers."

Perhaps, by then I will still have resisted the temptation to install a satellite dish. It would have been nice to have had Bernard Shaw and Peter Arnett live from Baghdad; it would have been convenient to have had some sports event not carried on a regular television channel; it would have been juicy to have caroused and fantasized and been enveloped by some erotic scenes played out by actors and actresses. But, that would have had little to do with my real powers and the Nature all around me that have always been mine for the asking.

What powers have I?

The garden must not lie fallow. There must be strawberries. There must be tomatoes and beans and potatoes and radishes and onions and corn and cucumbers and carrots and pumpkins and squash and watermelons. The orchard must not wither and die. There must be apples and cherries and pears. The livestock must be husbanded. The hooks in the meathouse must bear the weight of nourishment. The freezer on the back porch must be filled with provisions for all seasons.

The leather-bound books on the shelves on either side of the fireplace in the living room must not gather dust and sag of their own burdens. The piano brought up from Great-grandmother Cynthia's house downstream in Joshua Meadows must not remain untuned, unplayed, so unappreciated. It puzzles me. Why do I so often "give my heart away, a sordid boon?"

Not all of us are called. Maybe I'm presumptuous enough to think I am. Yet, there are more opportunities then we might suppose to become closer to a "true vocation," to keep ourselves from being "out of tune."

The joy I feel and see is not so much in apple orchards as it is in single apples, not so much in the paring of the outer skin, as in the discovery of the core, not nearly so much in the core as in the individual seed and the worlds contained inside. The power of one kernel of corn exploding into stalk weighted down with ears of sustenance, row on row, the power of one prayerful thought, translating into discourse with God are the joys of the Nature that is ours.

The problem, it seems to me, is our seduction by artificiality, of representation rather than presentation. There's a generation of youth at the end of the 20th century, members of which don't feel real unless they see events, even better, themselves on television. How sad.

True vocations are still possible, when the small voice inside calls me, I want to be sure to answer: "Here I am."

Spring is creeping in. Although the calendar won't formalize it until March 20, nature has never been comfortable with formalities. The hints are there. Little signs are appearing, indicating the irrepressible approach of the vernal equinox.

We knew it when the cattle had to be brought in off the road three times in one night. There was a glint in their eyes, dulled by winter. Mrs. Prather, our neighbor on the Cane Ridge Road who died in the spring of 1991 and whose farm sold at auction in late summer, had pitched in despite her years and helped Lalie round them up the first time they were out. Roger Wilson showed up the second time to lend a hand. Our other neighbor, Billy Dale, had already dressed for bed, but he came out with his flashlight and helped walk the cows, heavy with calf, and the two bulls back down the Plum Lick Road and into the main gate. The next day, on the way to Mt. Sterling, by the side of the road, a woodcutter was resting beside his chain saw. Thin, blue smoke curled up from the pile of smaller limbs he had trimmed away, the man meticulous, not wanting to leave behind unnecessary unsightliness. The man seemed most content, and yet it was another clear sign the season of winter would soon be turning to the season of spring.

A short distance away, on the other side of the highway, a woman and a child were out for a slow, contemplative walk along a portion of the former roadway. They seemed not at all concerned about traffic. The woman and the child maintained enough distance between them to make their walking smoother, yet friendly. Doves, too, unbothered by hunters, have been seeking crumbs along the sides of the roads. Grackles and their extended family of blackbirds thrash the air as they swarm from tree to tree. There are visions of robins returning, their scouts expected any day now.

Light takes on renewed vigor and texture. The cold glare of winter softens into the advancing warmth of spring. It comes gradually from the south, about 15 miles a day, according to naturalist Edwin Way Teale, and yet of that there is seldom predictability. Exactness, as calendars, doesn't suit the whims of the changing seasons.

JOSHUA

Easter morning on Plum Lick in the year 1992: the recent snow had melted; a few pockets of white clung stubbornly to the rock slabs and tables across the creek, where 200 years before, the trace provided the only way for travelers—no cars, no trucks, no tractors...no radios, no television...no refrigerators, no freezers...few, if any, medical microscopes...no vaccines...no airplanes...no helicopters to track down marijuana growing naturally among the Plum trees...no debate about legalizing marijuana...no contradictory programs, on the one hand supporting the growing of burley tobacco, on the other hand condemning its usage.

Great-great-great grandfather Joshua and great-great-great grandmother Polly Sr. witnessed their Easter mornings in the valley of the Plum trees seeded and ceded by the Indians, and the family tree Joshua and Polly Sr. planted at the log house had grown to eight generations of laughter and tears. The record of the many branches of the family begun in the 1790s would be computerized by 1992, and with the simple touch of keys, the names would spill out on parchment: Polly Jr. brought in the Hedges; Cynthia brought in the Crouchs; Bill brought in the Neals; Lucile brought in Samuel I, the son of the Reverend Dick; David brought in the Casales and the Cumbos; and Catherine brought in the O'Shields. One day, perhaps my grandson, Jay David will bring his sweetheart to a new Sycamore tree on Plum Lick Creek to carve her initials there; Ravy may bring in her swain to live and love on Plum Lick. In time, say, about 2,192, a writer will look back on 1992 for answers to questions about who they all were, what they said, what they did, how they loved, the quality of their thoughts, their gentleness, their disappointments, their triumphs, their hellos and their goodbyes.

Jay David, born in the month of April, would become another link in the chain winding through the generations of a people who've seen and felt on this spot of earth a place for roots. There are many families composing the quilted land. Not all, of course, have seen a hope for the future here, but many have, and it is to all of them *The View from Plum Lick* is dedicated, as well as to Lalie, whose courage and determined energies have made the writing of it such a joy. It is from within ourselves we discover the present and dream of the future. The past has served us well, but we labor now on the broadening shoulders of our forebears, the heritage they've given us. The future becomes our main challenge, for we do not wish to live for ourselves alone. Were we to be isolationist, we would die in time; our family connections would be broken, our dedicated efforts would become footnotes in dust on genealogical shelves, or lost in the labyrinths of computer software. Therein lies our willingness for change, for growth that is strong and filled with value in harmony with nature.

Who among us would have thrown the computer switch to halt the recent snow? Who among us would have damned the flash flood, which preceded the blinding pre-Easter snow storm? Those who would, simply do not understand or appreciate the proper, essential role nature plays in our lives today, our lives 200 years ago and our lives in the year 2192.

Concrete has its place. Here on the farm it has its proper function. But it is the soil, the grass and the animals by which we ensure our survival. Gravel pits and stone quarries are fine for building roads, for moving from "A" to "B," but the central question of mid-century remains in 1992: "Is this trip really necessary?" Beyond the richness of our blood, the strength of our bones, and the mobility of our entireness, there is also the quality of our spiritual lives deriving from the good earth.

We've grown accustomed to the jokes. We understand the derision springing from the increasingly dominant urban culture. Most of us in the valley of the Plum trees are quietly at work and have been for two centuries. Occasionally, one of us might feel a responsibility to write about it, to communicate to our brothers and sisters in town: "Your work is important, but so is ours. Kentucky's motto is fitting for the nation: 'United We Stand, Divided We Fall.' "

In that spirit, the voice of the sixth generation says to all living members of recent generations, "Be confident in this place, or whereever your place may be; there is God's work to be done; there is refreshment at the end of the day; and there is every reason to believe in the cause of the ninth generation, as well as succeeding generations spiralling through the 21st century toward the 22nd and beyond into infinity.

J. LARKINS

Many of the descriptions in this volume appeared earlier in "Kentucky Living," the monthly publication of the Kentucky Association of Electric Cooperatives, Inc., while others appeared in a weekly column entitled "Our Kentucky," which was syndicated to numerous newspapers in the commonwealth.

Permission was granted by the Louisville *Courier-Journal*, to reprint selections from *Joe Creason's Kentucky*, copyrighted (1972) by The Courier-Journal and Louisville Times.

Permission was granted by The University Press of Kentucky to reprint the opening lines of John Fox Jr.'s *Trail of the Lonesome Pine* (1984).

REFERENCES

1. John Donne, "A Valediction Forbidding Mourning," 1611.
2. William Wordsworth, Ode, "Intimations of Immortality from Recollections of Early Childhood," 1803.
3. Alfred Tennyson, "Serenade" from "Songs from the Princess," 1847.
4. Alfred Tennyson, "Crossing the Bar," 1889.
5. William Shakespeare, XCIV, "Sonnets," 1598.
6. The Holy Bible, I. Corinthians, Chapter III.
7. W.B. Yeats, "The Lake Isle of Innisfree," 1890.
8. John Milton, "II Peneroso, 1645.
9. William Blake, "The Lamb" from "Songs of Innocence," 1789.
10. William Wordsworth, Miscellaneous Sonnets, Part I, XXIII, 1807.

ACKNOWLEDGMENTS

The View from Plum Lick would not have been possible without the love and talents of many. I'll run the risk of naming some, while unavoidably leaving others out. Those not mentioned, I pray, will understand.

First of all my soul mate, Lalie, was the primary inspiration. Her complete name is Eulalie Anne Cumbo Dick, the daughter of another Eulalie from New Orleans and Woodville, Mississippi, Eulalie Bradford Harvey "Betty" Cumbo. The roots of Betty and Charles Cumbo reach back in four directions: England, Ireland, France and Sicily. The richness of their lives has involved many Kentuckians, Louisianians and Mississippians.

They gave Lalie generous portions of their remarkable talents in art and drafting but most important of all, a deep love for people. They didn't forget to include in her genes natural abilities preparing her for the most complicated word processing situations, type faces, and page composition. Lalie understands both the value of words and the space they occupy. She's every author's dream.

Our daughter, Ravy Bradford Dick, 9 years old in the summer of '92, suffered through all the neglect that goes with the writing, editing and publishing of a volume such as this. Then, there was Ravy's great great-grandmother, the mysterious Cynthia Hedges Kennedy Crouch, whose presence I would never have known without the diligent work of Donald Armstrong of Frankfort, a genealogist married to Anne, another descendant of Cynthia.

Such is Lalie's nature that she would insist that I also acknowledge the dedication of my first wife, Rose Ann Casale Dick, who raised four beautiful children while I was covering earthquakes and presidential campaigns. It was a marriage that lasted 25 years. It would take another book to tell that part of the story.

Without Betty Cumbo's brother, Audio Gray Harvey, his wife Louie and their son, John, there would have been no Plum Lick Farms as we know it today. Uncle Audio, a retired petroleum company engineer from Jackson, Mississippi, bought the Isaac Shelby Crouch house and surrounding land in 1985, and then sold it to Lalie and me. He had the financing capability that we sorely lacked.

At Host Creative Communications Printing in Lexington, Kentucky, Jim Host, Joseph E. Freeman, Dianna Moyer, Paulette Ball, Sharon Burke, Denise LeCompte, and Edmund Recktenwald were the cogs in the wheel that pulled everything together. It would not have happened without them.

Kenneth Cherry at the University Press of Kentucky provided inspired, unselfish editorial criticism. Because of his insightfulness we cut the manuscript in half and changed the title. Both recommendations resulted in a vastly improved finished work.

Gary Luhr, editor of "Kentucky Living," graciously gave us permission to use the title of my monthly column, "The View from Plum Lick," as well as many of the pieces appearing on the back page of the magazine during the past three years.

It was Gary Luhr who introduced us to Jackie Larkins, whose talent as an illustrator gives the reader a richness the words alone do not provide. Jackie is a discovery, and we are already grateful to him for his magic.

Finally there's the Commonwealth of Kentucky to give the foremost tribute, as well as prayerful thanks to the Great Creator who decided that this spot in the universe would receive such incredible riches. If *The View from Plum Lick* repays a portion of the divine debt, the author will rest easy each night by the side of the little stream hurrying to the ocean.

ABOUT THE AUTHOR

Born in Cincinnati, Ohio in 1930, David Dick was 18 months old when his father died and his mother returned with their three small children to her native Bourbon County, Kentucky.

David grew up on a farm, Mt. Auburn, only a few miles "across the watershed" from Plum Lick, where in the latter years of his life he would return to live on land purchased by his ancestor, Joshua, in the 1790's.

"It was a piece of green I carried with me on assignments for CBS News, and it was what kept me reasonably sane," says David, who retired from the network after 19 years. He covered stories in 22 countries and all the states in the United States except Alaska and Hawaii.

David received the Emmy for coverage of the shooting of Governor George Wallace in 1972. He was inducted into the Kentucky Journalism Hall of Fame in 1987.

Prior to CBS, David Dick was a reporter for WHAS Radio and Television in Louisville. He was educated at the North Middletown Consolidated High School in Bourbon County, and the University of Kentucky, where he earned his B.A. and M.A. in English literature.

Immediately following his retirement from CBS in 1985, David joined the faculty of the University of Kentucky. He became the director of the UK School of Journalism in 1987 and held that position for six years. He was University Orator from 1991 to 1997. He became professor emeritus of the University of Kentucky in 1996. He holds an honorary doctorate of the humanities from Cumberland College where he has also served as an adjunct professor in the Department of English.

He has been the publisher of a weekly newspaper, syndicated columnist for numerous Kentucky newspapers, and since 1989 a monthly columnist for "Kentucky Living," published by the Kentucky Association of Electric Cooperatives.

David and his wife, Eulalie ("Lalie"), a native of New Orleans and Woodville, Mississippi, live with their daughter, Ravy, in an 1850 house by the side of Plum Lick Creek in eastern Bourbon County.